Communications in Computer and Information Science 1647

More information about this series at https://link.springer.com/bookseries/7899

Karina Abad · Santiago Berrezueta (Eds.)

Doctoral Symposium on Information and Communication Technologies

Second Doctoral Symposium, DSICT 2022
Manta, Ecuador, October 12–14, 2022
Proceedings

Springer

Editors
Karina Abad
CEDIA
Cuenca, Ecuador

Santiago Berrezueta
CEDIA
Cuenca, Ecuador

Technische Universität München
Munich, Germany

ISSN 1865-0929 ISSN 1865-0937 (electronic)
Communications in Computer and Information Science
ISBN 978-3-031-18346-1 ISBN 978-3-031-18347-8 (eBook)
https://doi.org/10.1007/978-3-031-18347-8

This Springer imprint is published by the registered company Springer Nature Switzerland AG
The registered company address is: Gewerbestrasse 11, 6330 Cham, Switzerland

Preface

We are very pleased to introduce the proceedings of the second edition of the Doctoral Symposium on Information and Communication Technologies (DSICT 2022), which was held during October 12–14, 2022, in conjunction with 10th Ecuadorian Conference on Information and Communication Technologies (TICEC 2022).

The Doctoral Symposium on ICTs has become a prestigious annual event on areas of intelligent systems, artificial intelligence, ICTs, and their applications to the real world. This symposium not only showcased state-of-the-art methods and valuable experience but also provided the audience with a vision of further development in the fields of interest. More importantly, doctoral candidates benefited from the feedback of our international Program Committee and were able to expand their network considerably.

In addition to the presentation of the papers, the doctoral students shared the following:

- Summaries of their research with the motivation justifying the importance of the research problem,
- Research questions and hypotheses formulating what they want to achieve, solve, or demonstrate,
- Technical challenges associated with the research questions and the discussion of existing solutions with an explanation of why they do not solve the problem,
- Discussion on the originality of their contributions stating how the results go beyond existing approaches,
- Descriptions of the research methods including strategies for evaluating their work to provide credible evidence of the results, and
- Descriptions of the progress they have made so far towards completing the research.

One of the meaningful and valuable dimensions of this symposium is the way it brings together researchers, scientists, academics, and engineers in the field from different countries. The aim was to further increase the body of knowledge in this specific area by providing a forum to exchange ideas and discuss results, and to build international links.

The Program Committee of DSICT 2022 represented 27 countries. This certainly attests to the widespread, international importance of the theme of the symposium. Each paper was reviewed in a X-blind process by at least X members of the Program Committee and paper selection was based on originality, novelty, and rigorousness. After the reviews, 15 papers were accepted for presentation and publication in the proceedings. These papers provide good examples of current research on relevant topics, covering deep learning, data mining, data processing, human–computer interactions, natural language processing, expert systems, robotics, ambient intelligence, biomedical sensors and wearables systems, data science, ICTs applications, software development, and technology and the environment, to name a few.

We warmly thank and greatly appreciate the contributions from the authors, and we kindly invite all doctoral students involved in ICTs and related areas to contribute to future DSICT symposiums.

We believe this event will continue to help more doctoral students to share their research with the world and get more experience in the field.

October 2022   Karina Abad
                                                                              Santiago Berrezueta

Organization

Honorary Committee

Cecilia Paredes — CEDIA, Ecuador

Marco Zambrano — Universidad Laica Eloy Alfaro de Manabí, Ecuador

Juan Pablo Carvallo Vega — CEDIA, Ecuador

General Chairs

Karina Abad — CEDIA, Ecuador

Santiago Berrezueta — CEDIA, Ecuador and Technische Universität München, Germany

Program Committee Chairs

Karina Abad — CEDIA, Ecuador

Santiago Berrezueta — CEDIA, Ecuador and Technische Universität München, Germany

Program Committee

Agustin L. Herrera-May — Universidad Veracruzana, Mexico

Agustín Yagüe — Universidad Politécnica de Madrid, Spain

Alex Fernando Buitrago Hurtado — Universidad Externado de Colombia, Colombia

Alvaro Suarez — Universidad de Las Palmas de Gran Canaria, Spain

Angel Alberto Magrñan — Universidad de La Rioja, Spain

Arcangelo Castiglione — University of Salerno, Italy

Artur Rydosz — AGH University of Science and Technology, Poland

Belen Bermejo — University of the Balearic Islands, Spain

Belen Curto — Universidad de Salamanca, Spain

Carlos Abreu — Instituto Politécnico de Viana do Castelo, Portugal

Carme Quer — Universitat Politècnica de Catalunya, Spain

Cesar Azurdia-Meza — University of Chile, Chile

Che-Wei Lin — National Cheng Kung University, Taiwan

Christos Antonopoulos — University of Peloponnese, Greece

Claudia Marzi — Italian National Research Council, Italy

Cristian Vasar	Politehnica University of Timisoara, Romania
Dan Pescaru	Universitatea Politehnica din Timisoara, Romania
Darius Andriukaitis	Kaunas University of Technology, Lithuania
David Valiente	Miguel Hernandez University, Spain
Emil Pricop	Petroleum-Gas University of Ploiesti, Romania
Firas Raheem	University of Technology, Iraq
Francisco Prieto-Castrillo	Universidad Politécnica de Madrid, Spain
Gabor Sziebig	The Arctic University of Norway, Norway
George Adam	University of Thessaly, Greece
Gerasimos Vonitsanos	University of Patras, Greece
Giuseppe Ciaburro	Università degli Studi della Campania Luigi Vanvitelli, Italy
Hugo Almeida-Ferreira	Polytechnic Institute of Oporto, Portugal
Ibraheem Kasim Ibraheem	Baghdad University, Iraq
Ioan Viorel Banu	Gheorghe Asachi Technical University of Iasi, Romania
Iosif Szeidert	Politehnica University of Timisoara, Romania
Irina Georgiana Mocanu	Politehnica University of Bucharest, Romania
Isabel Sofia Sousa Brito	Instituto Politécnico de Beja, Portugal
Jari Hannu	University of Oulu, Finland
Javier Gomez	Universidad Autónoma de México, Mexico
Jerwin Prabu A	Bharati Robotic Systems India Pvt Ltd, India
John Castro	Universidad de Atacama, Chile
José Martinez-Carranza	Instituto Nacional de Astrofísica, Óptica y Electrónica, Mexico
José Olivas-Varela	Universidad de Castilla-La Mancha, Spain
José Joaquim de Moura Ramos	University of A Coruña, Spain
José Juan Pazos-Arias	Universidad de Vigo, Spain
Kiril Alexiev	Institute of Information and Communication Technologies, BAS, Bulgaria
Lidia Lopez	Barcelona Supercomputing Center, Spain
Lukasz Sobaszek	Lublin University of Technology, Poland
Marcin Ciecholewski	University of Gdansk, Poland
Marcin Górski	Silesian University of Technology, Poland
Marco Zappatore	University of Salento, Italy
Marco Antônio P. Araújo	Federal University of Juiz de Fora, Brazil
Marian Wysocki	Czestochowa University of Technology, Poland
Marija Seder	University of Zagreb, Croatia
Mariusz Kostrzewski	Warsaw University of Technology, Poland
Martín López-Nores	Universidad de Vigo, Spain
Modestos Stavrakis	University of the Aegean, Greece
Mohiuddin Ahmed	Edith Cowan University, Australia

Natasa Zivic	University of Siegen, Germany
Noman Naseer	Pusan University, South Korea
Noor Zaman	Taylor's University, Malaysia
Patricio Galdames	Universidad del Bio-Bio, Chile
Piotr Dziurdzia	AGH University of Science and Technology, Poland
Raúl Antonio Aguilar Vera	Universidad Autónoma de Yucatán, Mexico
Robert Alexandru Dobre	Politehnica University of Bucharest, Romania
Roberto Murphy	INAOE, Mexico
Rosaria Rucco	University of Naples Parthenope, Italy
Rostom Mabrouk	Bishop's University, Canada
Rui Zhao	University of Nebraska Omaha, USA
Ruoyu Su	Memorial University of Newfoundland, Canada
Samuel Ortega	University of Las Palmas de Gran Canaria, Spain
Sara Paiva	Oviedo University, Spain
Stavros Souravlas	University of Macedonia, Macedonia
Stefano Mariani	Università degli Studi di Modena, Italy
Tomasz Bieniek	Institute of Electron Technology, Poland
Valerio Baiocchi	Sapienza University of Rome, Italy
Vera Ferreira	Federal University of Pampa, Brazil
Wojciech Zabierowski	Lodz University of Technology, Poland
Yanhua Luo	University of New South Wales, Australia
Zoltán Adam Tamus	Budapest University of Technology, Hungary

Contents

Evaluating University Students' Information Literacy: An Approach from Task-Based Test Execution

Patricia Henríquez-Coronel[1]([✉]) [iD], Sebastián Lepe-Báez[2] [iD], and Genesis Armas-Bravo[1]

[1] Universidad Laica Eloy Alfaro de Manabí, Manta, Ecuador
patricia.henriquez@uleam.edu.ec
[2] Universidad Rovira i Virgili, Tarragona, Spain

Abstract. The results of a research whose main objective was to evaluate the information literacy (IL) of the students of the Universidad Laica Eloy Alfaro de Manabí - ULEAM are presented- through an instrument that measures the informational literacy shown by the execution of tasks at predetermined time intervals. It is a study with a quantitative approach and a descriptive scope that uses the survey as a data collection technique from a stratified randomly selected sample. The survey was designed and subsequently validated through two procedures: value judgment by experts and pilot testing to a group of 10 students. The survey was applied to a sample of 375 students during a period of 11 days. The results showed a low (3.55) IL for the studied group, with the students being more proficient at the information search skill. The competence results evidenced in the test tasks were similar to the self-perceived competence carried out in a previous study.

Keywords: Informational literacy · Students · Evaluation

1 Introduction

The knowledge economy has information and knowledge as the axis of productive activity, and technology and innovation as allies for its production, management, transfer and dissemination. The digital economy requires a workforce with digital skills, which is why governments and organizations around the world design policies and frameworks aimed at enhancing the digital skills of the workforce to improve economic growth and competitiveness [11]. The COVID pandemic fast-tracked digitization processes and with it the digital skills requirements of workers. A Salesforce research of more than 23.000 workers in 19 countries revealed that 76% of global workers say they feel unequipped and unprepared to operate in a digital-first world [40].

The pandemic accelerated the processes of digital transformation in all areas, especially in education. Lockdowns and school closures made basic digital skills a prerequisite for learning and skill acquisition [43]. Digitization of teaching and learning processes was accelerated at all levels [8, 35, 36, 38]. Many teachers had to learn about the use of online education tools while using them to remedy the lack of face-to face

K. Abad and S. Berrezueta (Eds.): DSICT 2022, CCIS 1647, pp. 1–13, 2022.
https://doi.org/10.1007/978-3-031-18347-8_1

classes. Before the pandemic, teachers' digital skills were at basic levels [2, 35, 36, 39, 44], becoming a need to develop them further [2, 31].

Regarding the students, various studies focused on their informational literacy and had been showing low or medium levels of achievement [1, 14, 25, 32, 41, 42], during the pandemic this reality was made evident, because the students, although they belong to the generation of digital natives, were not users of online education either and had to learn on the fly [27]. During the pandemic, the need for information literacy of students, focused on teaching and learning the appropriate skills for handling information through active processes was especially clear [13, 16, 33, 35]. Participation of teachers as responsible for their students achieving the key competencies related to handling information is most certainly needed [20]. International informational literacy standards such as ISTE [28] or DIGCOMP [7] consider information literacy as part of it and find it related to searching, evaluating, using, and creating information effectively. According to Pinto, Caballero, and Segura [38], informational competence is related to recognizing when they need information, where to locate it, how to evaluate its suitability, and how to use it appropriately according to the given problem. Several authors signal that the development of informational literacy plays an important role in the academic trajectory and has a positive impact on student performance [13, 16, 18, 29, 33, 35].

Nieto-Isidro, Martínez-Abad, Rodríguez-Conde [33], point out that there are few information literacy programs at educational levels prior to university, which is why they (universities) mostly assume the responsibility of developing informational literacy of their students through various training strategies [12, 19, 20], and teachers are key figures for the development of this competence in students [13, 18, 29]. Many authors have conducted research on self-perceived informational literacy and a few on informational literacy evidenced in testing task solving capabilities. In self-perceived competence studies [4, 10, 12, 13, 16, 20, 22, 24, 29, 30, 33, 35, 38, 45] the perceptions that students have about their own capacities for the search, evaluation, use and creation of information are measured. However, when tests are carried out based on tasks that students must perform to demonstrate their informational literacy, it has been found that self-perceived competence generally turns out to be overrated in relation to actual performance [13, 33].

This research presents the results of the measurement of the informational literacy of university students through the task tests. It aims to answer the following questions:

- What is the degree of competence students have when managing information?
- What is the degree of competence students have when searching for and locating information?
- Do students have the skills necessary to evaluate or distinguish one source of academic information from another?
- What is the degree of competence students possess in order to manage a significant amount of information?
- What is the degree of competence students have in order to share the knowledge they produce, in an appropriate way?

2 Methodology/Approach

The research was carried out under a quantitative, non-experimental descriptive approach [26], it seeks to evaluate, through the execution of tasks, the levels of informational literacy of the students of the Universidad Laica Eloy Alfaro de Manabí.

The task test technique was used, similar to the one proposed by Nielsen and Landaur [34] for web usability studies and which have been widely tested in different investigations [9, 17, 21].

The population consisted of 14.242 students enrolled at ULEAM, distributed among 20 faculties. The calculation of the sample of finite populations was carried out through the SurveyMonkey ® service, with a confidence level of 95% and an error of 5%, indicating a sample size of 375 students. The sampling was random, stratified, probabilistic, considering the faculty as the sample stratum. Thus, 20 strata corresponding to the 20 faculties of the ULEAM were used. The 375 responses to the test tasks were collected through the Google Forms® tool.

The test consists of five tasks[1] to be carried out in a preset time. These tasks were designed based on and then classified according to the area of competence, as shown in Table 1.

Table 1. Area of competition and task description.

Area of competition	Task description
Search of information	1. Identification of the abstract's keywords 2. Retrieval of a book in the virtual library e-libro ® of the ULEAM
Evaluation of information	3. Distinguish between different sources of information
Prosecution of information	4. Treatment of information for management of data
Communication of information	5. Elaboration of a mind map

The validation process for the tasks was carried out in two instances. First, a pilot of the test was made with a group of 10 students who joined voluntarily. The researchers watched as the students attempted to solve the tasks and recorded the time required for each task on the test. When the student finished each task, they were asked to assess the degree of clearness and unambiguity to which the task had been formulated, making sure the task's instructions left no doubts to the participants. The scale used for the assessment was from 1 to 5, with 1 being the lowest value and 5 the highest. This piloting made it possible to identify failures in the understanding of certain tasks and to estimate the average times required for the execution of said tasks. When the test was corrected taking into account the findings of the pilot, the second moment of validation began,

---

[1] The five tasks of the designed test were inspired in the issues formulated to determine the self-perceived informational literacy of the students of the ULEAM, previously in year 2019 within of the INCOTIC survey by ARGET research group from URV, widely reviewed in the scientific literature.

which consisted of an evaluation by three experts considering the criteria of content validity (relevance) and writing (clarity and unambiguity). Three experts participated, two of them experts in informational literacy and a third in quantitative methods. Finally, a quantitative assessment of the test's tasks was carried out based on the content assessment coefficient (CVC), obtaining a value of 0.85, together with an internal consistency analysis using Cronbach's Alpha coefficient, obtaining a result of 0.92. The application of the test was carried out during the month of December 2020, the online instrument enabled in the ULEAM virtual classroom platform was applied from Thursday 10 to Monday 21 of said month. The professors at the University, who participated in the massive application of the test to the students were trained by the researchers so that the process was always carried out under regular conditions: in the classrooms, in the foreseen time and through mobile or personal computer access.

An analytical rubric was designed [15], which established, based on the evaluation criteria of the area of competence (Table 1), a definition of quality in relation to the description of the expected performance and it established a 5-level scoring strategy (Poor = 1, Deficient = 2, Fair = 3, Satisfactory = 4, and Excellent = 5). For the interpretation of the values of the scale, the INCOTIC survey of the ARGET group of the URV was adapted, which distributes students into three levels of development of informational literacy (see Fig. 1): low, medium and high. The reason for adopting this scale is that in 2019 we had already used it in a previous study of self-perceived informational literacy with the same group of students at the same university and it could allow us to make comparisons in the future [23].

Informational literacy	Low	<3.75	Your informational literacy level is low, this indicates that often you may find difficulties in the search, evaluation, processing and communication of information. You should improve these useful competencies in order to better your learning process at university.
	Medium	3.76-4.50	Your informational literacy level is average, this indicates that you usually overcome the main obstacles in the search, evaluation, processing and communication of information. Still so, you should improve these useful competencies in order to better your learning process at university.
	High	>4.51	Your informational literacy level is high, which indicates that you usually

Fig. 1. Description and score of each one of the levels of informational literacy

The data stored in Google Forms®, was downloaded to calculate the averages of each sub area of competition. The data collected through the poll was processed with Microsoft Excel® to calculate figures, percentages, and distribution of frequencies.

3   Results

Before going into the detailed analysis of each individual research question, the general results of the 375 students were reviewed. The first task of the test referring to identifying keywords in an abstract obtained an average of 3.735 points out of 5. Similarly, the second task of the test referring to locating a book in the ULEAM virtual library showed an average of 3.941 out of 5, the third task concerning the validation of academic sources had an average of 3.662 out of 5, the fourth task pertaining to the treatment of information and data obtained an average of 3.456 out of 5, while the last task, referring to the elaboration of a mind map, presented an average of 2.980 out of 5, being by far the lowest score. Figure 2 represents the averages obtained in the different tasks carried out.

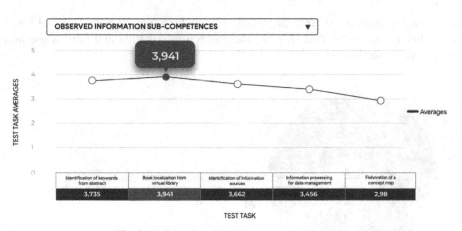

Fig. 2. Informational sub competence averages.

Let's now see the specific results from each one of the tasks in the Test.

3.1   What is the Degree of Competence Students Have When Managing Information?

Only 11.8% of the students managed to identify the three keywords of the abstract presented in the first task, a rather poor result. This low performance should be analyzed due to the importance of keywords to correctly perform Internet searches. 58.8% achieved the identification of two keywords, 20,6% only identified one of the three keywords, while 8.8% failed to identify all of the keywords, this means that 29.4% belong in the regular and poor levels of the rubric. Only 44 students out of 375 managed to identify the 3 key words for reading, from these answers a low reading comprehension could be inferred. (see Fig. 3).

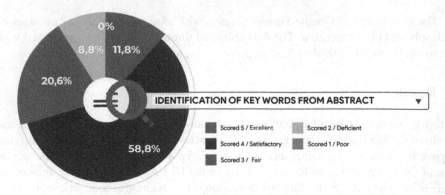

Fig. 3. Percentages of achievement obtained in task 1 of the Test

3.2 What is the Degree of Competence Students Have When Searching for and Locating Information?

To answer this question, students are asked to search for a specific book in the ULEAM virtual library: e-libro®. That is, place the retrieval information and find its use in a given context. (see Fig. 4).

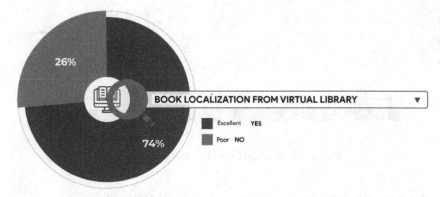

Fig. 4. Achievement percentages obtained in task 2 of the test.

Figure 4 shows that 74% of the students knew how to locate a book in the library, this task being the best performer within the evaluation of informational literacy applied to ULEAM students, on the other hand, 26% were unable to locate the requested book.

Figure 4 reveals that 74% of the students knew how to locate a book from the library, being this task of the test the most achieved among the informational digital competence evaluation applied to ULEAM's students, whilst a 26% didn't accomplished to locate the required book.

3.3 Do Students Have the Skills Necessary to Evaluate or Distinguish One Source of Academic Information from Another?

In this question, students were presented with different sources of digital information (conference proceedings, magazine articles, books and theses) which they had to identify precisely. Figure 5 shows that 41.2% of the students managed to accurately identify the source of information every time, 42.6% managed to identify two of the four sources of information and 16.2% managed to identify only one of the four sources of scientific information. Considering the scores associated with the regular and poor levels of the rubric, students in those categories account for 58.8% of the responses, that is, more than half of the students fall into misinformation by not being able to distinguish one source of academic information from another. In a global society where false information, predatory editorials, misleading information campaigns, among others, abound, students are required to be able to discriminate, compare and validate information. (see Fig. 5).

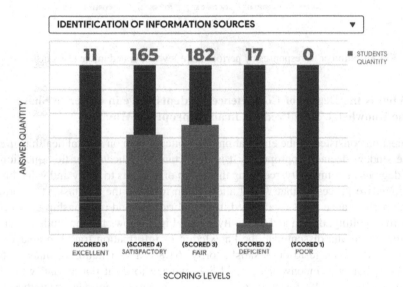

Fig. 5. Number of responses by level of performance obtained in task 3.

3.4 What is the Degree of Competence Students Possess in Order to Manage a Significant Amount of Information?

Through this question, students were asked to identify the essential fields to create a movie database. This ability is essential to manage the large volumes of data that circulate on the Internet. Figure 6 shows that only 2.9% of students have the ability to manage and process a significant amount of information, on the other hand, 44.1% managed to manage and process the data satisfactorily, 48.5% regularly and 4.4% managed to identify level and 4.4% managed to identify only one field to process the information for a database. This task obtained a low performance on average, being the information processing sub-competence less achieved by the students. (see Fig. 6).

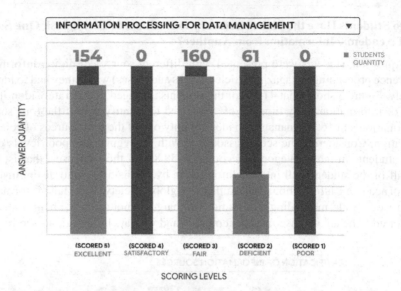

Fig. 6. Number of responses by performance level obtained in the test's task 4.

3.5 What is the Degree of Competence Students Have in Order to Share the Knowledge They Produce, in an Appropriate Way?

This question consisted of the elaboration of a concept map on mental health using any tool the student deemed appropriate. It is important to indicate that this question has higher degrees of complexity, requiring the group of students to apply and value higher-order cognitive processes that would allow them to solve the test task in accordance with the performance goals established in the rubric: use and relationship of concepts, link words, spelling, design and creativity. Thus, Fig. 6 shows that no student manages to communicate and disseminate the knowledge or information found in a successful manner, 19.1% manage to do it satisfactorily, 61.8% a vast majority, manage to do it regularly, but with inconveniences, 11.8% manage to do it poorly and with many inconveniences and 7.4% for their part, do not manage to disseminate or synthesize the knowledge or information found through the realization of a conceptual map. This turns out to be the lowest achievement level task. (see Fig. 7).

On the other hand, when reviewing the data in Fig. 1 processed in relation to the measure of central tendency (mean) and measure of dispersion (standard deviation), we can observe that the average performance in relation to the 5 tasks designed for informational literacy corresponds to 3.5548, therefore, the level of development of informational literacy of ULEAM students is at a regular/satisfactory level. When reviewing and comparing the standard deviation of the tasks of the applied test, 4 of the tasks of the test were considered, excluding task 2, since it corresponded to a dichotomous type question, whose results are polar adjusting to the extremes according to the rubric applied. It is observed Table 2. Data report, own elaboration. That the standard deviation of task 4 of the test is the lowest, showing a performance with a lower degree of dispersion. Task 3 of the test

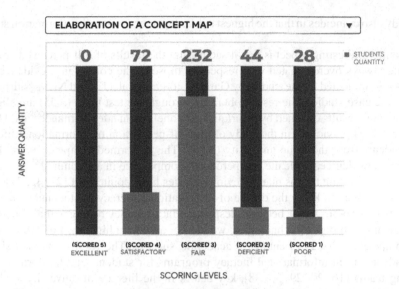

Fig. 7. Number of responses by performance level obtained in the test's task 5.

is the highest, showing a performance in a higher degree of dispersion, compared to the other tasks of the test.

Table 2. Data report, own elaboration.

Task	Half	Standard deviation
Task 1	3.735	0.785
Task 3	3.662	1.180
Task 4	3.456	0.633
Task 5	2.980	1.105

4   Discussion and Conclusions

According to the results obtained, the informational literacy of the ULEAM students in the test is found to be, according to the average of the means, of 3.5548. According to the scale used to interpret the test results, it would be a low informational literacy (<3.75), however, a deeper analysis allows us to see that the tasks best achieved are the two that belong to the sub-competence of information search, that would correspond to a medium competence (3.7 and 3.9 respectively), while those related to the evaluation, use and creation of information are poorly achieved and are of low grade (3.6, 3.4 and 2.98). These results also confirm previous findings [3, 5, 6, 25] on a low or medium level of self-perceived informational literacy in university students. Within this competence, this study also coincides in that the highest sub competence is usually information search [25].

Another interesting aspect is that it seems that the results of self-perceived competence are always overestimated with respect to those of the competence evidenced by test tasks, as indicated by the studies by García-Llorente et al. [13] and Nieto-Isidro et al. [33]. In the case studied, the results obtained through the test tasks (3.55) are slightly lower than the results obtained by Henríquez-Coronel, Fernández-Fernández and Usart-Rodríguez [23] previously in the study of the self-perception of informational literacy with students from the same university (3.77). The performed competence would be found in a low degree, while the self-perceived competence in a medium degree.

It is worth noting that as many previous studies have pointed out [27, 32, 37] there is an evident need to know the degree of informational literacy of students who are in university classrooms today, because, despite the fact that they belong to that generation that grew up with digital technologies, we cannot assume a high level of achievement in a competency that is essential for academic success. The results obtained should allow advancing in informational literacy programs for students and the formation of teaching teams [16, 20, 29, 33, 38], key actors in the literacy of university students. This study is interesting because it concludes the evaluation process of informational literacy evidenced in a task test, after having previously carried out the study of self-perceived competence with the same group of university students. However, it is limited to presenting the values obtained in relation to the degree of informational literacy of ULEAM students; future works could explore these data in relation to the conditioning factors of competence such as gender, age or the type of career studied, for a better characterization of the target group of literacy actions. Another interesting aspect would result from the exhaustive comparison of the two tests (self-perceived competence and performance proven competence) to determine the credibility they bring.

Acknowledgement. This article is part of the second author's research to obtain the degree of Doctor of Educational Technology, under Dr. Patricia Henriquez PhD mentorship, a scholar of the University Rovira i Virgili, Tarragona.

References

1. Acosta-Silva, D.: Following the competencies of digital natives: advances of a metasynthesis. Lat. Am. Sci. Mag. Soc. Child. Youth **15**(1), 471–489 (2017). https://doi.org/10.11600/169 2715x.1513014062016
2. Amhag, L., Hellstrom, L., Stigmar, M.: Teacher educators' use of digital tools and needs for digital competence in higher education. J. Digit. Learn. Teach. Educ. **35**(4), 203–220 (2019). https://doi.org/10.1080/21532974.2019.1646169
3. Avitia Carlos, P., Uriarte Ramirez, I.: Assessment of university students' digital skills: initial status and educational potential. Edutech. Electron. Mag. Technol. Educ. **61**(61), a366 (2017). https://doi.org/10.21556/edutec.2017.61.861
4. Brand-Gruwel, S., Kammerer, Y., Van Meeuwen, L., Van Gog, T.: Source evaluation of domain experts and novices during web search. J. Comput. Assist. Learn. **33**(3), 234–251 (2017). https://doi.org/10.1111/jcal.12162

5. Cando, J.M.B., Álvarez, R.R.: Characterization of the use of teaching aids for the teachers who they perform in the new physician training program. Cuban Mag. High. Med. Educ. **22**(3), 1–8 (2009)
6. Carrasco-Lozano, M.E.E, Sánchez-Olavarría, C., Carro-Olvera, A.: Digital skills in students of postgraduate education. Lasallian Mag. Res. **12**, 10–18. (2015). http://www.redalyc.org/articulo.oa?id=69542291002
7. Carter, S., Punie, Y., Vuorikari, R., Cabrera, M., O'Keeffe, W.: DigComp Into Action (2018). https://doi.org/10.2760/112945
8. Chakraborty, P., Mittal, P., Gupta, M.S., Yadav, S., Arora, A.: Opinion of students online education during the COVID-19 pandemic. Hum. Behav. Emerg. Technol. **3**(3), 357–365 (2021). https://doi.org/10.1002/hbe2.240
9. Chanchi, G. E., Alvarez, M.C., Countryside, W.Y.: Proposal for an Inspection Tool Based on Nielsen Usability Attributes, pp. 448–460. Association Iberian Systems and Technologies of Information (2020)
10. Comas, R., Sureda, J., Pastor, M., Morey, M.: The search for information for purposes academics among university students. Span. Mag. Doc. Sci. **34**(1), 44–64 (2011). https://doi.org/10.3989/redc.2011.1.769
11. Engen, B.K.: Understanding social and cultural aspects of teachers' digital competencies. Communicate **27**(61), 9–19 (2019). https://doi.org/10.3916/C61-2019-01
12. Franklin, K.Y., Faulkner, K., Ford-Baxter, T., Fu, S.: Redesigning an online information literacy tutorial for first-year undergraduate instruction. J. Acad. Librariansh. **47**(1) (2021). https://doi.org/10.1016/j.acalib.2020.102277
13. García- Llorente, H.J., Martínez-Abad, F., Rodríguez-Conde, M.J.: Assessment of observed and self-perceived information literacy in compulsory secondary education students from a Spanish region with a high performance in PISA. Electron. Mag. I Will Educate **24**(1) (2020). https://doi.org/10.15359/ree.24-1.2
14. García-Vandewalle García, J.M., García-Carmona, M., Trujillo Torres, J.M., Moya Fernández, P.: Analysis of digital competence of educators (DigCompEdu) in teacher trainees: the context of Melilla, Spain. Technol. Knowl. Learn. (2021). https://doi.org/10.1007/s10758-021-09546-x
15. Gatica-Lara, F., del Niño Jesús Uribarren-Berrueta, T.: How to create a rubric? Res. Med. Educ. **2**(5), 61–65 (2013). https://doi.org/10.1016/s2007-5057(13)72684-x
16. Gómez-Pablos, V.B., Muñoz-Repiso, A.G.V., Martín, S.C., González, M.C.: Evaluation of information literacy skills in students and a study of several influential variables. Mag. Complut. Educ. **31**(4), 517–528 (2020). https://doi.org/10.5209/rced.65835
17. Not Just Usability, Usability test in environments of Virtual reality. http://www.nosolousabilidad.com/articulos/test_usabilidad_realidad_virtual.htm. Accessed 18 May 2022
18. Gündüzalp, S.: 21st century skills for sustainable education: prediction level of teachers' information literacy skills on their digital literacy skills. Speech Commun. Sustain. Educ. **12**(1), 85–101 (2021). https://doi.org/10.2478/dcse-2021-0007
19. Guo, J., Huang, J.: Information literacy education during the pandemic: the cases of academic libraries in Chinese top universities. J. Acad. Librariansh. **47**(4), 102363 (2021). https://doi.org/10.1016/j.acalib.2021.102363
20. Hammonds, J.: Teaching the teachers to teach information literacy: to literature review. J. Acad. Librariansh. **46**(5) (2020). https://doi.org/10.1016/j.acalib.2020.102196
21. Hassan Montero, Y., Martin Fernández, F.: Method Test with Users. Not only Usability (2003)
22. Henkel, M., Grafmüller, S., Gros, D.: Comparing information literacy levels of Canadian and German university students. In: Chowdhury, G., McLeod, J., Gillet, V., Willett, P. (eds.) iConference 2018. LNCS, vol. 10766, pp. 464–475. Springer, Cham (2018). https://doi.org/10.1007/978-3-319-78105-1_51

23. Henríquez - Coronel, P., Fernández-Fernández, L., Usart - Rodríguez, M.: Factors Determinants in Digital Competition of Latin American University Students, pp. 521–532. Alfamed (2020). https://doi.org/10.3916/Alfamed2020
24. Henríquez Coronel, P.M., Fernández Fernández, I., Trampuz, J.P.: The evaluation of the self - perceived digital competence of ULEAM university students. Edutech. Electron. Mag. Technol. Educ. (2019). https://doi.org/10.21001/edutec.2019
25. Henríquez, P., Gisbert, M., Fernández, I.: The evaluation of the digital competence of students: a review Latin American case. Lat. Am. Mag. Commun. (137), 91–110 (2018). https://doi.org/10.16921/chasqui.v0i137.3511
26. Hernández Sampieri, R., Collado, F., C., Lucio, C.B., del Pilar, M.: Methodology of the Research, 5th edn., vol. fifth building. McGraw-Hill, New York (2015)
27. EDUCAUSE. The Difference Between Emergency Remote Teaching and Online Learning. https://er.educause.edu/articles/2020/3/the-difference-between-emergency-remote-teaching-and-online-learning. Accessed 10 May 2022
28. ISTE: ISTE Standards for Teachers, pp. 1–2 (2017). http://eduteka.icesi.edu.co/pdfdir/iste-estandares-teachers-2017.pdf
29. Komissarov, S., Murray, J.: Factors that influence undergraduate information-seeking behavior and opportunities for student success. J. Acad. Librariansh. **42**(4), 423–429 (2016). https://doi.org/10.1016/j.acalib.2016.04.007
30. Kultawanich, K., Koraneekij, P., Na-Songkhla, J.: Development and validation of the information literacy assessment in connectivism learning environment for undergraduate students. Proceeded – Soc. Behav. Sci. **174**, 1386–1390 (2015). https://doi.org/10.1016/J.SBSPRO.2015.01.764
31. Lakkala, M., Ilomaki, L.: A case study of developing ICT-supported pedagogy through a college practice transfer process. Comput. Educ. **90**, 1–12 (2015). https://doi.org/10.1016/j.compedu.2015.09.001
32. Marksbury, N., Arbelo Bryant, E.: Enter the twilight zone: the paradox of the digital native. Issues Inf. Syst. (2019). https://doi.org/10.48009/2_iis_2019_206-215
33. Nieto-Isidro, S., Martínez-Abad, F., Rodríguez-Conde, M.J.: Informational competence in primary education: diagnosis and effects of training in the teachers and students of Castile and Leon (Spain). Span. Mag. Doc. Sci. **44**(4) (2021). https://doi.org/10.3989/redc.2021.4.1818
34. Nielsen, J., Landauer, T.: A model mathematician of the search for usability problems. In: Proceedings of the INTERACT 1993 and CHI 1993 Conference on Human Factors in Computing Systems, pp. 206–213 (1993)
35. Nikou, S., Aavakare, M.: An assessment of the interplay between literacy and digital technology in higher education. Educ. Inf. Technol. **26**(4), 3893–3915 (2021). https://doi.org/10.1007/s10639-021-10451-0
36. Ogodo, J., Morris, D., Acubo, M.: Examining K-12 teachers' digital competency and technology self-efficacy during COVID-19 pandemic. J. High. Educ. Theory Pract. **21**(11) (2021). https://doi.org/10.33423/jhetp.v21i11.4660
37. Pérez Escoda, A., Rodríguez Count, M.J.: Evaluation of the competencies digital self-perceived of primary education teachers in Castile and Leon (Spain). Mag. Educ. Res. **34**(2), 399 (2016). https://doi.org/10.6018/rie.34.2.215121
38. Pinto, M., Caballero-Mariscal, D., Segura, A.: Experiences of information literacy and mobile technologies amongst undergraduates in times of COVID. A qualitative approach. Aslib J. Inf. Manag. **74**(2), 181–201 (2022). https://doi.org/10.1108/AJIM-10-2020-0333
39. Prendes, M.P., Gutiérrez, I., Martínez, F.: Digital competence: a need of the faculty university in the XXI century. Mag. Educ. Distance (RED) **56**, 1–22 (2018). https://doi.org/10.6018/red/56/7

40. Salesforce. 76% of employees do not feel prepared for the work of the future. https://www.salesforce.com/es/company/news-press/press-releases/2022/01/220127/. Accessed 28 June 2022
41. Scolari, C.A.: Beyond the myth of the "digital native": adolescents, collaborative cultures and transmedia skills. Nord. J. Digit. Lit. **14**, 164–174 (2019). https://doi.org/10.18261/ISSN.1891-943X-2019-03-04-06
42. Silva, J., Usart, M., Lázaro- Cantabrana, J.-L.: Teacher's digital competence among final year pedagogy students in Chile and Uruguay. Communicate **27**(61), 33–43 (2019). https://doi.org/10.3916/C61-2019-03
43. UNESCO: Global Education Monitoring Report 2021/2: Non-state actors in education: who do you choose? Who lose? 2nd edn. (2021). http://www.unesco.org/open-access/
44. Vázquez, E., Vélez, M.R., Zamora, L.C., Meneses, E.L.: Digital competence of student body of the University Catholic of Santiago de Guayaquil. Option **33**(83), 229–251 (2017). http://www.redalyc.org/pdf/310/31053772008.pdf
45. Walton, G., Hepworth, M.: A longitudinal study of changes in learners' cognitive states during and following an information literacy teaching intervention. J. Doc. **67**(3), 449–479 (2011). https://doi.org/10.1108/00220411111124541

Teaching Digital Competence in Higher Education. A Comprehensive Scientific Mapping Analysis with Rstudio

Andrés Cisneros-Barahona[1](✉), Luis Marqués Molías[2],
Gonzalo Samaniego Erazo[1], María Uvidia-Fassler[1],
Gabriela de la Cruz-Fernández[1], and Wilson Castro-Ortiz[1]

[1] Universidad Nacional de Chimborazo, Riobamba 060150, Ecuador
ascisneros@unach.edu.ec
[2] Universitat Rovira I Virgili, 43007 Tarragona, Spain

Abstract. Using the Bibliometrix module of the Rstudio software and the PRISMA Publication Guide, it was developed a scientific mapping of the scientific literature from the Scopus database about teaching digital competence (TDC) in universities. The review was delimited through Eric's thesaurus or its approximations and Boolean operators. The following research questions were raised: 1. ¿What is the scientific production per year, per author, affiliation, and country? 2. ¿Which are the main sources of scientific productions, their relevance and impact? 3. ¿Who are the authors with the most scientific productions identified in the search; the most cited; their production over time; their productivity and impact? 4. ¿In which countries does scientific production originate? 5. ¿What collaboration networks between countries, authors and institutions have been developed? and 6. ¿What are the most relevant publications? Spanish authors and institutions stand out in the study related to TDC in universities, expanding networks to Latin America, Europe, Anglo-Saxon countries, and the Asian continent. An adequate scientific mapping facilitates the review processes of scientific literature. The responsible action of researchers when integrating metadata in scientific productions allows a suitable use of exploitation tools and bibliometric analysis. In the future, it is proposed the need to develop studies aimed at the use of other tools that allow the generation of scientific maps in the context of TDC.

Keywords: Teacher training · ICT · Digital literacy · University · Bibliometrix · Scientific mapping

1 Introduction

Digital competence (DC) is related to the ability to explore and face technological situations in a flexible way, to analyze, select and critically evaluate information, to represent, solve problems and build shared and collaborative knowledge, at the same time as awareness of own personal responsibilities and respect for reciprocal rights/obligations are encouraged [1].

K. Abad and S. Berrezueta (Eds.): DSICT 2022, CCIS 1647, pp. 14–31, 2022.
https://doi.org/10.1007/978-3-031-18347-8_2

Emergency situations such as those of Covid-19 have questioned the DC of teachers and students, this has caused a sudden interest in learning how to use technology quickly to perform classroom tasks in each student's houses [2].

The teacher and researcher of the 21st century require DC to integrate the Information and Communication Technology (ICT) in the teaching and learning process, therefore these skills are getting relevant in all contexts [3, 4]. Specifically, universities should move from a non-systemic digitization to a true digital transformation, to take advantage of the potential of digital resources [5].

It is important to link the university with society, to promote the professional development of university professors and the digital literacy of their students, promoting collaborative learning and authorship [6]. Thus, one of the challenges lies in the importance that the university administrators give to the need to be part of the updating processes that help to better fulfill the tasks of teaching, research and management related to digital activities [2, 7–11].

Through the Bibliometrix module of the Web Rstudio application [12], it was developed a scientific mapping of the scientific literature from the Scopus platform about teaching digital competence (TDC) in higher education institutions, the research was delimited through key concepts, using the Education Resources Information Center (ERIC) thesaurus or its approximations as follows: "digital competences", "higher education", "university teachers" and "teaching"; the search was carried out in English and, by using "and" operator; finally, no time limit was specified until May 2022. The following research questions were considered: 1. ¿What is the scientific production per year, per author, affiliation and country, related to TDC in higher education institutions?; 2. ¿Which are the main sources of scientific productions, their relevance and impact?; 3. ¿Who are the authors with the most scientific productions identified in the search, the most cited, their production over time, their productivity and impact?; 4. ¿In which countries does the scientific production related to the topic mentioned originate? 5. ¿What collaboration networks between countries, authors and institutions have been developed related to TDC in universities? and 6. ¿What are the most relevant publications related to the topic? In the future, it is proposed the need to develop studies aimed at the use of other tools that allow the generation of scientific maps in the context of TDC.

2 Method

Through the Bibliometrix computer module of the Rstudio application [12] and through the Preferred Reporting Items for Systematic Reviews and Meta-Analyses - PRISMA publication guide, a systematic literature review (SLR) founded on the scientific mapping and the meta-analysis (MA) [13]. The objective was to analyze the scientific production from the Scopus database, about the digital competence of university teachers, taking into account the following research variables: 1. Year of publication of the works; 2. Scientific production by author, affiliation and country; 3. Source of scientific production, 4. Relevance of scientific production; 5. Impact of scientific production; 6. Authors with more scientific productions identified in the search; 7. Most cited authors; 8. Production of the authors over time; 9. Productivity of the authors; 10. Impact of the authors;

11. Countries where production originates; 12. Collaboration networks between countries; 13. Collaboration networks between authors; 14. Collaboration networks between institutions and, 15. Most cited publications.

At the beginning, the research was delimited through key concepts, using ERIC thesaurus or its approximations, through a controlled vocabulary of descriptors [14–17], as follows: "digital competencies" as a fundamental aspect, "higher education", "university teachers" and "teaching"; the search was performed in English and by using "and" operator; finally, no time limit was specified until May 2022. It is necessary to extend this research towards the use of other tools that allow the generation of scientific maps in the context of TDC.

3   Results

The result of the extraction, based on the search criteria determined in Fig. 1, permitted to obtain the references in the Scopus database according to Fig. 2, and thus answer the research questions.

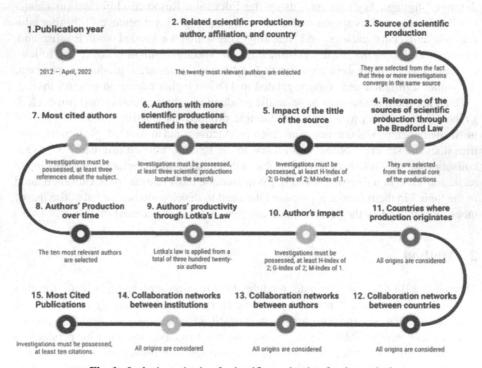

Fig. 1. Inclusion criteria of scientific production for the analysis

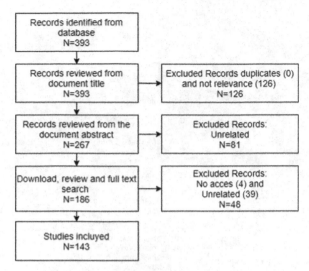

Fig. 2. References located in SCOPUS from the PRISMA methodology.

3.1 Scientific Production per Year

The search was carried out without establishing exclusion criteria regarding temporality, even until May 2022, that is, the total production of research related to the topic mentioned.

The results obtained are presented in Fig. 3.

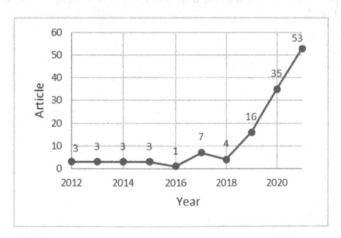

Fig. 3. Scientific production located in Scopus through the years.

3.2 Related Scientific Production by Author, Affiliation, and Country

The 20 most relevant authors were established as inclusion criteria. The results obtained are presented in Fig. 4.

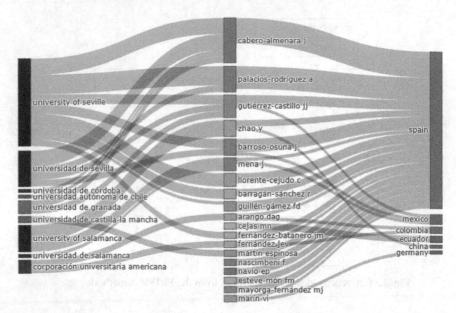

Fig. 4. Relationship of scientific production between author, affiliation, and country (Rstudio).

3.3 Data Sources

Source of Scientific Production. To determine the most relevant sources, at least 3 productions per source were established as inclusion criteria. The results obtained are presented in Fig. 5.

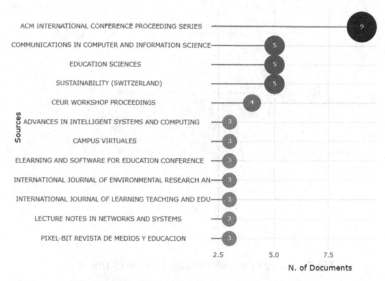

Fig. 5. Scientific production by source (Rstudio).

Relevance of the Origins of Sources Through the Grouping of Scientific Production by the Bradford's Law. Figure 6 shows the grouping of sources of scientific production through Bradford's law.

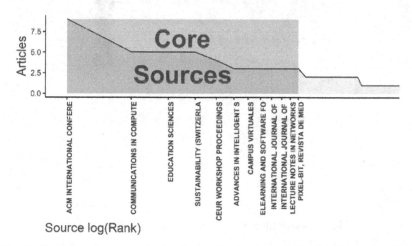

Fig. 6. Grouping of sources of scientific production through Bradford's law (Rstudio).

Impact of the Source Title

H-Index of the Source Title. In Fig. 7 it is shown the source titles with at least an H-Index of 2.

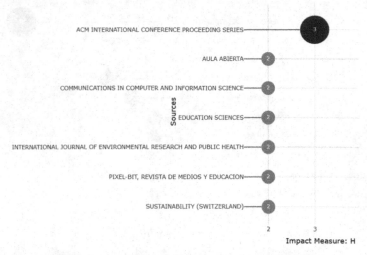

Fig. 7. Source titles with H-Index of at least 2 (Rstudio).

G-Index of the Source Title. In Fig. 8 you can see the source titles with at least one G-Index of 2.

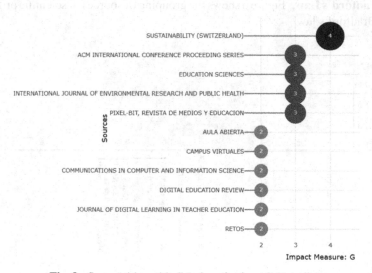

Fig. 8. Source titles with G-Index of at least 2 (Rstudio).

3.4   Authors

Authors with More Productions Located in the Search. The most relevant authors are revealed with the most productions located in Fig. 9 according to the defined search criteria, it is established at least 3 productions per researcher.

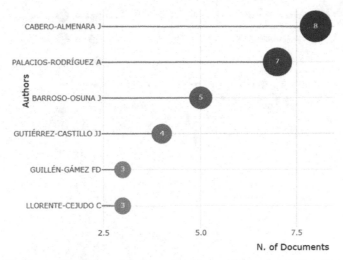

Fig. 9. Authors with more productions located in the search (Rstudio).

Most Cited Authors. Figure 10 shows the number of authors with at least 3 citations according to the productions located in the search.

Fig. 10. Most cited authors

Production of Authors over Time. Figure 11 distinguishes the production of the ten most relevant authors over time.

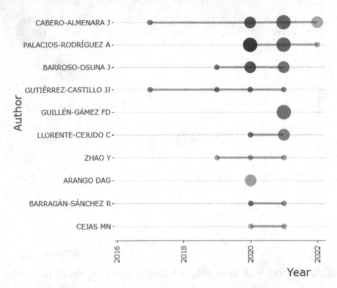

Fig. 11. Authors' production over the time (Rstudio).

Productivity of Authors Through Lotka's Law. Figure 12 shows the productivity of authors through Lotka's Law based on the scientific productions located in the search.

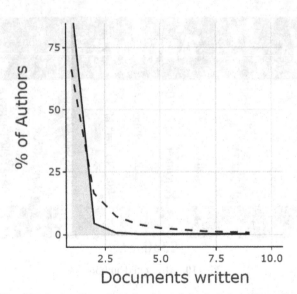

Fig. 12. Authors' productivity through Lotka's Law (Rstudio).

3.4.1 Impact of the Author

Author's H-Index. Figure 13 shows the authors with at least one H-Index of 2 based on the search carried out.

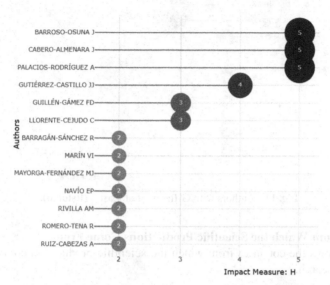

Fig. 13. Authors with an H-Index of at least 2 (Rstudio).

Author's G-Index. Figure 14 shows the authors with at least one G-Index of 2 based on the search carried out.

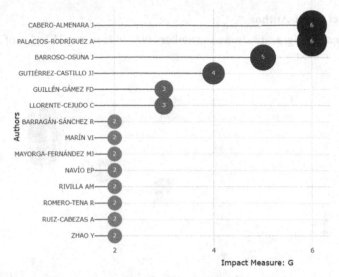

Fig. 14. Authors with G-Index of at least 2 (Rstudio).

Countries from Which the Scientific Productions Come From

Figure 15 shows the countries from which the scientific productions come from, as a result of the search.

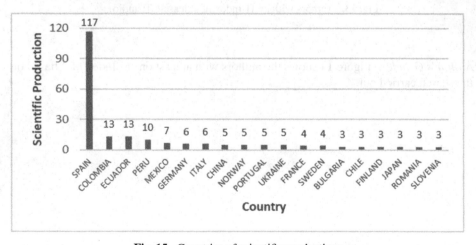

Fig. 15. Countries of scientific productions.

3.5 Collaboration Networks

Collaboration Networks Between Countries. In Fig. 16 it is presented a scheme of collaboration networks between researchers from various countries related to the topic of this study that has been collected based on the established search criteria.

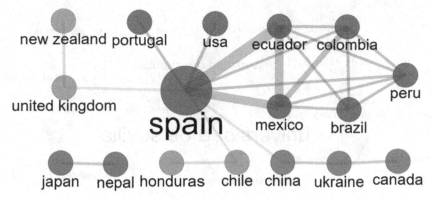

Fig. 16. Collaboration networks between countries (Rstudio).

Collaboration Networks Between Authors. In Fig. 17 it is observed a scheme of collaboration networks between researchers according to the topic of this study that has been collected based on the established search criteria.

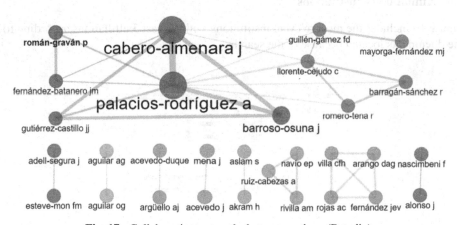

Fig. 17. Collaboration networks between authors (Rstudio).

Collaboration Networks Between Institutions. In Fig. 18 it is noticed a scheme of collaboration networks between institutions based on the topic of this study that has been gathered according to the established search criteria.

Fig. 18. Collaboration networks between institutions (Rstudio).

3.6 Affiliation of Institutions

Figure 19 includes the most relevant institutions with at least 3 affiliations according to the documents located because of the search.

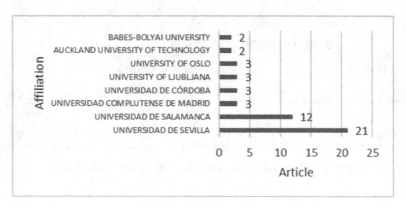

Fig. 19. Affiliation of institutions.

4 Discussion

Revision performed identifies that as an average per year there are 12.80 productions, with a standard deviation of 17.40, and an annual growth rate of 17.46%. A significant increase in publications can be observed since the year 2019. The year of greatest production is 2021 with 53 works of the totality, the year 2016, is the year of least production with just one scientific product.

There is a relationship between the authors and institutions that are disaggregated around the world, with the country where the works originate. Collaboration networks integrated by groups of researchers of various nationalities are discovered, among which Spanish authors stand out (48% of all productions have affiliation of Spanish institutions), the existence of a group of researchers is evidenced which extends from the Sevilla University to the University of Córdoba, the University of Cantabria and the University of Valencia; also to the Autonomous University of Chile and the University of Granada; finally to the Complutense University of Madrid and the University of Jaume I.

The 12.60% of the sources, that means 12 titles include at least 3 scientific publications about the subject settled, which are the following: ACM International Conference Proceeding Series; Communications in Computer and Information Science; Education Sciences (Q2); Sustainability (Switzerland) (Q2); CEUR Workshop Proceedings; Advances in Intelligent Systems and Computing (Q4); Campus Virtuales (Q1); Elearning and Software for Education Conference; International Journal of Environmental Research and Public Health (Q2); International Journal of Learning (Q4), Lecture Notes in Networks and Systems (Q4) and Pixel-Bit, Revista de Medios y Educación (Q2). Highlighting the ACM International Conference Proceeding Series source with 9 publications representing 6.3% of all documents and the Communications in Computer and Information Science, Education Sciences (Q2) and Sustainability (Q2) sources, with 5 publications each, equivalent to 3.5% individually of all productions.

Through Bradford's law [18–22] we can identify a group of just 12 sources out of a total of 95, this means 12.60% of all the sources that host to one third of the total localized productions (49 of a total of 143 productions): ACM International Conference Proceeding Series; Communications in Computer and Information Science; Education Sciences (Q2); Sustainability (Switzerland) (Q2); CEUR Workshop Proceedings; Advances in Intelligent Systems and Computing (Q4); Campus Virtuales (Q1); Elearning and Software for Education Conference; International Journal of Environmental Research and Public Health (Q2); International Journal of Learning (Q4); Lecture Notes in Networks and Systems (Q4); and Pixel-Bit Revista de Medios y Educación (Q2).

There are data sources that have an H-Index of at least 2 and that have a G-Index of at least 2 (Table 1):

Table 1. Author local impact

Source	H-Index	G-Index
Sustainability (Q2)	2	4
ACM International Conference Proceeding Series	3	3
Education Sciences (Q2)	2	3
Aula Abierta (Q3)	2	2
Communications in Computer and Information Science;	2	2
International Journal of Environmental Research and Public Health (Q2)	2	3
Pixel-Bit Revista de Medios y Educación (Q2)	2	3

This research network extends mostly through authors of Spanish origin with affiliation to the University of Seville. It is stated a list of 7 authors with at least 3 productions according to the inclusion (Table 2):

Table 2. Authors with at least 3 productions

Author	Orcid ID
Cabero-Almenara J.	0000-0002-1133-6031
Palacios-Rodriguez A.	0000-0002-0689-6317
Barroso-Osuna J.	0000-0003-0139-9140
Gutiérrez-Castillo J.	0000-0002-7536-2976
Guillén-Gamez F.	0000-0001-6470-526X
Llorente-Cejudo C.	0000-0002-4281-928X
Zhao Y.	0000-0001-5956-4546

According to Lokta's law analysis [18–20, 23–25] it is shown that, out of a total of 376 authors, only 1 author has 9 productions (0.25% of authors), only 1 author has 8 productions (0.25% of authors), only 1 author has 7 productions (0.25% of authors), only 1 author has 5 productions (0.25% of authors) and only 1 author has 4 productions (0.25% of authors), 3 authors have 3 productions (0.75% of authors); 18 authors have 2 productions (4.48% authors) and 376 authors have only one production (93.53% of authors). This means that approximately 6.5% of the works repeat authorship of at least 2 authors.

There are 13 authors who have one H-Index [26–29] of at least 2 and one G-Index [27, 28, 30] of at least 2 (Table 3).

Table 3. Author local impact

Author	Orcid ID	H-Index	G-Index
Cabero-Almenara J.	0000-0002-1133-6031	5	6
Palacios-Rodriguez A.	0000-0002-0689-6317	5	6
Barroso-Osuna J.	0000-0003-0139-9140	5	5
Gutiérrez-Castillo J.	0000-0002-7536-2976	4	4
Guillén-Gamez F.	0000-0001-6470-526X	3	3
Llorente-Cejudo C.	0000-0002-4281-928X	3	3
Barragán-Sánchez R.	0000-0001-6336-2728	2	2
Marín-Díaz V.	0000-0001-9836-2584	2	2
Mayorga-Fernández M.	0000-0003-3749-1264	2	2
Navio E.	0000-0001-8688-9602	2	2
Rivilla A.	0000-0002-1483-0668	2	2
Romero-Tena R.	0000-0001-9886-8403	2	2
Ruiz-Cabezas A.	0000-0002-2977-0485	2	2

There are at least 3 scientific productions affiliated to 6 institutions: the University of Seville, the University of Salamanca, the Complutense University of Madrid, the University of Córdoba, the University of Ljubljana and the University of Oslo. The University of Seville stands out with 21 publications.

The most relevant document is the article: Educating online student teachers to master professional digital competence: The TPACK-framework goes online, [31] with a total of 56 citations; and determines how online teacher education programs can enhance innovative ways of teaching and learning with information and communication technologies (ICTs).

It is necessary to extend this research towards the use of other tools that allow the generation of scientific maps in the context of TDC.

5 Conclusions

The analysis of scientific production per year denotes a sustained growth from the year 2019, in general, it is observed that this fact is related to the processes implemented at the educational level due to the pandemic caused by Covid 19.

It is identified a barely group of 14% of sources that host one third of the total productions that have been located in this investigation and that finally are the central nucleus of the works.

There is a large number of authors who publish a small number of works individually, while only 7% of authors have more than two publications located in the search. Likewise, there are a small number of data sources and authors that are relevant with significant H, G and M indices about the settled topic.

Almost half of all the authors are from Spain, thus, the study of this subject extends at the Ibero-American level from Spain to countries such as Ecuador, Colombia, Mexico, Brazil, Peru, Chile and Honduras; at European level it is stated a network between Spain, United Kingdom, Ukraine, Portugal and New Zealand, of Anglo-Saxon level a research network is appreciated extending from Spain to the United States and Canada. There is also a network of work between institutions and researchers from Nepal and Japan, however, these works are carried out in isolation.

The variables detailed through Software Rstudio through the Bibliometrix module help to simplify the review processes of scientific literature specially in the phase of selection and analysis of documents of any field of knowledge.

The responsible action of researchers when integrate metadata in scientific productions allows an adequate use of exploitation tools, generation of scientific maps and bibliometric analysis, in addition to contributing to the internationalization processes of higher education institutions, because this information is part of the analysis in the consolidation of the different quality rankings at a local, regional, and global level.

References

1. Calvani, A., Cartelli, A., Fini, A., Ranieri, M.: Models and instruments for assessing digital competence at school. J. e-Learn. Knowl. Soc. **4**, 44–56 (2008). https://doi.org/10.1017/cbo 9780511554445.007
2. Cuadrado, A.M.M., Sánchez, L.P., de la Torre, M.J.: Teachers digital competences in Digcomp-based university environments. Educ. em Rev. **36**, 1–21 (2020). https://doi.org/10.1590/0104-4060.75866
3. Bond, M., Marín, V.I., Dolch, C., Bedenlier, S., Zawacki-Richter, O.: Digital transformation in German higher education: student and teacher perceptions and usage of digital media. Int. J. Educ. Technol. High. Educ. **15**(1), 1–20 (2018). https://doi.org/10.1186/s41239-018-0130-1
4. Cabero-Almenara, J., Barroso-Osuna, J., Palacios-Rodríguez, A.: Digital competences of educators in Health Sciences: their relationship with some variables | Estudio de la competencia digital docente en Ciencias de la Salud. Su relación con algunas variables. Educ. Medica. **22**, 94–98 (2021). https://doi.org/10.1016/j.edumed.2020.11.014
5. García-Peñalvo, F.J., Corell, A., Abella-García, V., Grande, M.: Online assessment in higher education in the time of COVID-19. Educ. Knowl. Soc. **21**, 26 (2020). https://doi.org/10.14201/eks.23013
6. Domingo-Coscollola, M., Bosco, A., Segovia, S.C., Valero, J.A.S.: Fostering teacher's digital competence at university: the perception of students and teachers. Rev. Investig. Educ. **38**, 167–182 (2020). https://doi.org/10.6018/rie.340551
7. Esteve-Mon, F.M., Gisbert-Cervera, M., Lázaro-Cantabrana, J.L.: La competencia digital de los futuros docentes: ¿Cómo se ven los actuales estudiantes de educación? Perspect. Educ. **55**, 38–54 (2016). https://doi.org/10.4151/07189729-vol.55-iss.2-art.412
8. Gallardo, E., Marqués, L., Gisbert-Cervera, M.: Importance of ICT competences within the framework of Edutec. Rev. Electrónica Tecnol. Educ. **36**, 1–15 (2011)
9. Silva, J., Salinas, J.: Innovando con TIC en la formación inicial docente: aspectos teóricos y casos concretos. Univ. Santiago Chile y Enlaces Mineduc. **277** (2014)
10. Silva Quiroz, J., Miranda Arredondo, P.: Presencia de la competencia digital docente en los programas de formación inicial en universidades públicas chilenas. Rev. Estud. y Exp. en Educ. **19**, 149–165 (2020). https://doi.org/10.21703/rexe.20201941silva9

11. Silva, J., Miranda, P., Gisbert, M., Morales, J., Onetto, A.: Indicadores para evaluar la competencia digital docente en la formación inicial en el contexto Chileno – Uruguayo. Rev. Latinoam. Tecnol. Educ. **15**, 141–154 (2016). https://doi.org/10.17398/1695
12. Aria, M., Cuccurullo, C.: Bibliometrix: an R-tool for comprehensive science mapping analysis. J. Informetr. **11**, 959–975 (2017). https://doi.org/10.1016/j.joi.2017.08.007
13. Urrutia, G., Bonfill, X.: PRISMA declaration: a proposal to improve the publication oy systematic reviews and meta-analyses (2010). http://es.cochrane.org/sites/es.cochrane.org/files/public/uploads/PRISMA_Spanish.pdf
14. Blanco, S.A., Martín Álvarez, R.: Tesauros: ¡menuda palabrota! No todo es clínica. Actual. en Med. Fam. **15**, 509–515 (2019)
15. Ferreras, D.M.: Los tesauros (2009)
16. Torres, Á.: Thesaurus: Palabra clave. https://www.revistacomunicar.com/wp/escuela-de-autores/thesaurus-palabra-clave/
17. Tous, M.G., Salim Mattar, V.: The keys of the key words in scientific articles. Rev. MVZ Córdoba. **17**, 7–9 (2012)
18. Falcato, P.: La ley de Bradford y sus aplicaciones: una introducción. Universidad de Buenos Aires, Buenos Aires (1989)
19. Gorbea-Portal, S., Quesada, E.S.: Las supuestas «Leyes» métricas de la información. Rev. Gen. Inf. y Doc. **7**, 87–93 (1997)
20. Sembay, M., Luiz Pinto, A., Jerónimo De Macedo, D., Moreiro-González, J.A.: Aplicação da Lei de Bradford a pesquisas relacionadas a Open Government. An. Doc. **23**, 1–10 (2020). https://doi.org/10.6018/analesdoc.326771
21. Urbizagástegui Alvarado, R.: Una revisión crítica de la Ley de Bradford. Investig. Bibl. Arch. Bibl. e Inf. **10**, 16–26 (1996). https://doi.org/10.22201/iibi.0187358xp.1996.20.3835
22. Alvarado, R.U.: El crecimiento de la literatura sobre la ley de Bradford. Investig. Bibl. **30**, 51–72 (2016). https://doi.org/10.1016/j.ibbai.2016.02.003
23. Urbizagástegui Alvarado, R.: La ley de Lotka y la literatura de bibliometría. Investig. Bibl. Arch. Bibl. e Inf. **13**, 125–141 (1999). https://doi.org/10.22201/iibi.0187358xp.1999.27.3913
24. Urbizagástegui Alvarado, R.: The Scientific Productivity of Authors: an Application Model of Lotka's Law By the Generalized Inverse Power Method. Redalyc (2005)
25. Urbizagástegui Alvarado, R., Suárez, J.: La teoría epidémica en la literatura sobre la Ley de Lotka. Investig. Bibl. **22**, 91–111 (2008). https://doi.org/10.22201/iibi.0187358xp.2008.46.16942
26. Alonso, S., Cabrerizo, F.J., Herrera-Viedma, E., Herrera, F.: h-Index: a review focused in its variants, computation and standardization for different scientific fields. J. Informetr. **3**, 273–289 (2009). https://doi.org/10.1016/j.joi.2009.04.001
27. Byl, L., et al.: White paper: measuring research output through bibliometrics. Univ. Waterloo. 1–35 (2016). https://doi.org/10.13140/RG.2.1.3302.5680
28. Hirsch, J.E.: An index to quantify an individual's scientific research output. Proc. Natl. Acad. Sci. U.S.A. **102**, 16569–16572 (2005). https://doi.org/10.1073/pnas.0507655102
29. Mazurek, J.: A modification to Hirsch index allowing comparisons across different scientific fields. Curr. Sci. **114**, 2238–2239 (2018)
30. Eggue, L.: Theory and practise of the G-index. Scientometrics **69**, 131–152 (2006)
31. Tømte, C., Enochsson, A.B., Buskqvist, U., Kårstein, A.: Educating online student teachers to master professional digital competence: the TPACK-framework goes online. Comput. Educ. **84**, 26–35 (2015). https://doi.org/10.1016/j.compedu.2015.01.005

Decision Making by Applying Z-Numbers

Johnny Bajaña Zajia[1,2]([✉]) [ID], J. A. Morente-Molinera[1] [ID], Inés Amaya Díaz[3] [ID], and E. Herrera-Viedma[1,4] [ID]

[1] University of Granada, Granada, Spain
jbajana@correo.ugr.es, {jamoren,viedma}@decsai.ugr.es
[2] Universidad Técnica de Cotopaxi, Cotopaxi, Ecuador
[3] Universidad Técnica de Babahoyo, Los Ríos, Ecuador
iamaya@utb.edu.ec
[4] Department of Electrical and Computer Engineering, King Abdulaziz University, Jeddah, Saudi Arabia

Abstract. The article presents a model for selecting the recruitment of a soccer player for a Spanish Second Division soccer team. Considering that this is a very complex model, which can be approached from several aspects, this paper is limited only to the criteria related to the recruitment or disposition of the player. Decision making (DM) is still an open question. Zadeh has developed Z-number for modelling fuzzy numbers with the degree of confidence. In this paper, a new DM method based on Z-number is proposed to deal with linguistic decision making problems. The decision making process can be easily carried out using Z-number calculations. A numerical example on DM is used to exemplify the effectiveness of the proposed method. The Z-numbers in the decision making matrix are converted to the crisp numbers for decision making, which is very important for deciding in soccer injury situations.

Keywords: Decision-making · Z-number · Fuzzy set · Triangular fuzzy number

1 Introduction

The ability to respond flexibly to changing circumstances is fundamental to the adaptive behaviour of humans and to artificial systems, such as software- and hardware-level DSSs. Decision making is an important source of both theoretical activities (e.g., in economics, computer science, and AI) and practical challenges (e.g., in business, politics and conflict resolution, investments and insurance, voting and consumer behaviour, and medicine). These interests have led to a wide divergence in research on decision processes. Of course, there have been important attempts to develop domain-independent perspectives, such as behaviour-based decision models (e.g., heuristics and biases and prospect theory) and information processing approaches (e.g., neural networks and cognitive

Supported by University of Granada.

architectures). However, these attempts tend to occur from only one point of view and do not create a single point of view.

To favour the use of group knowledge and experience in real situations, many group decision making (GDM) methods have been presented. These have different approaches, such as aggregation of the preferences of different decision makers [23] or group consensus convergence [20–22]. The goal of reaching group consensus is to arrive at a solution that is preferred or accepted by the majority or all decision makers [25]. To accelerate the arrival of group consensus, multi-criteria group decision-making method for heterogeneous and dynamic contexts using multi-granular fuzzy linguistic modelling and consensus measures [24]. A group is usually considered to be satisfied with a generated solution when the predetermined group consensus level is reached [27]. This seems to show that a high level of group consensus indicates high group satisfaction with the GDM.

The remainder of the paper is organized as follows: Sect. 2 discuses some definitions and concepts. In Sect. 3 the proposed method of decision making using Z-number is discussed. Section 4 contains an example to illustrate the proposed approach. At last, a conclusions is made in the Sect. 5.

2 Background Information

2.1 Essential Definitions

Fuzzy Subset
The theory of fuzzy subsets has been created to model human knowledge and perception. The specificity of fuzzy logic is its ability to bridge the gap between articulated linguistic descriptions and numerical models of systems [30].

Let E be a set with finite or infinite. Let A be a set contained in E. Then the set of ordered pair $(x, \mu_A(x)))$ gives the fuzzy subset A of E, where x is an element in E and $\mu_A(x)$ is the degree of membership of x in E.

Fuzzy Number
A fuzzy number is a generalization of a regular, real number and are very useful to represent data corresponding to uncertain situations.

There are several methods to classify or order the fuzzy numbers. The concept of probability measure was used to determine the order of the fuzzy numbers considering the mean and dispersion of the alternatives [31]. In addition, a computational approach was proposed to rank the alternatives using fuzzy numbers [32].

It refers to a connected set of possible values, where each possible value has its own weight between 0 and 1. A fuzzy number is thus a special case of a convex, normalized fuzzy set of the real line.

Triangular Fuzzy Number
The fuzzy set theory is first introduced by Prof. Zadeh [18]. Then, many scholars from around the world used it in different fields of study. A triangular fuzzy number (TFN) that is known as a type of trapezoidal fuzzy number wide-spread

employed in the literature. The mathematical membership function $\mu_o : R \rightarrow [0, 1]$, the values between 0 and 1 represent partial membership, where the higher the value, the stronger the degree of membership, that is defined for the TFNs $\bar{o} = (a, b, c)$ is given as follows [19].

$$(a_1, b_1, c_1) \oplus (a_2, b_2, c_2) = (a_1 + a_2, b_1 + b_2, c_1 + c_2) \tag{1}$$

$$(a_1, b_1, c_1) - (a_2, b_2, c_2) = (a_1 - a_2, b_1 - b_2, c_1 - c_2) \tag{2}$$

$$\frac{a_1, b_1, c_1}{a_2, b_2, c_2} = \left(\frac{a_1}{c_2}, \frac{b_1}{b_2}, \frac{c_1}{a_2} \right) \tag{3}$$

$$(a_1, b_1, c_1)^{-1} = \left(\frac{1}{c_1}, \frac{1}{b_1}, \frac{1}{a_1} \right) \tag{4}$$

The above operational rules are addition, subtraction, multiplication, division and reciprocity of fuzzy numbers, respectively (Fig. 1).

A fuzzy number $\widetilde{A} = (a, b, c)$ is called triangular fuzzy number if its membership function is given by

$$\mu_A(X) = \begin{cases} 0, & x < a \\ \dfrac{x - a}{b - a}, & a \leq x \leq b \\ \dfrac{c - x}{c - b}, & a \leq x \leq b \\ 1, & x > c \end{cases} \tag{5}$$

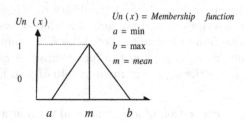

$Un(x)$ = Membership function
a = min
b = max
m = mean

Fig. 1. Triangular fuzzy number $A = (a_1, a_2, a_3)$

2.2   Z-Numbers

Decisions are based on information. To be useful, information must be reliable. Basically, the concept of a Z-number relates to the issue of reliability of information. A Z-number, Z, has two components, Z = (A, B). The first component, A, is a restriction (constraint) on the values which a real-valued uncertain variable, X, is allowed to take. The second component, B, is a measure of reliability (certainty) of the first component. Typically, A and B are described in a natural language. Example: (about 45 min, very sure). An important issue relates to computation with Z-numbers. Examples: What is the sum of (about 45 min, very sure) and (about 30 min, sure)? What is the square root of (approximately 100, likely)? Computation with Z-numbers falls within the province of Computing with Words (CW or CWW) [13]. In this note, the concept of a Z-number is introduced and methods of computation with Z-numbers are outlined. The concept of a Z-number has a potential for many applications, especially in the realms of economics, decision analysis, risk assessment, prediction, anticipation and rule-based characterization of imprecise functions and relations [6,9,16].

Linguistic Variable

Linguistic variable [8] is a variable whose values are not numbers but words or sentences in a natural or artificial language. The concept of fuzzy linguistic variable is a staple of the type-1 fuzzy set theory. It has the remarkable property of putting together symbols and the meaning of those symbols as proper elements of a computational system. Essentially, the linguistic variable concept introduces two levels for manipulating words, the syntactic or symbolic level, where the names of the words are given and certain operations can be defined working on those symbols to generate new symbols, and the semantic or meaning level, where type-1 fuzzy sets are introduced to give the meaning of each symbolic word. Both levels are expressed explicitly in of a linguistic variable given by Zadeh.

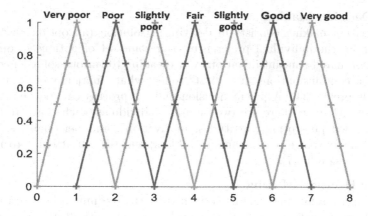

Fig. 2. Membership function of five levels of linguistic variables

2.3   Decision-Making

Decision making has been historically addressed by multiple disciplines, from the classical ones such as philosophy, statistics, mathematics and economics, to the most recent ones such as Artificial Intelligence. Decision-making methods often apply fuzzy sets in their calculations. In [33] a decision method was presented that represented uncertain quantities as fuzzy sets and subsequently obtained an optimal alternative.

The theories and models developed aim at rational support for complex decision making [27]. They include typical activities such as:

a) Defining the decision making problem.
b) Analyse the problem and identify solution alternatives $X = x_1, ... x_n (n \geq 2)$
c) Establish evaluation criterion(s).
d) Evaluate alternatives.
e) Rank and select the best alternative.
f) Implement and follow up.

When the number of criteria satisfy that $C = c_1, c_2, ... c_m (m \geq 2)$ it is considered a multi-criteria decision making problem (21). When the number of experts is such that $K = k_1, k_2, ... k_n (n \geq 2)$ it is considered a group decision making problem [28].

Decision-making can be defined, in very general terms, as a process or set of processes that result in the selection of an element among a set of possible alternatives. Within this general definition, the processes can be natural and conscious, as in the deliberate choice between alternatives, but also unconscious or artificial (as in an expert system that provides decision support). Moreover, decisions can refer to what to do (action), but also to what to believe (opinion).

Group Decision-Making

Group decision making consists in deriving a solution (an option or a set of options) from the individual preferences over some set of options in question. The solution may be meant in various ways leading to various solution concept. Basically, it contains options that "best" reflect what a majority of the involved individuals prefer [34]. A group decision-making process can be defined as a decision situation: (i) there are two or more individuals, each characterized by his or her own perceptions, attitudes, motivations, and personalities; (ii) all recognize the existence of a common problem; and (iii) all attempt to reach a collective decision [5, 17].

Dynamic Decision-Making

Dynamic decision making (DDM) is defined by three common features: a series of actions must be taken over time to achieve some overall goal, the actions are interdependent so that later decisions depend on earlier actions, and the environment changes both spontaneously and as a consequence of earlier actions [2]. Dynamic decision tasks differ from sequential decision tasks [3] in that the former are primarily concerned with controlling dynamic systems over time, whereas the latter are more concerned with sequential search for information to be used in making decisions.

Group decision-making processes are usually divided into two processes: the consensus process and the selection process. Both processes are executed sequentially to obtain the alternative solution. The consensus process, in which the individuals in the group argue and reason their opinions with the objective of reaching the highest level of agreement, is carried out first. This process is usually coordinated by a moderator, whose objective is to direct the negotiation and help individuals to bring positions closer together. At all times, the degree of existing agreement is obtained, so that if this is satisfactory, this process is concluded and the selection process begins, whose objective is to find out which is the alternative solution, considering the preferences communicated by the individuals of the group. If this is not the case, the individuals are urged to discuss again and modify their opinions in order to bring their positions closer together. Thus, we can define group decision making as the iterative and dynamic procedure in which a group of individuals modify their initial opinions until their positions on the best decision are sufficiently close. When this occurs, the selection process is carried out to find out which is the consensus solution [29].

Decision Support Systems

A DSS is defined [4] as an interactive computer-based system that supports rather than replaces decision-makers, uses data and models to solve problems with different degrees of structure and focuses on the effectiveness rather than the efficiency of decision processes (facilitates the decision process).

3 Methodology

3.1 Build the Fuzzy Decision-Making Matrix

Let the matrix M be the decision making matrix, m is the basic element of matrix, where $m_{ij} = Z_{ij}(\widetilde{A}, \widetilde{B}), i = 1, ..., m; j = 1, ...n$ and $Z_{ij}(\widetilde{A}, \widetilde{B})$ is the evaluation of the jth criteria for the ith selection. $\widetilde{A}$ and $\widetilde{B}$ is respectively the constraint and reliability of a Z-number. The knowledge, for example, if an opinion is expressed as "The price of soccer players is high, most likely." then the opinion can be described with Z-number $(H; VH)$ [10,12,14].

3.2 Convert Linguistic Value into Numerical Value

Some knowledge/opinions are presented as linguistic value, in order to deal with this linguistic value, these linguistic variables should be converted into numerical values under the frame of fuzzy set which is described by Fig. 2. For example, if the $Z - number$ is $(G; VG)$ with linguistic value, then according the membership function of linguistic, the numerical value is $((5, 7, 9); (7, 9, 9))$ [11,13].

3.3 Normalize the Fuzzy Decision-Making Matrix

Using the linear scale transformation, which enables decision makers to transform TFNs into the closed interval $[0, 1]$. The evaluation criterion may be either benefit criterion (i.e., the larger the rating, the greater the preference) or cost criterion (e.g., the smaller the rating, the greater the preference), and the normalization formulas are different for cost and benefit criteria [1]. The normalized fuzzy decision matrix $\widetilde{R} = [\widetilde{r}_{ij}]_{mxn}$ can be computed by:

$$\widetilde{r_{ij}} = \left(\frac{l_{ij}}{u_j}, \frac{m_{ij}}{u_j}, \frac{u_{ij}}{u_j}\right) \, and \, j \in B \tag{6}$$

$$\widetilde{r_{ij}} = \left(\frac{l^-_j}{u_j}, \frac{l^-_j}{m_j}, \frac{l^-_j}{l_j}\right) \, and \, j \in C \tag{7}$$

where B in Eq. (7) are the sets of benefit criteria and C in Eq. (8) and are the sets of cost criteria.

3.4   Convert the Z-Numbers to Crisp Number

Let $m_{ij} = Z_{ij}(\widetilde{A}, \widetilde{B}), i = 1, ..., m; j = 1, ...n,$ $\widetilde{A} = a_l^{ij}, a_m^{ij}, a_u^{ij},$ $\widetilde{R} = r_{ij}^l, m_{ij}^m, r_{ij}^u,$ the combination between Restriction $\widetilde{A}$ and Reliability $\widetilde{R}$ can be denoted by the following equation according to the canonical representation of multiplication operation on t riangular fuzzy number.

$$w(Z_{ij}) = w(\widetilde{A}, \widetilde{R})$$
$$w(Z_{ij}) = \widetilde{A} \otimes \widetilde{R}$$
$$w(Z_{ij}) = (a_{ij}^l, a_{ij}^m, a_{ij}^u) \otimes (r_{ij}^l, r_{ij}^m, r_{ij}^u)$$
$$w(Z_{ij}) = (a_{ij}^l + 4X a_{ij}^m + a_{ij}^u) \otimes (r_{ij}^l + 4X r_{ij}^m, r_{ij}^u)$$

3.5   The Weight of Alternatives

The weight of each alternative can be defined as follows:

$$priority = \sum w(Z_a)(wZ_f) \tag{8}$$

where Z_a is the weight of the criteria, and Z_f is the value of each criteria.

4   Illustrative Example

In the following, we show an example of football player selection, to illustrate the procedure of the proposed approach. There are four different options, namely Player 1, Player 2, Player 3 and Player 4. Three main criteria are taken into account (price of the player, time without injury and number of goals scored). For each player, depending on the particular case, the price (taken from the German transfermarkt.com website) is the most significant element, which can be described by the linguistic variable "Very high". Similarly, the length of time without injury and the number of goals are also described by the linguistic notion of Z-number. The evaluation of the linguistic criteria of the four players can be described in Table 1.

Based to the membership function given by Eq. (1) and described by Fig. 2, the linguistic variable can be converted into a numerical value, which is described in Table 2.

Table 1. Decision matrix with linguistic values

	Price (Million USD)	Time without injury (Months)	Goals (Amount)
Player 1	((4, 5, 6), VH)	((7, 10, 12), M)	((7, 8, 9), VH)
Player 2	((6, 7, 8), H)	((6, 7, 8), VH)	((7, 8, 10), H)
Player 3	((4, 5, 6), H)	((4, 5, 6), H)	((1, 2, 3), M)
Player 4	((3, 4, 5), H)	((10, 11, 12), H)	((5, 6, 7), H)

Table 2. Decision matrix with numerical values

	Price (Million USD)	Time without injury (Months)	Goals (Amount)
Player 1	((4, 5, 6), (0.75, 1, 1))	((7, 10, 12), (0.25, 0.5, 0.75))	((7, 8, 9), (0.75, 1, 1))
Player 2	((6, 7, 8), (0.5, 0.75, 1))	((6, 7, 8), (0.75, 1, 1))	((7, 8, 10), (0.5, 0.75, 1))
Player 3	((4, 5, 6), (0.5, 0.75, 1))	((4, 5, 6), (0.5, 0.75, 1))	((1, 2, 3), (0.25, 0.5, 0.75))
Player 4	((3, 4, 5), (0.5, 0.75, 1))	((10, 11, 12), (0.5, 0.75, 1))	((5, 6, 7), (0.5, 0.75, 1))

The third step consists of normalising the fuzzy data to facilitate the mathematical calculations in the decision process according to Eqs. (6) and (7). The price and goal criteria are cost criteria, while the non-injury time criterion belongs to the profit criterion. The standardised decision matrix is presented in Table 3.

Table 3. Normalized decision matrix

	Price (Million USD)	Time without injury (Months)	Goals (Amount)
Player 1	((0.25, 0.38, 0.5), (0.75, 1, 1))	((0, 0.17, 0.42), (0.25, 0.5, 0.75))	((0.7, 0.8, 0.9), (0.75, 1, 1))
Player 2	((0, 0.13, 0.25), (0.5, 0.75, 1))	((0.33, 0.42, 0.5), (0.75, 1, 1))	((0.7, 0.8, 0.1), (0.5, 0.75, 1))
Player 3	((0.25, 0.38, 0.5), (0.5, 0.75, 1))	((0, 0.17, 0.42), (0.5, 0.75, 1))	((0.1, 0.2, 0.3), (0.25, 0.5, 0.75))
Player 4	((0.38, 0.5, 0.63), (0.5, 0.75, 1))	((0, 0.08, 0.17), (0.5, 0.75, 1))	((0.5, 0.6, 0.7), (0.5, 0.75, 1))

The fourth step consists of converting the Z numbers to crisp numbers according to the triangular fuzzy number multiplication operation. The result of the normalized matrix is detailed in Table 4 and Table 5.

Table 4. Decision matrix which combines the restraint and reliability of z-numbers

	Price (Million USD)	Time without injury (Months)	Goals (Amount)
Player 1	(0.25, 0.38, 0.5) ⊗ (0.75, 1, 1)	(0, 0.17, 0.42) ⊗ (0.25, 0.5, 0.75)	(0.7, 0.8, 0.9) ⊗ (0.75, 1, 1)
Player 2	(0, 0.13, 0.25) ⊗ (0.5, 0.75, 1)	(0.33, 0.42, 0.5) ⊗ (0.75, 1, 1)	(0.7, 0.8, 0.1) ⊗ (0.5, 0.75, 1)
Player 3	(0.25, 0.38, 0.5) ⊗ (0.5, 0.75, 1)	(0, 0.17, 0.42) ⊗ (0.50, 0.75, 1)	(0.1, 0.2, 0.3) ⊗ (0.25, 0.5, 0.75)
Player 4	(0.38, 0.5, 0.63) ⊗ (0.5, 0.75, 1)	(0, 0.08, 0.17) ⊗ (0.5, 0.75, 1)	(0.5, 0.6, 0.7) ⊗ (0.5, 0.75, 1)

To conclude, after normalising the weights of the criteria, according to Eq. (4), the final priority weights of the four players are obtained, which are shown in Table 6. The result can be seen in Table 6. The result can be depicted in Fig. 3.

Table 5. Decision matrix with crisp numbers

	Price (Million USD)	Time without injury (Months)	Goals (Amount)
Player 1	0.36	0.09	0.77
Player 2	0.09	0.40	0.50
Player 3	0.28	0.14	0.10
Player 4	0.38	0.06	0.45

Table 6. The weight of players selection

	Price (Million USD)	Time without injury (Months)	Goals amount	Priority weight
Player 1	0.36	0.09	0.77	0.41
Player 2	0.09	0.40	0.50	0.33
Player 3	0.28	0.14	0.10	0.17
Player 4	0.38	0.06	0.45	0.30

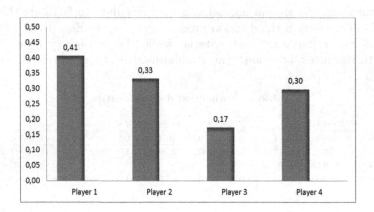

Fig. 3. The weight of players selection

5   Discussion and Conclusions

Decision-making has been the subject of intense research in recent decades, and fuzzy sets have been applied in multiple decision making processes, since uncertainty and complexity are phenomena present in the real world. But the problem is that the reliability of the information is not efficiently taken into account.

Many more complicated cases still need to be considered in the future, such as uncertain weights of criteria problems, etc., the calculation with Z-numbers requires further study in wider fields.

The presented case demonstrates that the developed method using Z-numbers is a great option for approaching and solving problems related to the selection of soccer players.

The proposal made by Zadeh, about Z numbers are a new vision, which has more capacity to describe the uncertainty. In this paper, we solve the decision making using Z-number, and a method is proposed to deal with Z-number. Finally, the Z numbers of the decision matrix are converted to crisp numbers. In the following, simple additive weighting methods can be used to solve multi-criteria fuzzy decision making.

Before concluding, the method is demonstrated with a numerical example to illustrate the proposed procedure. Analysing the results of the example detailed in Chapter III, it is evident that one of the criteria, the number of goals scored, has a strong influence on the final decision process, players 1 and 3 have very similar values in the criteria of price and time without injury, however, when applying the decision making process, there is a marked difference in the order and its influence on the final decision, using the risk analysis of the criteria.

Acknowledgment. The authors would like to acknowledge al CITIC-UGR and also the financial support from the Universidad Técnica de Cotopaxi. This work was supported by the project B-TIC-590-UGR20 co-funded by the Programa Operativo FEDER 2014-2020 and the Regional Ministry of Economy, Knowledge, Enterprise and Universities (CECEU) of Andalusia, by the China Scholarship Council (CSC), and by the project PID2019-103880RBI00 funded by MCIN/AEI/10.13039/501100011033.

References

1. Perfilieva, I.: Fuzzy transforms: theory and applications. Fuzzy Sets Syst. (157), 993–1023 (2006)
2. Edwards, W.: Dynamic decision theory and probabilistic information processing. J. Hum. Factors 59–73 (1962)
3. Diederich, A.: Decision and Choice: Sequential Decision Making. International Encyclopedia of the Social and Behavioral Sciences: Methodology, Mathematics, and Computer Science. Pergamon, Amsterdam (2001)
4. Eom, S., Kim, E.: A survey of decision support system applications (1995–2001). J. Oper. Res. Soc. **57**(11), 1264 (2006)
5. Bui, T.X.: Co-oP: A Group Decision Support System for Cooperative Multiple Criteria Group Decision Making. Springer, Heidelberg (1987). https://doi.org/10.1007/3-540-18753-7
6. Zadeh, L.A.: Inf. Sci. Int. J. **181**(14), 2923–2932 (2011)
7. Lotfi, A., Zadeh, L.A.: The concept of a linguistic variable and its application to approximate reasoning. Part I. Inf. Sci. **8**(199), 249 (1975)
8. Nurnadiah, Z., Abdullah, L.: A new linguistic variable in interval type-2 fuzzy entropy weight of a decision making method. Procedia Comput. Sci. **24**, 42–53 (2013)

9. Aliev, R.A., Alizadeh, A.V., Huseynov, O.H., Jabbarova, K.I.: Z-number based linear programming. Int. J. Intell. Syst. **30**, 563–589 (2015)
10. Casasnovas, J., Riera, J.V.: On the addition of discrete fuzzy numbers. WSEAS Trans. Math. **5**, 549–554
11. Hanss, M.: Applied Fuzzy Arithmetic. An Introduction with Engineering Applications. Springer, Heidelberg (2005). https://doi.org/10.1007/b138914
12. Kang, B., Wei, D., Li, Y., Deng, Y.: Decision making using Z-numbers under uncertain environment. J. Comput. Inf. Syst. **8**, 2807–2814
13. Pal, S.K., Banerjee, R., Dutta, S., Sarma, S.: An insight into the Z-number approach to CWW. Fundamenta Informaticae 197–229 (2013)
14. Bingyi, K., Daijun, W., Ya, L., Yong, D.: A method of converting Z-number to classical fuzzy number. J. Inf. Comput. Sci. **9**(3), 703–709 (2012)
15. Jiang, W., Xie, Ch., Luo, Y., Tang, Y.: Ranking Z-numbers with an improved ranking method for generalized fuzzy numbers. J. Intell. Fuzzy Syst. **32**, 1931–1943 (2017)
16. Li, Y., Garg, H., Deng, Y.: A new uncertainty measure of discrete Z-numbers. Int. J. Fuzzy Syst. **22**(3), 760–776 (2020). https://doi.org/10.1007/s40815-020-00819-8
17. Li, Y., Garg, H., Deng, Y.: Decision making procedure based on Jaccard similarity measure with Z-numbers. Sci. - Technol. 561–574 (2017)
18. Zadeh, L.: Fuzzy sets. Inf. Control **8**, 338–353 (1965)
19. Chang, D.: Applications of the extent analysis method on fuzzy AHP. Eur. J. Oper. Res. **95**, 649–655 (1996)
20. Hou, F., Triantaphyllou, E.: An iterative approach for achieving consensus when ranking a finite set of alternatives by a group of experts. Eur. J. Oper. Res. **275**(2), 570–579 (2019)
21. Zhang, Z., Pedrycz, W.: Goal programming approaches to managing consistency and consensus for intuitionistic multiplicative preference relations in group decision making. IEEE Trans. Fuzzy Syst. **26**(6), 3261–3275 (2018)
22. Wan, S., Wang, F., Dong, J.: A group decision-making method considering both the group consensus and multiplicative consistency of interval-valued intuitionistic fuzzy preference relations. Inf. Sci. **466**, 109–128 (2018)
23. Liu, P.: Multiple attribute group decision making method based on interval-valued intuitionistic fuzzy power Heronian aggregation operators. Comput. Ind. Eng. **108**, 199–212 (2017)
24. Morente-Molinera, J.A., Wu, X., Morfeq, A., Al-Hmouz, R., Herrera-Viedma, E.: A novel multi-criteria group decision-making method for heterogeneous and dynamic contexts using multi-granular fuzzy linguistic modelling and consensus measures. Inf. Fusion **53**, 240–250 (2020)
25. Herrera-Viedma, E., Cabrerizo, F., Kacprzyk, J., Pedrycz, W.: A review of soft consensus models in a fuzzy environment. Inf. Fusion **17**, 4–13 (2014)
26. Dong, Y., Zha, Q., Zhang, H., Herrera, F.: Consensus reaching and strategic manipulation in group decision making with trust relationships. IEEE Trans. Syst. Man Cybern.: Syst. **51**, 6304–6318 (2021)
27. Herrera, F., Martinez, L., Sanchez, P.: Managing non-homogeneous information in group decision making. Eur. J. Oper. Res. **166**, 115–132 (2005)
28. Sailunaz, K., Alhajj, R.: Emotion and sentiment analysis from Twitter text. J. Comput. Sci. **36** (2019)

29. Callejas, E.: Toma de decisiones en grupo en ambientes multicriterio, heterogéneos y lingüísticos (2020). Universidad Nacional de Educación a Distancia (España). Escuela Internacional de Doctorado. Programa de Doctorado en Ingeniería de Sistemas y Control

30. Dubois, D., Nguyen, H.T., Prade, H., Sugeno, M.: The Real Contribution of Fuzzy Systems. Fuzzy Systems: Modelling and Control, pp. 8–10. Kluwer, Boston (1998)

31. Lee, E., Li, R.: Comparison of fuzzy numbers based on the probability measure of fuzzy events. Comput. Math. Appl. **15**, 887–896 (1988)

32. Dias, O.: Ranking alternatives using fuzzy numbers: a computational approach. Fuzzy Sets Syst. **56**, 247–252 (1993)

33. Jain, R.: Decision-making in the presence of fuzzy variables. IEEE Trans. Syst. Man Cybern. **6**, 698–703 (1976)

34. Kacprzyk, J.: Group decision making with a fuzzy linguistic majority. Fuzzy Sets Syst. **18**, 105–118 (1986)

Comparative Analysis of the Performance of Machine Learning Techniques Applied to Real and Synthetic Fraud-Oriented Datasets

Marco Sánchez[1] and Luis Urquiza-Aguiar[2][(✉)]

[1] Departamento de Informática y Ciencias de la Computación,
Escuela Politécnica Nacional, Ladrón de Guevara E11-253, Quito 170517, Ecuador
marco.sanchez01@epn.edu.ec
[2] Departamento de Electrónica, Telecomunicaciones y Redes de Información,
Escuela Politécnica Nacional, Ladrón de Guevara E11-253, Quito 170517, Ecuador
luis.urquiza@epn.edu.ec

Abstract. One of the most critical resources today is information, an intangible asset that has become a vital research source. On many occasions, access to data becomes a complex and challenging task. For many organizations sharing information, it is often a risk in terms of security and privacy, especially if the data is sensitive. In response to this problem, synthetic data emerges as a valid alternative, generated by different methods and techniques from an original or real dataset, allowing sharing of information very close to reality. In this work, an experiment is carried out that allows validating the efficiency of synthetic versus real datasets by applying a model that predicts possible fraud cases in a dataset based on machine learning algorithms LDA and Random Forest or Gradient Boosting. We compared the prediction performance of our model over the real and synthetic datasets using metric ROC-AUC curves. Our results show a similar behavior among the data sets in our model, suggesting a promising path in the use of synthetic data sets for this kind of applications.

Keywords: Fraud · Real and synthetic dataset · Classification methods · AUC-ROC · Topic modeling

1 Introduction

Fraud is a global concern that affects both public and private institutions, and it encompasses a wide range of illegal actions, including deliberate deceit or misrepresentation. The Association of Certified Fraud Examiners (ACFE) defines fraud as "any purposeful or deliberate act of depriving someone of property or money by cunning, deception, or other unfair acts." [1].

According to a Price Waterhouse Coopers investigation, 30% of the organizations examined have already been victims of fraud. Furthermore, 80% of their fraud was done within the company's ranks, particularly in administrative departments such as accounting, operations, sales, and management, not to mention customer service relationships [3]. Often unknown within a corporation, fraud-related practices define a sequence of anomalies and illegal acts defined by fraudsters' purposeful deceit. Most discovered abnormalities result from a lack of internal control systems, and in such cases, fraudsters perpetrate fraud by leveraging the flaws [4]. Because humans commit fraud, it is closely related to their behavior. Therefore, understanding the motivations of perpetrators or their psychological and personality traits that lead them to cross ethical boundaries can provide a new perspective for fraud detection [5]. There is agreement that prevention should be a primary approach to reducing fraud through effective risk management. Avoiding fraud saves time and money since detecting it after it has occurred makes it almost impossible to recover what was stolen. To increase fraud prevention, companies must identify those factors that drive people to commit fraud and understand this behavior [6]. Numerous theories have tried to explain this issue, being Cressey's Fraud Triangle Theory (FTT) and Wolf and Hermanson's Fraud Diamond Theory (FDT) [7], the most referenced in this field. Both techniques examine in-depth the invoices that motivate committing fraud.

One of the most difficult challenges to the investigation and study of fraud is the lack of access to data linked to this issue. Except for studies conducted by private entities such as the Federal Bureau of Investigation (FBI) and ACFE, information with evidence of fraudulent activities associated with fraud theory, in which communications related to pressure, opportunity, and rationalization are observed, is incipient in the scientific community. They were successful in obtaining data related to this topic of research. For the development of fraud prevention methods, fraud-related data is essential. Actual datasets are scarce due to infringements of copyright and intellectual property. Due to the difficulties of acquiring this sensitive information, the fabrication of synthetic data is a viable approach for acquiring fraud data. According to several experts, synthetic data is the key to making ML and AI quicker and their algorithms more effective at predicting fraudulent behavior, particularly when acquiring actual data is costly or difficult [8].

The scientific community often employs synthetic data production. These data are often created to fit particular criteria not present in the original data. Researchers may manipulate data more freely and test a broader range of settings and scenarios in their applications by creating synthetic datasets [9]. In experimental investigations, synthetic datasets that follow statistical distributions and data from real-world applications are used as test datasets. Synthetic datasets allow testing the behavior of an algorithm or data structure under specific conditions or in extreme situations. Also, for testing scalability, synthetic datasets are often suitable [10].

This article analyzes the validity of synthetic data generated through neural networks and tools available on the internet, which synthesize data based directly on real data of interest. The real data was obtained through simulation with students from the Escuela Politécnica Nacional (EPN). Validation of the use of synthetic data for research requires a comparison of results derived from synthetic data with those based on original data.

Through a model that allows detecting suspected fraud behaviors which use a theory to analyze this phenomenon from the point of view of human behavior known as FTT, plus modeling of topics and automatic learning algorithms as classification methods allows alerting on the possibility of fraud in a dataset. This model will be used to carry out a comparative study of real and synthetic datasets. In this work, the validation of three datasets generated by different methods is carried out using the mentioned model, in which topic modeling is applied, which is a widely used approach in text mining and provides a complete representation of a corpus through the inference of latent content variables called topics. This technique assigns a probability to a text or document belonging to a specific topic [11]. Different classification methods will use the probability that a document belongs to a topic to identify which technique is more compatible with topic modeling and efficiently identify phrases suspected of fraud. The AUC-ROC curve was used to measure the classification models' performance. As a result, it was observed that the Random Forest (RF) and Gradient Boosting algorithms were the most efficient in predicting possible fraud cases, and these methods will be used to compare the datasets under study.

The rest of this paper is organized as follows: Sect. 2 presents a review of the literature in the area of dataset comparison. Section 3 describes the data preparation and the methodology used in this work. Next, Sect. 4 presents the experiment and the results. Finally, Sect. 5 presents the conclusions and future work.

2   Related Work

Many areas of study use synthetically generated data, from data mining to software engineering to artificial intelligence. However, few works are in charge of comparative analysis of synthetic datasets against real datasets based on their performance applying classification methods. In this sense, the following studies were found in the literature contributing to this topic of study.

In [12], signal detection performance based on synthetic training data is compared with the performance of real-world training images. With synthetic and real data and a configurable number of training samples, Viola-Jones detectors are constructed for 4 distinct traffic lights. We test and evaluate detectors. The goal of [13] is to investigate whether synthetic data can be used as a reliable substitute for real-world data in machine learning systems. This research evaluates the performance of synthetic datasets when used to train machine learning models. Using three object identification methods, [14] verified the synthetic data for model pretraining and data augmentation to examine the synthetic dataset's utility. Our findings demonstrate that the synthetic dataset considerably enhances model pretraining and data augmentation for small and medium-sized real-world datasets, illustrating the utility and promise of synthetic data in aerial imagery. In [15], they validate five studies on the omission of suggested medicine, the influence of time to procedure, and hospitalization measures on survival after discharge, imaging risks, and diabetes therapies. Institutional review board (IRB) approval was acquired to utilize real data, allowing real and synthetic data comparison. These studies evaluated the accuracy and precision of synthetic patient data-based estimations. On the other hand [13], experimented with studying the validity of performing machine learning on synthetic data. They compared evaluation metrics from machine learning models trained on synthetic data with metrics from machine learning models trained on the corresponding real data, by generating a fully synthetic dataset through subsampling a synthetically generated population and generating a partially synthetic dataset by obtaining the values of sensitive attributes.

The authors of [16] studied these techniques using different dataset synthesizers such as linear regression, decision tree, random forest, and neural network. They evaluated the effectiveness of these techniques towards the amounts of utility they preserve and the disclosure risks they suffer. The features of the synthetic data are compared to those of the original data in the work proposed by [17], and a model demonstrating how the synthetic data may be utilized to create and improve a standard learning analysis is shown. [9], a method for producing synthetic microdata utilizing the publicly accessible tool Benerator to introduce a new domain for data generation based on census-based personal information is discussed. In addition, they examine the distributions of the original and synthetic data, revealing that the synthetic dataset maintains a high degree of accuracy in contrast to the original distribution. In this work [18], the authors analyze a cancer clinical trial to show how synthetic data may be used to get the same conclusions from real data. These findings imply that synthetic data may act as a stand-in for real data, increasing the accessibility of relevant clinical trial data to researchers. Unlike previous research, our work will compare and evaluate the performance of different synthetic datasets to identify if they can be a reliable replacement for actual data by using a tool that detects possible fraud cases. This model identifies suspicious fraud behaviors in a data set through topic modeling techniques and classification methods, which, aligned with the FTT, allow addressing this phenomenon from a sociological point of view, associating the different behaviors found to the vertices of this theory.

3   Methodology

3.1   Dataset Selection

Finding evidence confirming the occurrence of fraud becomes challenging when studying and analyzing this phenomenon. Whether due to its importance or sensitivity, the corporations and organizations that own this source of information protect it. Often due to their confidentiality rules, which restrict access to this resource. Researchers typically use real data for analysis and experimentation in their research. However, synthetically generated datasets can solve this problem when access to this information is limited or non-existent [19,20]. For this work, two synthetic datasets were generated from a real fraud-oriented dataset created at the EPN. This was done through a controlled experiment with EPN students, for which a data dictionary called "Textual Survey Word List 103115" was used, acquired from the company Audinet [21], which contains words related to the three vertices of the FTT, "Pressure, Opportunity and Rationalization," Which was used to create this initial or real dataset containing phrases related to fraud. This real dataset, named for this paper "Students", comprises 14,226 records balanced in two classes fraud and non-fraud (7113×7113). Each sentence belongs to one of two classes: fraud, represented by a 1, or not fraud, represented by a 0. This initial dataset served as a seed to feed a neural network and tools available on the internet to generate two synthetic datasets, which were used to feed the model to predict possible cases of fraud mentioned above.

3.2   Generating Synthetic Data

To analyze any phenomenon that needs to be studied, it is recommended to have real data. However, in the absence of this resource, the data generated synthetically by some simulation tool becomes a valid alternative. The generation of synthetic data is a complex task and demands resources for its execution, so it is necessary to use an adequate methodology that optimizes this work and establishes an adequate procedure that allows the execution of the related tasks. The methodology proposed by Lundin et al. [22] was taken as a reference for the generation of synthetic datasets, adapting it to the required needs and depending on the tools used. Different strategies were used to generate the synthetic datasets, and as requirements, the characteristics of the real dataset were established as functional parameters, referring to the number of records and classes used. The first synthetic dataset, named "WebScraping", was constructed from the use of various keywords related and unrelated to the FTT, in the same proportion as the real dataset (7113×7113) for fraud and non-fraud, respectively, using the phrases related to fraud; the dictionary "Textual Survey Word List 103115" and for phrases not related to fraud words not related to this phenomenon. Using different online tools to generate text, like [23–25]; Phrases were obtained that included the selected keywords. These tools allow sentences to be generated from a specific word with a well-defined grammatical and semantic structure. Finally, a web scraping tool, "Firefox Addon," allows us to save the generated results and export them in CSV format for processing. The process followed to generate this dataset is shown in Fig. 1.

For the second synthetic dataset, named "Neural-Networks," the methodology established by [2] was used, in which a portion of sentences of the real or initial dataset "Students," was used as input for generating text related and not related to fraud, which, as in the previous synthetic dataset "WebScraping," kept the same parameters in which the real dataset was built. The next step is to review the data collected using [22] exploratory data analysis (EDA). In addition, essential characteristics are identified and valuable parameters for fraud detection. Next, relevant parameters are identified in the input data, and one way to identify these parameters is to study the characteristics necessary for fraud

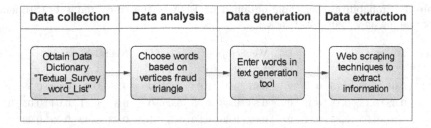

Fig. 1. Flow chart used to generate the synthetic dataset named "WebScraping".

detection. These features must-have properties related to the FTT. The result of this stage will allow the identification of a suitable profile to analyze fraudulent activities. Finally, the real dataset will be downsampled to balance the minority class with the majority class. The initial dataset, composed of phrases identified as fraud and non-fraud, will be the input for the text generation algorithms by applying deep learning algorithms such as recurrent neural networks (RNN) and long short-term memory (LSTM). The process followed to generate this dataset is shown in Fig. 2.

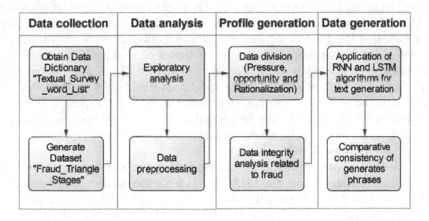

Fig. 2. Flow chart used to generate the synthetic dataset named "Neural-Networks".

3.3   Topic Modeling and Classification Methods Used in Real and Synthetic Datasets

Taking as reference the model proposed by [26], in which they propose identifying hidden patterns within a dataset that may be related to fraud. To achieve this, they develop a model to predict if a specific phrase belongs to one of these categories (pressure, opportunity, rationalization, and others). If it matches one

Table 1. Probabilities per topic obtained by LDA of the study datasets (Students, WebScraping and Neural-Networks).

Docs	Students				DT	WebScraping				DT	Neural-Networks				DT
	1	2	3	4		1	2	3	4		1	2	3	4	
0	0.08	0.08	0.75	0.08	2	0.91	0.03	0.03	0.03	0	0.36	0.03	0.03	0.58	3
1	0.62	0.13	0.13	0.13	0	0.83	0.06	0.05	0.05	0	0.6	0.31	0.04	0.05	0
2	0.05	0.05	0.85	0.05	2	0.02	0.66	0.02	0.3	1	0.93	0.02	0.02	0.02	0
3	0.05	0.05	0.85	0.05	2	0.89	0.04	0.04	0.04	0	0.56	0.04	0.37	0.04	0
4	0.06	0.06	0.56	0.31	2	0.95	0.02	0.02	0.02	0	0.02	0.02	0.74	0.23	2
...	...	...	...	...	...	...	...	...	...	...	...	...	...	...	...
14222	0.05	0.05	0.25	0.65	3	0.02	0.02	0.68	0.28	2	0.04	0.19	0.04	0.73	3
14223	0.08	0.08	0.42	0.42	2	0.2	0.04	0.26	0.49	3	0.4	0.07	0.07	0.47	3
14224	0.04	0.04	0.04	0.89	3	0.34	0.03	0.61	0.03	2	0.05	0.05	0.05	0.85	3
14225	0.06	0.06	0.06	0.81	3	0.75	0.02	0.2	0.02	0	0.25	0.05	0.05	0.65	3
14226	0.06	0.06	0.06	0.81	3	0.44	0.15	0.39	0.02	0	0.5	0.06	0.06	0.37	0

of the first three, this phrase is suspected of fraud. To detect suspicious patterns related to fraud, in a first phase, they perform topic modeling (unsupervised learning) on an unstructured dataset [27]. They select Latent Dirichlet Allocation (LDA) as the best topic model. Then, based on the resulting coherence value, which indicates the level of semantic similarity between words on a topic [28], they determine the appropriate number of topics or k value. This value is an input parameter needed to obtain a topic model in LDA. They determine a value of k = 4 in their study. Once the appropriate value of k is obtained, LDA is applied to the study corpus, and we proceed to extract the probabilities that the documents belong to specific topics, values provided by the algorithm that will be useful to feed classification methods and try to predict phrases related to fraud, as can be seen in the Table 1.

In a second phase, with the probabilities that the documents belong to a specific topic (obtained from the LDA model) from the datasets, the records are labeled with 1 or 0 to indicate whether or not it is related to fraud, respectively. Documents grouped by dominant topic (DT) and their indicator related to fraud or no fraud are selected to build new datasets (T1, T2, T3, and T4), as can be seen in the Tables 2, 3 and 4, related with the different study datasets "Students, WebScraping and Neural-Networks". This new representation of the datasets will be used as input for different classification algorithms, whose resulting prediction models will be used later to measure their performance and compare them. To compare the classifiers, it is essential to choose a good metric; they selected the area under the curve (AUC) since it is trendy when it is necessary to classify predictions and not necessarily obtain well-defined probabilities [29]. Random Forest (RF) and Gradient Boosting (GB) were the most efficient classification methods.

Table 2. Segmentation of probabilities by Dominant Topic (DT) and labeling fraud = 1 and no fraud = 0 (Students Dataset).

DT 1				F	DT 2				F	DT 3				F	DT 4				F
1	2	3	4		1	2	3	4		1	2	3	4		1	2	3	4	
0.62	0.13	0.13	0.13	1	0.05	0.62	0.28	0.05	1	0.08	0.08	0.75	0.08	1	0.06	0.38	0.06	0.49	1
0.5	0.17	0.29	0.04	1	0.05	0.65	0.25	0.05	1	0.05	0.05	0.85	0.05	1	0.04	0.05	0.21	0.71	1
0.44	0.29	0.24	0.03	1	0.04	0.45	0.34	0.18	1	0.05	0.05	0.85	0.05	1	0.13	0.13	0.13	0.62	1
0.6	0.31	0.04	0.04	1	0.44	0.45	0.06	0.06	1	0.06	0.06	0.56	0.31	1	0.21	0.23	0.04	0.52	1
0.62	0.13	0.13	0.13	1	0.35	0.53	0.06	0.06	1	0.06	0.06	0.81	0.06	1	0.06	0.06	0.31	0.56	1
...	...	...	...	...	...	...	...	...	...	...	...	...	...	...	...	...	...	...	...
0.56	0.06	0.06	0.31	0	0.05	0.52	0.05	0.38	0	0.06	0.06	0.56	0.31	0	0.08	0.08	0.08	0.75	0
0.42	0.08	0.08	0.42	0	0.08	0.42	0.08	0.42	0	0.03	0.16	0.41	0.41	0	0.05	0.05	0.25	0.65	0
0.25	0.25	0.25	0.25	0	0.08	0.42	0.08	0.42	0	0.08	0.08	0.42	0.42	0	0.04	0.04	0.04	0.89	0
0.46	0.06	0.07	0.41	0	0.06	0.56	0.06	0.31	0	0.06	0.29	0.33	0.31	0	0.06	0.06	0.06	0.81	0
0.42	0.08	0.08	0.42	0	0.08	0.42	0.08	0.42	0	0.08	0.08	0.42	0.42	0	0.06	0.06	0.06	0.81	0

Table 3. Segmentation of probabilities by Dominant Topic (DT) and labeling fraud = 1 and no fraud = 0 (WebScraping Dataset).

DT 1				F	DT 2				F	DT 3				F	DT 4				F
1	2	3	4		1	2	3	4		1	2	3	4		1	2	3	4	
0.91	0.03	0.03	0.03	1	0.02	0.66	0.02	0.03	1	0.41	0.05	0.49	0.05	1	0.07	0.06	0.06	0.81	1
0.84	0.06	0.05	0.05	1	0.07	0.8	0.06	0.06	1	0.02	0.21	0.74	0.02	1	0.41	0.01	0.01	0.57	1
0.89	0.04	0.04	0.04	1	0.37	0.46	0.03	0.14	1	0.05	0.44	0.45	0.05	1	0.02	0.02	0.47	0.49	1
0.95	0.02	0.02	0.02	1	0.04	0.88	0.04	0.04	1	0.38	0.18	0.42	0.02	1	0.13	0.13	0.13	0.62	1
0.87	0.04	0.04	0.04	1	0.04	0.9	0.03	0.03	1	0.32	0.19	0.45	0.04	1	0.33	0.19	0.01	0.46	1
...	...	...	...	...	...	...	...	...	...	...	...	...	...	...	...	...	...	...	...
0.84	0.05	0.06	0.05	0	0.04	0.58	0.04	0.34	0	0.04	0.04	0.69	0.22	0	0.04	0.21	0.04	0.71	0
0.92	0.03	0.03	0.03	0	0.03	0.64	0.32	0.02	0	0.08	0.08	0.74	0.1	0	0.08	0.08	0.09	0.75	0
0.89	0.04	0.04	0.04	0	0.05	0.84	0.05	0.05	0	0.34	0.05	0.56	0.05	0	0.05	0.25	0.05	0.65	0
0.75	0.02	0.02	0.02	0	0.04	0.88	0.04	0.04	0	0.02	0.02	0.68	0.28	0	0.05	0.05	0.05	0.85	0
0.44	0.15	0.39	0.02	0	0.02	0.94	0.02	0.02	0	0.34	0.03	0.61	0.03	0	0.2	0.04	0.26	0.49	0

Table 4. Segmentation of probabilities by Dominant Topic (DT) and labeling fraud = 1 and no fraud = 0 (Neural-Networks Dataset).

DT 1				F	DT 2				F	DT 3				F	DT 4				F
1	2	3	4		1	2	3	4		1	2	3	4		1	2	3	4	
0.91	0.03	0.03	0.03	1	0.02	0.66	0.02	0.3	1	0.02	0.02	0.74	0.23	1	0.6	0.03	0.03	0.58	1
0.83	0.06	0.05	0.05	1	0.07	0.8	0.06	0.06	1	0.39	0.03	0.56	0.03	1	0.06	0.07	0.07	0.8	1
0.89	0.04	0.04	0.04	1	0.37	0.46	0.03	0.14	1	0.36	0.19	0.41	0.04	1	0.03	0.23	0.35	0.39	1
0.95	0.02	0.02	0.01	1	0.04	0.88	0.04	0.04	1	0.03	0.92	0.03	0.31	1	0.03	0.03	0.03	0.9	1
0.87	0.04	0.04	0.05	1	0.04	0.9	0.03	0.03	1	0.12	0.02	0.6	0.25	1	0.31	0.2	0.02	0.46	1
...	...	...	...	...	...	...	...	...	...	...	...	...	...	...	...	...	...	...	...
0.84	0.05	0.06	0.05	0	0.04	0.58	0.04	0.34	0	0.03	0.03	0.54	0.39	0	0.08	0.36	0.08	0.47	0
0.92	0.03	0.03	0.02	0	0.03	0.64	0.32	0.02	0	0.03	0.03	0.63	0.31	0	0.04	0.19	0.04	0.73	0
0.88	0.04	0.04	0.04	0	0.05	0.84	0.05	0.05	0	0.08	0.08	0.42	0.42	0	0.4	0.07	0.07	0.47	0
0.75	0.02	0.2	0.02	0	0.04	0.87	0.04	0.04	0	0.31	0.06	0.32	0.31	0	0.05	0.05	0.05	0.85	0
0.44	0.15	0.39	0.02	0	0.02	0.95	0.02	0.02	0	0.05	0.05	0.47	0.42	0	0.25	0.05	0.05	0.65	0

4   Results

The comparison of the classifiers if the classes are balanced and also there is no certainty that the classifier has chosen the best decision threshold, it is better to work with the AUC metric, which is equivalent to the probability that the classifier assigns the highest score to relevant classes compared to irrelevant ones [30]. The receiver operating characteristic (ROC) is a curve representing the rate of true positives against the rate of false positives, where the area determines the model's performance under the curve. The closer the AUC score is to 1, the better the model will distinguish between classes. In this work, the ROC curve was used to represent the performance of different machine learning models.

Once the model has been applied to the different study datasets, it can be seen that there is similar behavior of the classifiers in the ROC-AUC curves by topic. In topics 0, 2, and 3, the performance values of the RF and GB algorithms obtained are very similar with imperceptible differences, while in topic one, these differences are a little more visible, without this affecting the final average performance, as can be seen in Fig. 3.

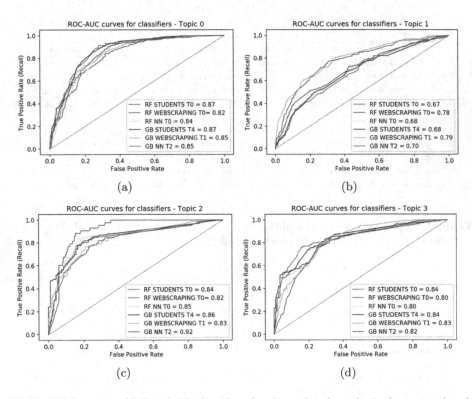

Fig. 3. ROC curves of RF and GB classifiers for the real and synthetic datasets related to each dominant topic. (**a**) DT 1. (**b**) DT 2. (**c**) DT 3. (**a**) DT 4.

In this context, about the real dataset "Students," it was observed that the RF and the GB obtained an average AUC of 0.81 and 0.81, respectively, while the synthetic dataset generated by internet "WebScraping" had a similar behavior when applying RF and GB, obtaining performance values with an average AUC of 0.81 and 0.83, respectively. Finally, in the second synthetic dataset, "Neural-Networks," generated by deep learning, it can be seen that the RF and GB obtain an average AUC of 0.79 and 0.82, respectively, as can be seen in the Table 5.

Table 5. Performance, measured with AUC, of RF and GB when classifying a document related or not to fraud within the study datasets (Students, WebScraping and Neuronal-Networks). T1, T2, T3, and T4 correspond to new datasets, each corresponding to a learned dominant topic of LDA.

CM(AUC)	Students				M	WebScraping				M	Neural-Networks				M
	T1	T2	T3	T4		T1	T2	T3	T4		T1	T2	T3	T4	
Random Forest	0.87	0.67	0.84	0.84	**0.81**	0.82	0.78	0.82	0.80	**0.81**	0.84	0.68	0.85	0.80	**0.79**
Gradient Boosting	0.87	0.68	0.86	0.84	**0.81**	0.85	0.79	0.83	0.83	**0.83**	0.85	0.70	0.92	0.82	**0.82**

These results suggest a similar behavior in the datasets analyzed based on the performance averages of the classifiers used, as can be seen in Fig. 4. Therefore, since synthetic datasets can be a very close alternative to the original data, it is feasible to produce a dataset that helps protect and protect information when it is confidential and difficult to access.

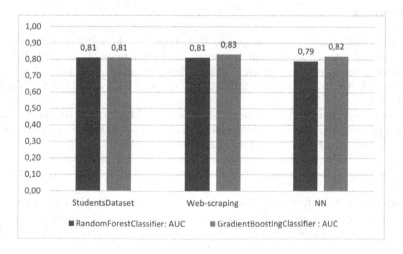

Fig. 4. Best metrics obtained by the algorithms (Random Forest and Gradient Boosting) applied to the study datasets.

5 Conclusions

This work shows that the performance obtained by a detector of fraud-suspicious behavior based on machine learning algorithms used on the real dataset is similar to that obtained from synthetic datasets. These findings suggest that the results of models built using synthetic datasets may reflect behaviors obtained as if real data had been used. If more work supports this hypothesis, researchers can generate or use synthetic datasets with complete confidence that their results will have scientific validity. Synthetic datasets preserve the privacy and confidentiality of the information, allowing the development of predictive models to discover patterns without the need to reveal confidential data, minimizing the risk of access to real data. It should also be mentioned that adequate evaluation metrics, which show the real behavior of the classifiers used, are essential since selecting the wrong one can be misleading in determining how the model behaves. In this case, according to the results obtained from the performance comparison, synthetic data is recommended to predict phrases suspected of fraud. As future work, it is proposed to carry out tests of the model for detecting fraud by applying deep learning algorithms and testing it with real and synthetic data to evaluate the performance and analyze if there is an improvement versus the classification methods.

Acknowledgements. This work was sponsored by the Vicerrectorado de Investigación, Innovación y Vinculación from Escuela Politécnica Nacional. Marco Sánchez is the beneficiary of a teaching assistant fellowship from Escuela Politécnica Nacional for doctoral studies in Computer Science.

References

1. Sanchez, M., Torres, J., Zambrano, P., Flores, P.: FraudFind: financial fraud detection by analyzing human behavior. In: Proceedings of the 2018 IEEE 8th Annual Computing and Communication Workshop and Conference (CCWC), Las Vegas, NV, USA, 8–10 January 2018 (2018). https://doi.org/10.1109/CCWC.2018.8301739
2. Sánchez, M., Olmedo, V., Narvaez, C., Hernández, M., Urquiza-Aguiar, L.: Generation of a synthetic dataset for the study of fraud through deep learning techniques. Int. J. Adv. Sci. Eng. Inf. Technol. **11**, 2534–2542 (2021)
3. PwC (This Link Contains Information about FRAUD). https://www.pwc.com/gx/en/forensics/global-economic-crime-and-fraud-survey-2018.pdf. Accessed 8 Sept 2021
4. Panigrahi, P.K.: A framework for discovering internal financial fraud using analytics. In: Proceedings of the 2011 International Conference on Communication Systems and Network Technologies, Katra, India, 3–5 June 2011, pp. 323–327 (2011)
5. Sayal, K., Singh, G.: What role does human behaviour play in corporate frauds? Econ. Political Wkly **5** (2020)
6. Ruankaew, T.: The fraud factors. Int. J. Manag. Adm. Sci. (IJMAS) **2**, 1–5 (2013)
7. Mansor, N., Abdullahi, R.: Fraud triangle theory and fraud diamond theory. Understanding the convergent and divergent for future research. Int. J. Acad. Res. Account. Financ. Manag. Sci. **1**, 38–45 (2015)

8. Guan, S.Y.J., Li, R., Zhang, X.: A method for generating synthetic electronic medical record text. IEEE/ACM Trans. Comput. Biol. Bioinform. https://doi.org/10.1109/tcbb.2019.2948985. Accedido 06 Nov 2019
9. Ayala-Rivera, V., Mcdonagh, P., Cerqueus, T., Murphy, L.: Synthetic Data Generation using Benerator Tool (2013)
10. Brinkhoff, T.: Real and Synthetic Test Datasets (2009)
11. Kherwa, P., Bansal, P.: Topic modeling: a comprehensive review. ICST Trans. Scalable Inf. Syst. **7**, 159623 (2018). https://doi.org/10.4108/eai.13-7-2018.159623
12. Møgelmose, A., Trivedi, M., Moeslund, T.: Learning to detect traffic signs: comparative evaluation of synthetic and real-world datasets. In: Proceedings - International Conference on Pattern Recognition, pp. 3452–3455 (2012)
13. Heyburn, R., et al.: Machine learning using synthetic and real data: similarity of evaluation metrics for different healthcare datasets and for different algorithms. In: Data Science and Knowledge Engineering for Sensing Decision Support, pp. 1281–1291 (2018). https://doi.org/10.1142/9789813273238_0160
14. He, B., Li, X., Huang, B., Gu, E., Guo, W., Wu, L.: UnityShip: a large-scale synthetic dataset for ship recognition in aerial images. Remote Sens. **13**, 4999 (2021)
15. Reiner-Benaim, A.: Analyzing medical research results based on synthetic data and their relation to real data results: systematic comparison from five observational studies. JMIR Med. Inform. **8**, 16492 (2020)
16. Dandekar, A., Zen, R.A.M., Bressan, S.: A comparative study of synthetic dataset generation techniques. In: Hartmann, S., Ma, H., Hameurlain, A., Pernul, G., Wagner, R.R. (eds.) DEXA 2018. LNCS, vol. 11030, pp. 387–395. Springer, Cham (2018). https://doi.org/10.1007/978-3-319-98812-2_35
17. Dorodchi, M., Al-Hossami, E., Benedict, A., Demeter, E.: Using synthetic data generators to promote open science in higher education learning analytics (2019)
18. Azizi, Z., Zheng, C., Mosquera, L., Pilote, L., El Emam, K.: Can synthetic data be a proxy for real clinical trial data? A validation study. BMJ Open **11** (2021)
19. Santos Brito, Y., Santos, C., Paula Mendonca, S., Araujo, T., Freitas, A., Meiguins, B.: A prototype application to generate synthetic datasets for information visualization evaluations. In: Proceedings of the 2018 22nd International Conference Information Visualisation (IV), Fisciano, Italy, 10–13 July 2018 (2018). https://doi.org/10.1109/iV.2018.00036
20. Redpath, R., Srinivasan, B.: Criteria for a comparative study of visualization techniques in data mining. In: Abraham, A., Franke, K., Köppen, M. (eds.) Intelligent Systems Design and Applications. ASC, vol. 23, pp. 609–620. Springer, Heidelberg (2003). https://doi.org/10.1007/978-3-540-44999-7_58
21. AudiNet (Using Key Word Analysis of an Organization's Big Data For Error and Fraud Detection). https://www.auditnet.org/key-word-analytics. Accessed 8 Sept 2021
22. Lundin, H.K.E., Jonsson, E.: A synthetic fraud data generation methodology. Accessed 07 July 2020
23. Randomwordgenerator (Random Word Generator). https://www.randomwordgenerator.org. Accessed 8 Sept 2021
24. Reverso (Reverso Context). https://context.reverso.net/traduccion/ingles-espanol. Accessed 8 Sept 2021
25. Sentencedict (Sentence Dict). https://sentencedict.com/. Accessed 8 Sept 2021
26. Sánchez-Aguayo, M., Urquiza-Aguiar, L., Estrada-Jiménez, J.: Predictive fraud analysis applying the fraud triangle theory through data mining techniques. Appl. Sci. **12** (2022). https://www.mdpi.com/2076-3417/12/7/3382

27. Ozyirmidokuz, E.: Mining unstructured Turkish economy news articles. Procedia Econ. Financ. **16**, 320–328 (2014). https://doi.org/10.1016/S2212-5671(14)00809-0
28. Tresnasari, N., Adji, T., Permanasari, A.: Social-child-case document clustering based on topic modeling using latent Dirichlet allocation. IJCCS Indonesian J. Comput. Cybern. Syst. **14**, 179 (2020). https://doi.org/10.22146/ijccs.54507
29. AUC (AUC). https://neptune.ai/blog/f1-score-accuracy-roc-auc-pr-au. Accessed 15 July 2021
30. Straube, S., Krell, M.: How to evaluate an agent's behavior to infrequent events?-Reliable performance estimation insensitive to class distribution. Front. Comput. Neurosci. **8**, 43 (2014). https://www.frontiersin.org/article/10.3389/fncom.2014.00043. Accessed 23 Mar 2022

Academic Management in Higher Education 4.0 Facing the Challenges of Industry 4.0

Milton Labanda-Jaramillo[1,2,3,4](✉) iD, María de los Angeles Coloma[1,2,4] iD, and Gloria Cecibel Michay[1,2,4] iD

[1] Universidad Nacional de Loja, Loja, Ecuador
{miltonlab,maria.coloma,cecibel.michay}@unl.edu.ec
[2] Research Group GITED, Facultad de Educación, Murcia, Spain
[3] Research Group GITIC, Facultad de la Energía, Loja, Ecuador
[4] Universidad Nacional Yacambú, Barquisimeto, Venezuela

Abstract. Industry 4.0 promotes the digital transformation of education, innovative, flexible, personalized learning; and requires transformations both methodological, curricular, as well as management. The present study intends to establish certain characteristics of the academic director in the area of Education, projected towards the fourth industrial revolution, for which the quantitative research approach supported by a semi-structured online questionnaire was used as a structured instrument in the 4 dimensions of the framework of enabling components of Education 4.0. The population was made up of the academic directors of the Facultad de la Educación, el Arte y las Comunicaciones of the Universidad Nacional de Loja. Among the main results, it was obtained that the competencies that the academic directors consider to be a priority are teamwork, innovation and participation in collaborative networks; The teaching role stands out as a manager of access to knowledge with 53%; 53.8% of academic directors use cloud computing as an information management mechanism and 46.22% of them affirm that 50% of their career information is digitized; 76.9% of the population requires training in matters related to Culture 4.0, while 58.3% consider that digital gaps and dehumanization are the main risks in Education 4.0. It is concluded that Education 4.0 is an unfinished field that includes not only technological but also organizational aspects with challenges and risks for contemporary society.

Keywords: Academic management · Education 4.0 · Industry 4.0

1 Introduction

Higher Education Institutions, organizations dedicated to the training of human talents based on the themes and problems of society, which are developed in the present and are projected into the future, seek to provide skills, mentality and talent so that professionals of the future can deal with change and transformations in an agile way, being the teachers of this third level of education, primary actors who must mediate the learning of the future. Some of the skills that, in this prospective line, the curricula and study plans must consider include: creativity for complex challenges in a collaborative manner, emotional intelligence and critical thinking, innovation and entrepreneurship, agile methodologies, sustainable mentality, handling design and programming of new technologies.

Teaching-learning experiences with real enterprises; the new role of the teacher as mentor and advisor; technology as an enabling tool for learning, networking, the collective construction of knowledge; the development of processes that combine online and face-to-face training; the design of study programs that take advantage of and face the challenges of Industry 4.0; all this makes us think that we are witnessing the birth of a new educational model in collaboration between higher education institutions, the employer sector and industry 4.0.

Education 4.0 developed within the challenges of Industry 4.0, considers the technologies that foster innovative, flexible, personalized learning based on data analytics, virtual realities, gamification, augmented reality, artificial intelligence, learning mobile, 3D printing, real-time interaction from any latitude, adaptive learning. This model also considers that the new university teacher must develop their capacity for adaptation, innovation and constant learning to face an educational system open to other contexts where the knowledge of the teacher and the student, as well as the development of their skills, it traverses and is configured in other spaces, other formal and informal spheres, in which access to knowledge and information, as well as its construction, are unfinished.

In this sense, at the present time, the academic directors of the universities need to align their management in the perspective of the challenges posed by the fourth industrial revolution; due to this, the present study that is part of the progress of the doctoral thesis work "Theoretical approach on intermediate management in Higher Education Institutions from an Open Innovation approach" intends to pay for the search for findings that contribute to the construction of trajectories training for management personnel of educational institutions, capable of renewing their management and making decisions that respond to the institutional transformation agenda and the demands of the productive sector that interacts with higher education. Therefore, the questions that provoked this research are: How should academic managers be prepared to take on the challenges of Education 4.0 in the face of the reality of Industry 4.0? What should be the priorities of the university academic manager with respect to the digital transformation of education? And what should be the concerns and risks that should be the attention of the academic directors of the universities?

2   Literature Review

2.1   The Arrival of the Fourth Industrial Revolution or Industry 4.0

The phenomenon of Industry 4.0 (I4.0) or the fourth industrial revolution (4RI) has repercussions in all areas, and education is no exception, which is why it is now necessary to rethink an education that responds to this new reality. In this context, according to [1], a 4.0 education uses digital technologies as the main means of learning and communication, uses the Internet as a common global space for education, and takes advantage of the knowledge generated worldwide; students connect internationally to educate themselves and work.

In addition, the profile of this new student uses teaching-learning processes that go beyond what he learns in the classroom, uses a greater number of languages than just his mother tongue, requires strong computer skills, takes advantage of technology to facilitate the processes of learning and knowledge management, and requires ways of thinking that understand transdisciplinarity, among others.

In the accelerated dynamics of this revolution, it seems that the world becomes flat and that its complexities are part of the educational and working life of people. These processes take place in learning and work flows. Offices, factories, and universities are part of these flows, but they are not necessarily the only or most important places. Work and education take place in any place, time, and in various contexts.

Going along with the reflection of [2], I4.0 offers many possibilities for innovation through a set of products and services that will also require a set of new approaches in areas such as talent, cyber risk and competitive disruption, where the core base of primary discussion will be how does it affect the educational system? as well as what is the type of learning that should circulate in the classrooms? in a world that is increasingly closer to global digitization.

2.2 Education 4.0

For the author Lase cited in [3], education 4.0 is the response to the needs of the new industrial revolution I4.0, where technology and people converge to create new, creative and innovative opportunities and as concluded in documentary research there is evidence of a close relationship between I4.0 and education, since it must be at the forefront of what the industry demands and its evolution, always trying to implement technological tools in the teaching-learning process to encourage the student in research and innovation and thus meet the demand of organizations.

However, in chapter seventeen of the book [4] entitled "Education 4.0, origin for its foundation", after sustained research, it is concluded that Education 4.0 lacks a theoretical and methodological definition for its foundation, being its main promoters entrepreneurs and leaders in the industrial sector, therefore considered a fruitful subject for educational research; On the other hand, it is determined that I4.0 and Education 4.0 maintain an epistemic relationship, since Education 4.0 originated from the demands produced by the emerging fourth industrial revolution, which requires the formation of qualified human capital. For decision-making and the use of disruptive technology.

In the same way, in the aforementioned study, it is concluded that Education 4.0 is an eclectic educational trend because it applies different perspectives and innovative learning strategies, without creating its own; Finally, it is established that Education 4.0 is a pragmatic educational trend because it is more concerned with methods than with theories, that is, it uses learning methodologies ignoring its epistemic support.

From the pedagogical point of view, according to the recent study and proposal of a framework linked to open innovation in the context of higher education [5], it is considered that the generation of knowledge in Education 4.0 transcends pedagogy and andragogy towards an approach that combines *heutagogy, peeragogy* and *cybergogy*.

Through heutagogy, Education 4.0 promotes self-learning based on student-centered humanist and constructivist principles for learning and teaching, self-reflection and metacognition are encouraged, or the understanding of the learning process itself. Peeragogy is an old concept that has been reconsidered with the arrival of Education 4.0; refers to the basis of collaborative learning and refers to the set of teaching techniques that promote peer learning. Likewise, cybergogy has emerged thanks to technological advances and the evolution of the Internet that have favored the educational offer, studies such as [6] define cybergogy as the learning strategies promoted by Information Technology Technologies. -Training and Communication (ICT) that offer learning experiences that go beyond the limits of time and space.

2.3 Higher Education 4.0 and Open Innovation

As we have appreciated, Education 4.0 is a response, without a doubt, on the one hand to the need for technological evolution that the 4RI means, where humans and technology are aligned to allow new possibilities, according to [7] then the digital transformation of the Education appears as the number one challenge for Education 4.0, however, as [8] concludes, the most complex challenges are associated with: the change in social practices and the culture of educational centers, universities and public administrations, the training and awareness-raising for teachers and management teams, encouragement and development of the talent of teachers who will make the educational revolution possible and, of course, resource management.

Higher Education Institutions train people with relevant skills on the issues and problems that are developed in the present and are projected into the future, where they seek to provide skills, mentality and talent so that the professionals of the future can face agile the change, being the teachers of higher education who must mediate the learning of the future. Some of the skills, which, in this prospective line, should be included in the curricula should be: creativity for complex challenges in a collaborative way, emotional intelligence and critical thinking, innovation and entrepreneurship, agile methodologies, sustainable mentality, design and programming management of new technologies.

With real entrepreneurship experiences; the new role of the teacher as mentor and advisor; technology as an enabling tool for learning, networking, the collective construction of knowledge; the development of processes that combine online and face-to-face training; the design of study programs that take into account taking advantage of and facing the challenges of I4.0; All this makes us think that we are witnessing the birth of a new institutional model in collaboration between higher education institutions, the employer sector and I4.0.

Knowledge in I4.0 has no borders, therefore the teacher must bring to the classroom the experience, practices, tools, challenges to teach by doing. The role of teachers has been more impacted, especially in young people for the professions of the future. It must have the support of the state, the formation of the future must take place in real collaboration between education, the I4.0 sector and the state in order to build real and virtual spaces for the development of talent with cutting-edge technology. The curriculum must also include the reality of the market and digital transformation.

The innovation that opens possibilities to make the transition from the current higher education system, from people and from institutions towards what new educational models demand; the current actor of Higher Education 4.0 must therefore develop his capacity for adaptation, innovation and constant learning to face an educational system open to other contexts where the knowledge of the teacher and the student, as well as the development of these, crosses and is configured in other spaces, other formal and informal areas, in which access to knowledge and information as well as its construction, are unfinished.

2.4   Academic Management 4.0 in Higher Education

The new institutional order in higher education poses interesting challenges to academic management, a function that is oriented towards educational processes that today go beyond disciplinarity in essentially theoretical teaching, with atomized contents unrelated to real problems and with informational educational practices that encourage repetitive and contemplative learning. With the concern of university directors in decision-making and the development of a new global vision, framed in the context of information and discussion of ideas to lead the institutional project, the experts' recommendation is that HEIs include by for example, subjects on culture 4.0, technological trends and needs in study plans and programs, as well as taking advantage of digital innovation that creates different and better ways of carrying out the higher education project.

The technologies have an impact, of course, on the daily actions of interaction and interrelation, this raises the development of new managerial and operational skills, in the process flows, in the form and acceleration of learning, use in the consolidation and construction of benefits. social networks, social networks, methodologies based on interaction that transfer part of the teaching process outside the classroom so that it is enriched by technologies and use class time for complex cognitive processes that favor meaningful learning.

Academic management 4.0 in higher education assumes skills that had already been defined for leaders in this field of human achievement, and adds skills that were not so necessary before, but are now essential for this new culture. What is needed is a reconversion of academic management models and their consequent assumption in vision and practice from culture 4.0. Culture 4.0 of a new world order that has humanization as its center of transformations, in which the essential search is the conscious and balanced integral human development. It also contemplates challenges and concerns about the principles and ethics of development, such as how to achieve greater individual and collective well-being? How to reach socially agreed innovation? how not to affect the natural human development and evolution? privacy, the accelerated affectation of the global ecosystem, how humanism is affected.

This 4.0 culture must be led by a leader with a profile that values access to information, knowledge and new forms of interaction, a leader who is informed knows how information is sought, processed and interpreted. It is important to consider the ability to lead and accelerate performance, integrate and strengthen work groups, foster learning capacity, foster entrepreneurial spirit, assess the performance of high-potential talent from within and outside institutions, in this way, build a culture that fosters the development of academic actors with shared purposes. In short, the leadership of academic management must drive higher education institutions towards culture 4.0, turning leaders mainly into managers of organizational change.

Academic management is oriented towards culture 4.0 and must promote the institutional conditions that allow an integrated and comprehensive response involving institutional actors, public sectors and civil society. The incorporation of this logic of connection and networking that culture 4.0 brings is under human control and is the responsibility of the leaders and the decisions that each one makes as an academic and citizen.

In addition, the academic leader of Higher Education 4.0 is characterized by the fact that he understands the new socio-educational order that has raised the incorporation of technologies into the field of HEIs marked not only by access to information and knowledge, but primarily by cooperation in the management, decision-making and distribution of services. The leader of education 4.0 guides the development of 21st century skills, such as creativity, assertive communication, teamwork, creative thinking, innovation, constitution and participation in work and collaboration networks, emotional intelligence and resilience.

There is literature that highlights the change in functions and professions due to the emergence of new skills and where the impact of I4.0 on people and the institution underlies. The axes of the 4RI technologies (IoT, BigData, Augmented Reality) require special emphasis on the development of skills such as critical thinking, understanding and analysis skills, integrating the literacy of new technological and communication media in educational programs, include learning in practice that favors the development of interpersonal competencies such as collaboration, teamwork, adaptive responses, broaden the base of learning (lifelong and for life), integrate interdisciplinary training that allows the development of competencies and knowledge in a variety of areas such as complex thinking, critical thinking, team management, negotiation and coordination, emotional intelligence, judgment and decision making, information processing, active listening and cognitive flexibility.

Regarding the challenges and fears, an aspect that worries in the Academy 4.0 is the risk in the inequalities generated by access to technology and automation due to limited qualifications, due to work environments in accelerated change of relationships and technology, mainly due to information security, there is the risk of not having arguments to overcome the conservative culture of the academy and dehumanize the interaction process.

3 Methodology

The present quantitative research was carried out through an exploration with the help of a survey applied to a sample of university academic directors and managers in functions belonging to the Facultad de la Educación, el Arte y las Comunicaciones de la Universidad Nacional de Loja.

The survey was implemented through a questionnaire structured by a set of questions framed within the four component enablers of the Education 4.0 vision, which comprise the framework designed and cited in the studies [5, 9] and [10] namely: (1) the main soft and hard skills to develop; (2) the learning methods to be taken into account in the new teaching-learning dynamics; (3) the application of current and emerging ICT for technology-based solutions using existing tools and platforms, and (4) the use of innovative infrastructure to improve pedagogical procedures and management processes at two levels, the classroom/home and the institutional.

The questionnaire used was configured through a set of 8 questions categorized within each of the enabling components of Education 4.0 (2 for each component) cited in the previous paragraph.

4   Results and Discussion

4.1   Component: Competencies

The population of academic directors investigated shows that the activities that generate the greatest satisfaction in them are those related to the presentation of research results (11 of 13) as evidenced in Fig. 1. Findings that are corroborated with [11] where teaching and research remain at the center of the concerns of academic directors, since such a study indicates that teaching (giving a lecture, preparing for a lecture) and research (developing a research project, publishing books and papers, and supervising doctoral students) are the activities that most satisfy this group of academic directors.

Based on these findings, the present investigation can be extended to the determination of the activities of greater satisfaction in the academic managers but including new variables such as age, gender and the rank or category of teacher, in a similar way. As analyzed in the study by [12], where it is determined that the younger the teachers, the greater satisfaction with the research is demonstrated, as well as the almost obvious statement that satisfaction with the research is related to the teacher category: the higher the category, the higher the level of satisfaction with the research.

Regarding the priority of the skills that the leader of academic management 4.0 should possess in a Higher Education Institution, most of the researched population states that Teamwork, Innovation and participation in collaborative networks are the ones that should be prioritized according to what is synthesized in Table 1.

These results highlight the relevance of competencies related to collaborative intelligence between machines and humans as one of the cores of I4.0, because as Wilson and Daugherty point out cited in [13] through this intelligence, Humans and Artificial Intelligences actively enhance their complementary strengths, the leadership, teamwork, creativity, and social skills of the former, and the speed, scalability, and quantitative capabilities of the latter.

Likewise, it is important to highlight the relationship of the most outstanding competencies in our study with the qualifications expected from the directors of Education 4.0 schools at work [14] whose study group consisted of 10 teachers who work precisely in the Faculty of Education and the Faculty of Open Education, Anadolu University, Turkey, in the academic year 2019–2020; where we can relate: 1) the competence of participation in work networks and collaboration with the skills of cooperation and communication and 2) the competence of innovation we can relate it to the technical skills of being innovative and supporting innovative ideas and on the technological skills side with adapting innovation in their own school or department.

4.2   Component: Learning Methods

The role of the teacher as manager of access to knowledge and Mediator stands out in a very notable way, having been selected by 53% and 23.1% respectively, as can be seen in Fig. 2 a situation that can be substantiated with what [15] mentions "The role of teachers, which should focus on guiding and supporting students by generating the conditions to build their own knowledge." (pp. 73), a statement that is corroborated by [16] when concluding in their analysis that what is important is learning and the conversion of

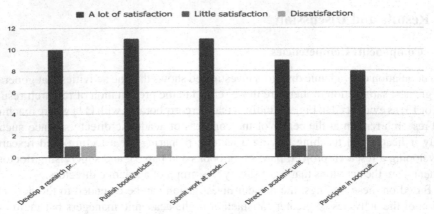

Fig. 1. Answers to the question: select the level of satisfaction generated in you by each of the academic activities listed below.

Table 1. Priority of competencies of the leader of university academic management 4.0

Academic management leader competence	Priority levels							
	8	7	6	5	4	3	2	1
Creativity	5	1	–	–	2	3	–	–
Assertive communication	6	1	–	–	2	1	1	1
Teamwork	7	1	–	–	1	2	–	2
Creative thinking	6	2	–	–	1	2	–	1
Innovation	7	1	–	–	1	2	1	–
Participation in work and collaboration networks	7	–	–	–	1	2	–	1
Emotional intelligence	4	3	–	–	–	3	–	–
Resilience	8	2	–	–	1	3	–	–

the role of the teacher to a mediator and manager of knowledge, which converges with the idea that the teacher in the higher education 4.0 is a mediator and manager of opportunities, sources, networks and access to knowledge that allow developing the skills of its students.

Finally, it is worth noting that the 4.0 teacher not only fulfills this task in the classroom, but also through digital educational platforms, online courses and materials; making possible the involvement of their students with other students from other parts of the country or the world, thus enhancing their skills and knowledge [1].

One of the most relevant findings is the fact that more than half of those surveyed, 58.3% specifically, have stated that they have included more than 3 subjects related to digital technologies in their curricular designs, fully corroborating the study [17] where more than 53% state that it is necessary to promote an environment in which new technologies are promoted as part of the academic curriculum, a situation that is already

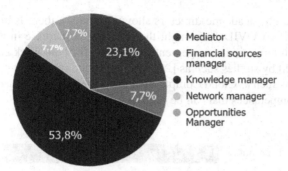

Fig. 2. Answers to the question: what is the teaching role that you consider should prevail in Education 4.0?

reflected in Higher Education Institutions such as the University Regional public in Chile where as a result of the study [18] the relationship that exists between the different engineering programs in the university of study that links the I4.0 in their study plans was determined. Undoubtedly, the increased computerization requires changes in the design, structure and curricular itineraries, appearing the so-called interactive curricula based on digital interaction, a model that, as described in [19], has the characteristic of generating a hidden curriculum that fosters a digital-mediated learning, concluding in the same study that we are facing the first version of curricular innovation based on smart technologies within the university 4.0 model, which has undoubtedly improved digitalized technologies and practices (Fig. 3).

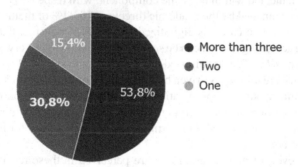

Fig. 3. Answers to the question: how many subjects directly related to digital tools or technologies does the last study plan of your career contain?

4.3 Component: Information and Communication Technologies

Designing the curriculum in order to promote the development of skills will contribute to reducing the education-work gap and will avoid wasting the new opportunities generated by the disruptive changes of the Fourth Industrial Revolution, argues [20]. Based on this and according to the findings of the present investigation, regarding the technologies of greater attention by academic directors shown in Fig. 4., there is no doubt that the pandemic caused by COVID-19 brought the exponential increase in the use of cloud computing as an information management mechanism for both work and personal use, which is supported by studies such as [21] where it is confirmed that cooperative work supported by skills such as Cloud Computing and the digital competence of information processing are competences that can be used in Education 4.0.

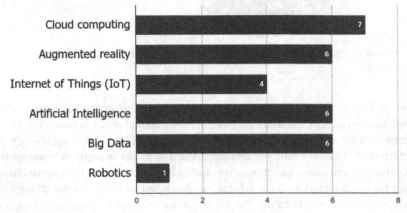

Fig. 4. Answers to the question: select the Industry 4.0 technologies that you are using or that you consider using in the future, either within the curricular designs or in your management activities.

On the other hand and within the same component, with respect to the digitalization of the information managed by the academic directors, 46.22% of them affirm that 50% of the information of their career is digitalized while 30.8% consider that about 75% is already digitized according to what can be seen in Fig. 4., showing a very good projection towards education and I 4.0, as manifested in the results of the study [22] without a doubt The fourth industrial revolution is driven by digital transformation, which implies certain competitive advantages such as optimization of processes, dynamic economies, adequate decision-making, among others, ratifying the need to generate a culture of change in educational centers to take digital transformation as an opportunity for improvement in all organizational areas.

Despite the levels of digitalization that are perceived in these results, it should be taken into account that digital transformation constitutes a challenge for HEIs and that, according to the conclusions of [23], the development of a strategy is a necessary task and that it should be assumed by the managerial levels of the university and whose application is also constituted in a process of organizational change.

4.4   Component: Infrastructure

According to Fig. 5, the preferences of the training topics, Innovative Leadership (69.2%) and Culture 4.0 (76.9%), requested by the academic managers, denote their concern for the development and institutional quality, which can be sustained in the study of [24] applied to 52 duly accredited Chilean HEIs, in whose results it is determined that

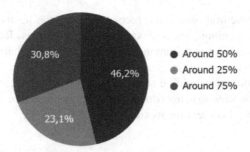

Fig. 5. Answers to the question: approximately in what percentage do you consider that the information of your career is digitized?

transformational leadership has a significant influence (test $t = 13.691$; $p < 0,01$) on the innovative culture, the latter being a determining variable of the quality of the institutions (test $t = 3.264$; $p < 0.01$). Since today's leaders need to assume complex roles, in tune with the adaptability of changes and innovation, supported by ethical principles, social responsibility, with global, inclusive and multicultural characteristics, since the current dynamics demand shared leadership in multidisciplinary work teams with delegation of functions and remote leadership as well [25] (Fig. 6).

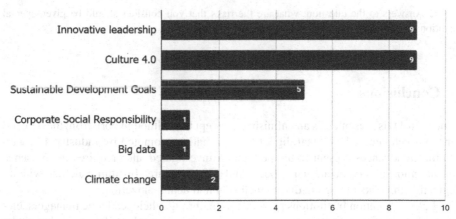

Fig. 6. Answers to the question: select from the following list of organizational aspects, those that you would be interested in including in future curricular or continuous training proposals for your career?

Within Education 4.0 arising from the fourth industrial revolution, according to the population of academic managers addressed, it is necessary to manage digital gaps on the one hand and dehumanization on the other as imminent risks. With respect to digital divides, we can find support in what [26] asserts, who concludes that the rapid diffusion of ICTs in contemporary societies continues to restructure the contours of digital divides at a national, regional and global scale, and that to mitigate them it is necessary to look at them in an inclusive, fair and ethical way, thinking critically about how 4.0 technologies operate and are appropriate, particularly those that are new, such as AI, through the multiple layers of structural inequality, recognizing increasing the complexity of the social fabric and its economic and sociocultural particularities. Regarding the second concern, according to [27], the dehumanization implicit in the characteristics of the 4.0 revolution is presented as one of the greatest challenges to be solved, explaining that the fourth industrial revolution would be successful if the person were the main center of attention. Since the theories up to now do not speak about the nature of the transformation but rather about an ideal context for its success simply (Fig. 7).

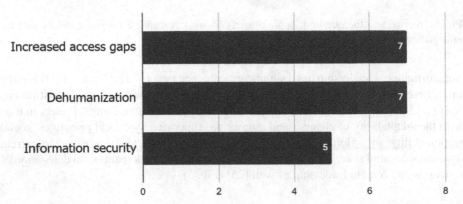

Fig. 7. Answers to the question: what are the risks that you consider should be given special attention in the fourth industrial revolution?

5   Conclusions

Education 4.0 is presented as an unfinished concept that, although born from the demand for the accelerated educational digital transformation promoted by Industry 4.0, with significant advances present in the population investigated, also requires the presence and attention of organizational aspects and infrastructure. Institutional, not without neglecting the risks of gaps in digital inclusion and dehumanization.

Higher Education Institutions must integrate, through their academic managers, elements that contribute to the construction of new educational models considering the relevance of their academic offer, which will have to be in tune with the needs of digital transformation that the sector requires. Influenced by the characteristics of the fourth industrial revolution. In this new 4.0 reality, there is a need to train educational actors in skills related to leadership, resilience, and management of change and transformation within the institution, to name a few.

References

1. Huerta Jiménez, C.S., Velázquez Albo, M.: Education 4.0 as a response to industry 4.0: an analytical-descriptive study. Latin Sci. **5**, 1042–1054 (2021). https://doi.org/10.37811/cl_rcm. v5i1.310

2. Espinoza Ordóñez, W.A., Labanda-Jaramillo, M., Michay Caraguay, G.C.: The fourth industrial revolution (2020). https://www.uny.edu.ve/wp-content/uploads/2020/12/Revista-DIC-2020-1.pdf

3. Ulloa-Duque, G.S., Torres-Mansur, S.M., López-Piñón, D.C.: Industry 4.0 in higher education (2022). http://www.web.facpya.uanl.mx/vinculategica/Vinculategica6_2/31_Ulloa_Torres_Lopez.pdf

4. REDINE: Contributions of Digital Technology in Educational and Social Development. Adaya Press (2020)

5. Miranda, J., Ramírez-Montoya, M.S., Molina, A.: Education 4.0 reference framework for the design of teaching-learning systems: two case studies involving collaborative networks and open innovation. In: Camarinha-Matos, L.M., Boucher, X., Afsarmanesh, H. (eds.) PRO-VE 2021. IAICT, vol. 629, pp. 692–701. Springer, Cham (2021). https://doi.org/10.1007/978-3-030-85969-5_65

6. Daud, W., Teck, W.K., Ghani, M.T.A., Ramli, S.: The needs analysis of developing mobile learning application for cybergogical teaching and learning of Arabic language proficiency. Int. J. Acad. Res. Bus. Soc. Sci. **9**, 33–46 (2019)

7. Pérez-Romero, P., Rivera Zárate, I., Hernández Bolaños, M.: Education 4.0 in a simple way, September 2019

8. Morales Galván, P., Guzmán Villalón, M.T., Medina Torres, M.G.: Proposal for an educational model for its integration into education 4.0 (2019). https://www.anfei.mx/revista/index.php/revista/article/viewFile/600/1237

9. Miranda, J., Lopez, C.S., Navarro, S., Bustamante, M.R., Molina, J.M., Molina, A.: Open innovation laboratories as enabling resources to reach the vision of education 4.0. In: 2019 IEEE International Conference on Engineering, Technology and Innovation (ICE/ITMC), pp. 1–7. IEEE, Valbonne Sophia-Antipolis (2019). https://doi.org/10.1109/ICE.2019.8792595

10. Miranda, J., et al.: The core components of education 4.0 in higher education: three case studies in engineering education. Comput. Electr. Eng. **93**, 107278 (2021). https://doi.org/10.1016/j.compeleceng.2021.107278

11. Santiago, R., Carvalho, T., Amaral, A., Meek, V.L.: Changing patterns in the middle management of higher education institutions: the case of Portugal. High. Educ. **52**, 215–250 (2006). https://doi.org/10.1007/s10734-004-2747-3

12. Oshagbemi, T.: How satisfied are academics with their primary tasks of teaching, re-search and administration and management? Int. J. Sustain. High. Educ. **1**, 124–136 (2000). https://doi.org/10.1108/1467630010371876

13. De-la-Calle-Durán, M.-C., Rodríguez-Sánchez, J.-L., González-Torres, T.: Talent skills in Industry 4.0, demand vs. supply: a case of study of the Rey Juan Carlos University, Spain. Form. Univ. **15**, 19–32 (2022). https://doi.org/10.4067/S0718-50062022000100019

14. Himmetoglu, B., Aydug, D., Bayrak, C.: Education 4.0: defining the teacher, the student and the school manager aspects of the revolution. Turk. Online J. Distance Educ. 12–28 (2020). https://doi.org/10.17718/tojde.770896

15. Bañuelos Márquez, A.M.: Education 4.0 in university institutions. In: REDINE (Coord.) Contributions of Digital Technology in Educational and Social Development, pp. 70–79 (2020)

16. Muñoz-Guevara, E., Velázquez-García, G., Barragán-López, J.F.: Analysis of the technological evolution towards education 4.0 and the virtualization of higher education (2021). https://www.revista-transdigital.org/index.php/transdigital/article/view/86/148

17. Carbajal-Amaya, R.V.: The university of the future and the revolution 4.0. towards an innovative university. Prospective analysis. You Fall **11**, 15–26 (2020). https://doi.org/10.22458/caes.v11i2.3321

18. Garcés, G., Peña, C.: Adjust engineering education to industry 4.0: a vision from the curricular development and the laboratory. REXE **19**, 129–148 (2020). https://doi.org/10.21703/rexe. 20201940garces7
19. Pedroza Flores, R.: The university 4.0 with intelligent curriculum 1.0 in the fourth industrial revolution/the university 4.0 with intelligent curriculum 1.0 in the fourth industrial revolution. RIDE **9**, 168–194 (2018). https://doi.org/10.23913/ride.v9i17.377
20. Annone, M.E.: The 4.0 revolution and the design of the university curriculum (2019). http://revista-ideides.com/785-2/
21. Fidalgo-Blanco, Á., Sein-Echaluce, M.L., García-Peñalvo, F.J.: Method based on education 4.0 to improve learning: lessons learned from COVID-19. ITEN **25** (2022). https://doi.org/10.5944/ried.25.2.32320
22. Gonzalez, Y.: Qualification of human talent against the 4.0 organization and its innovations. Spaces **41** (2020). National Open and Distance University, Colombia, https://doi.org/10.48082/spaces-a20v41n49p18
23. Kopp, M., Gröblinger, O., Adams, S.: Five common assumptions that prevent digital transformation at higher education institutions, Valencia, Spain, March 2019. https://doi.org/10.21125/inted.2019.0445
24. Pedraja-Rejas, L., Rodríguez-Ponce, E., Muñoz-Fritis, C.: Transformational leadership and innovative culture: effects on institutional quality. RVG **26**, 1004–1018 (2021). https://doi.org/10.52080/rvgluz.26.96.2
25. Flores Arocutipa, J.P., Manrique Nugent, M.A.L., Serna Silva, G.J., Aybar Bellido, I.E.: Leadership in times of the 4th industrial revolution. RVG **26**, 1096–1107 (2021). https://doi.org/10.52080/rvgluz.26.96.7
26. Lombana Bermudez, A.: The evolution of digital divides and the rise of artificial intelligence (AI). Mex. Mag. Distance Bac. **10**, 17–25 (2018). https://doi.org/10.22201/cuaed.20074751e.2018.20.65884
27. Salavert, J.M.: Industry 4.0 and dehumanization: the rise of psychosocial risks in a changing and tireless environment. https://revista.aem.es/noticia/industria-40-y-deshumanizacion-el-auge-de-psychosocial-risks-in-a-changing-and-untiring-environment. Accessed 07 July 2022

Linear Regression Analysis of Heart Rate While Learning the Soccer Technique of Driving. A Case Study

Luis Arturo Espín Pazmiño[1,2](✉) iD

[1] Facultad de Informática, Universidad de La Plata, Calle 50 &, Av. 120, La Plata, Provincia de Buenos Aires, Argentina
luis.espinp@ug.edu.ec
[2] Facultad de Ciencias Matemáticas y Físicas Cdla, Universidad de Guayaquil, Salvador Allende. Av. Delta y Av. Kennedy, Guayaquil, Ecuador

Abstract. Soccer ball driving with both profiles and edges, based on the development of an application using virtual environments in Python. In the article, as an advance of a doctoral thesis, a case study is presented, concerning the analysis of heart rate data of an 11-year-old participant in several training sessions, while learning one of the techniques. Heart rate is one of the physiological parameters directly related to people's emotional behavior in the different activities carried out, in this case, in learning physical movements in a specific sport. Over a month, with 20 training sessions for 15 min each, the participant was asked to perform the same technique in three specific scenarios each day. They downloaded the sensor data after each training session for data collection with the optical heart rate sensor using the Polar Verity Sense bracelet, with excellent fit and precision. For data analysis, developing a Python application with several packages/libraries, such as the pip tool, allowed the creation of two-dimensional scatters plots with a machine learning prediction model based on linear regression.

Keywords: Heart rate · Linear regression · Soccer techniques · Python · Machine learning

1 Introduction

In a world as competitive as sports, any detail, no matter how small, makes a big difference; the data offered by the different sensors and other means provide an extra competitive advantage that can be differential. The use of wearables, cameras, and various software offers a variety of data that can be processed and analyzed, giving way to a new stage where the other actors linked to sport can improve their training and decision-making capabilities. Technology has reached the sports industry and impacted the results of teams and athletes due to improved techniques, new training methods, and predictive data analysis [1].

Emotional states can generate stereotyped or automatic responses to different situations due to their functional nature. However, dynamic behavior is more specific by

K. Abad and S. Berrezueta (Eds.): DSICT 2022, CCIS 1647, pp. 71–82, 2022.
https://doi.org/10.1007/978-3-031-18347-8_6

performing a task for which the individual trained or has generated hours of training and put into practice in the analysis of a situation where the decisions making were almost immediately; the non-interference of the emotional state is caused, at least on a not so decisive level [2].

Distinctive, generalized affective reaction patterns usually show common character-istics in all human beings. These emotions are joy, sadness, anger, surprise, fear, and disgust. We can even defend that they are characterized by a series of physiological or motor reactions of their own [3]. Within a dimensional analysis of emotions, the varia-tion of the physiological activity is identified, specifically of the heart rate; according to the study, it decreases, has a slight increase, or the indices of this indicator rise.

Coping with pressure and anxiety is an ineluctable demand of sports performance. Heart rate variability (HRV) Biofeedback (BFB) shall be used as a tool for self regulating physiological responses resulting in improved psycho physiological interactions. For further analysis, the study has been designed to examine the relationship between anxiety and performance and also effectiveness of biofeedback protocol to create stress-eliciting situation in basketball players. The support the idea that HRV BFB lowers the anxiety and thus there seems to be a potential association between HRV BFB and performance optimization [4]. The importance of anxiety and other emotional and personality factors in sports competition has been recognized for many years. Stress refers to a complex psychobiological process that consists of three major elements: stressors, perceptions or appraisals of danger, and emotional reactions [5].

Were revealed the bigger meanings of LF/HF in athletes with average level of stress resistance for concerning to athletes of high level of stress resistance indicates the ampli-fication of sympathetic and weakening of parasympathetic link of autonomic nervous system. The athletes with high stress resistance level has high of level of heart rate vari-ability and low of centralization of heart rate regulation for compared to athletes with average level of stress resistance [6].

As a variable to assess parasympathetic activity, the square root of the mean of the differences in the sum of the squares between adjacent RR intervals (RMSSD) was calculated, together with the stress score (SS) as an indicator of sympathetic activity.The analysis of this monitoring would serve to detect possible fatigue states in the early stages and to modify, if necessary, the training load planning in preparation [7].

Machine learning represents a large field presented in information technology, statis-tics, probability, artificial intelligence, psychology, neurobiology and many other disci-plines. With machine learning the problems can be solved simply by building a model that is a good representation of a selected dataset. In regression analysis the goal is to pre-dict a continuous target variable, whereas another area called classification is predicting a label from a finite set [8].

2   Methods and Materials

2.1   Competitor

For the study, a male competitor was monitored, who at the time of the experiment was 11 years old and three months old, weighing 32 kg. And height of 136 cm, for an entire month that included twenty training sessions. Each training session was planned to consider the practice of the technique of driving the ball with both profiles and edges [9], in a time of fifteen minutes, with three pre-established scenarios of five minutes, respectively. Each day, before data collection, the participant performed a brief directed warm-up with the respective elongation movements to reduce the probability of injury. The participant was informed about the procedure that would be followed, with the consent of his legal guardian, to conduct this case study (Fig. 1).

Fig. 1. Participant in several training sessions with the bracelet.

2.2 Type of Study

This case study is of an evaluative type since it implies description and explanation to reach judgments about the reality under investigation [10], the data collection technique was applied through the optical heart rate sensor; for For processing, an interface with Python programming language was used and by the inductive method, based on premises and identified patterns, hypotheses that described the experiment were presented in a general way.

2.3 Procedure

Type of Data: The data compared is primary since it was taken in real-time using the Polar Verity Sense optical heart rate sensor [11] with a storage option (Fig. 2), to later be loaded as a.csv file in the application developed for this study and be presented in a graphical interface, for consultation, visualization, and analysis.

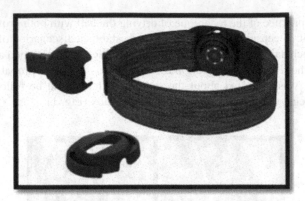

Fig. 2. Polar verity sense - optical heart rate sensor band.

The variation per second of cardiac performance in beats per minute throughout the development of each training session was recorded. According to the Polar Flow sensor application version 6.6.0, for the analysis and the age, weight, and height of the participant, the essential data considered in the study were the following (Table 1):

Table 1. According to the participant, heart rate indicators were obtained from the sensor application.

Indicator	Data
Maximum heart rate	200 bpm
Resting heart rate	55 bpm
Aerobic threshold	150 bpm
The anaerobic threshold	180 bpm

The experiment created three specific scenarios divided into the established fifteen minutes (five minutes for each system) of applying the defined technique for driving the ball. In the first scenario, the participant had to move the ball with both profiles and edges in a single direction and avoid touching the disks that delimited the route and space. In the second scenario, the participant had to practice driving the ball with both profiles and edges, back and forth, avoiding touching the discs that delimited the route and space. However, in this scenario, the participant was instructed to control the time that would be taken in the development of the exercise; in this way, it creates a moment of emotional stress. In the third scenario, the participant had to apply the technique of driving the ball with both profiles and edges in a single direction, avoiding touching the discs that delimited the route, and in the end, culminating the action with the variant of trying, with a shot to the arch, knock down a cone located in the angle 5 m from where the conduction ended.

Information, establishing a model of emotional behavior. The three scenarios presented moments of emotional stress and decision-making, where the participant had to carry out the exercise, apply the technique in the correct way possible, and try not to make coordination errors in the face of the different variants. The ball conduction technique with both profiles and edges [9], established for this experiment, was conduction avoiding contact with the discs that marked the route, constantly entering with the inner edge of the profile of the side in action, and leaving with the outer edge of the other shape, repeating the exercise successively. For the participant, the driving technique used in this experiment was known and had previously been trained; in this case, the main objective was to improve the application of the method, seek a relationship with the collection of heart rate data and evaluate said rate (Fig. 3).

Fig. 3. Participant in one of the training sessions applying the ball driving technique exercise with both profiles and edges.

3   Description and Development of the Application

The development of the application to the current product went through two phases defined according to the main objective of correlating emotional states by monitoring the participant's heart rate with the learning of the established soccer technique. The model used was Supervised Machine Learning algorithms [8], precisely Simple Linear Regression, since, after the systematic review of the proposal, it was concluded as the most feasible and convenient technique.

Initially, it was considered to use the data that would be loaded in a.csv file to generate the graphs of each of the training sessions, identifying the heart rate in unit bpm, as the dependent variable (Y) and the time in unit minutes, as the independent variable (X), these being the data that were used for the construction of the application in its two phases (Fig. 4).

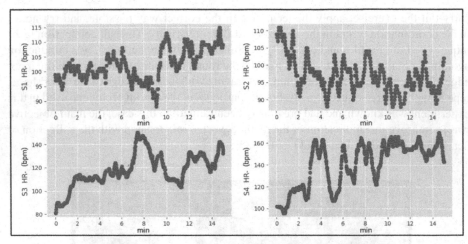

Fig. 4. Recording of the heart rate (bpm) (Y) of the training sessions (S1–S4), for 15 min (X), in a graph generated by the application - first phase.

In a second phase, for this case study and with a view to testing in groups, modifications were made, using the linear regression algorithm for machine learning, with the technique of supervised machine learning algorithms, which allowed us to approximate the dependency relationship between the established variables of heart rate and time, thus obtaining the automatic generation of the line, to receive prediction trends in the monitoring of learning techniques in individual participants.

The development environment used for programming was Visual Studio [12], the same one that allowed for creating the application and making the respective tests and iterations. For data manipulation, calculation, and analysis with the Python programming language, several libraries were imported, such as NumPy and its Pandas extension [13]; for the graphical interface, the standard library for Python was used, which is Tkinter; The Matplotlib [14] library was used to create graphs, and to fulfill the objective of model inference, the Scikit-learn machine learning library [15] was used, which facilitates the preprocessing, training, optimization and optimization stages.

4   Results

4.1   Based on Linear Regression Analysis

According to the graphs of prediction trends applying the linear regression technique, it can be verified that, of the 20 training sessions, 17 sessions presented a positive slope (m), that is, a straight line with an increasing function, whereas $x2 > x1 \rightarrow f(x2) > f(x1)$, three sessions had a slope (m) negative, that is, a decreasing function.

In general terms, it can be inferred that, in aerobic-type training for learning soccer techniques, by creating different scenarios with variables of emotional impact, the prediction model indicates the increase in heart rate; in this case, a study in 85% of the training sessions.

Likewise, random factors should be considered to obtain a relationship between the prediction trend and the learning of the technique (Figs. 5, 6, 7, 8 and 9).

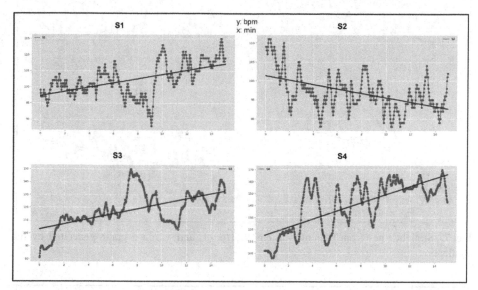

Fig. 5. Straight lines from training sessions 1, 2, 3, and 4, in a graph generated by the application.

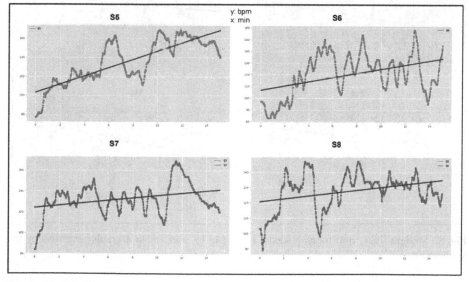

Fig. 6. Straight lines from training sessions 5, 6, 7, and 8, in a graph generated by the application.

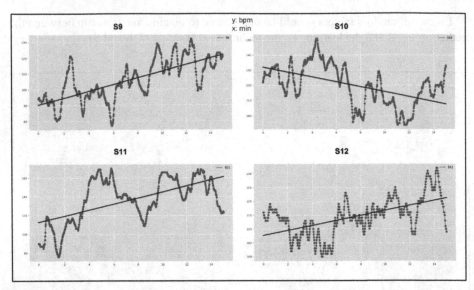

Fig. 7. Straight lines from training sessions 9, 10, 11, and 12, in a graph generated by the application.

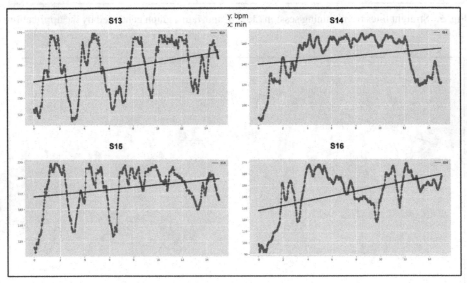

Fig. 8. Straight lines from training sessions 12, 14, 15, and 16, in a graph generated by the application.

4.2   Based on the Heart Rate Data Obtained in the Training Sessions

These data were obtained in the prototype of the application in the first phase, where the graphs generated by the application in each training session showed that the heart

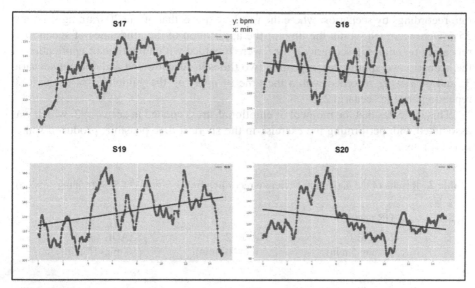

Fig. 9. Straight lines from training sessions 17, 18, 19, and 20, in a graph generated by the application.

rate range in which the training sessions were developed was from 80 to 170 bpm, which indicates that, in no session, the participant reached the maximum heart rate, nor the anaerobic heart rate threshold (200 bpm and 180 bpm, respectively). Regarding the aerobic threshold of heart rate (150 bpm), in 6 sessions, this data was not reached; in all the other sessions, work was done above the aerobic threshold at some point of the established time.

The average heart rate in the 20 training sessions was 128 bpm; only in training session 15 the average heart rate exceeds the heart rate aerobic threshold of 150 bpm to 154 bpm, so it is concluded that the training sessions of learning the technique of driving the ball with both profiles and edges, were strictly aerobic.

A statistical analysis of the data showed that the mean minimum heart rate of the 20 training sessions was 91 bpm. In contrast, the mean maximum speed of all the training sessions was 154 bpm, with a standard deviation of 21.9 and a coefficient of variation of 0.17; these results demonstrate that the relative spread of the data set is reliable for estimating the interpretation of the experiment.

4.3 Based on the Scenarios Established by Time

The training time for the technique of driving the soccer ball, using both profiles and the external and internal edges, was divided into three parts: five minutes for each piece. Three different scenarios were designated in each period; the first scenario presented minimal complexity and had the objective of applying the technique by the route traced by disks; the second scenario aimed to use the tone correctly in the shortest time possible; and the third scenario, the technique was applied, culminating the exercise with an archery attempt to knock down a cone. Table 2 - shows the results of the maximum heart rate recordings by scenarios, where the results express that of the 20 training sessions, 25% were recorded within the time of the application of the guidelines of scenario 1, repeating two times in scenario 2; 50% were recorded within the time of application of the scenario two approaches, repeating two times in scenario one and once in scenario 3; and 40% were recorded within the time of applying the guidelines of scenario 3, repeating once in scenario 2.

This indicates that the moment of emotional stress created in scenario 2, which was associated with performing the exercise in the shortest time possible, produced spikes in heart rate.

Table 2. Results of the maximum heart rate recording by scenarios. (*T.S. = training session)

T. S	HR max		
	STAGE 1 [0 min–5 min]	STAGE 2 (5 min–10 min)	STAGE 3 (10 min–15 min)
1			X
2	X		
3		X	
4			X
5		X	X
6			X
7			X
8	X	X	
9			X
10	X		
11		X	
12			X
13	X	X	
14		X	
15	X		
16			X
17		X	
18		X	
19		X	
20		X	

5 Discussion

The initial contribution of this case was the participant's heart rate recorded concerning time in the training of a soccer technique processed in a Python application with the simple linear regression technique of supervised machine learning and that, according to the prediction trends, generated a value criterion, on the other hand, in test time and with a systematic review of heart rate data in aerobic load physical training, the next version for the application is to be included in the model, the distribution of data according to emotional states, based on the representation of the Watson & Tellegen model of positive and negative affect [16].

From another point of view, the learning of the specific soccer technique in predefined experimental scenarios to a participant in the formative stage, through an application and the monitoring of the heart rate, relevant data in the regulation of emotional behavior, was also analyzed by carrying out training sessions in controlled scenarios, where there was no more significant inference of pressure and stress from external factors other than the variants of the instructions in each of the designs, the role of the coach, and the participant's mood.

For an analysis improvement in future advances in the application of this doctoral thesis study, concerning the emotional behavior of the participants, in addition to the heart rate, the electrical conductivity of the skin will be included as a variable in the data collection (GSR), an appropriate option for this type of study, with the variant of applying multiple linear regression to the model. The idea is that this model is available to make predictions of new training sessions with groups at different levels of training in learning soccer techniques, that it is capable of searching for an ideal method including variables of emotional impact and control of dynamic behavior, considering the data used in this study. Discuss the implications of these findings and suggestions for future research.

References

1. Fava, L., Vilches, D., Ferraresso, A., Boccalari, E., Díaz, J.: Inteligencia y tecnologías aplicadas al deporte de alto rendimiento. Red de Universidades con Carreras en Informática (RedUNCI), pp. 698–702 (2020)
2. Espín Pazmiño, L., Enderica Malo, M.: Influencia emocional en árbitros de fútbol aplicando tecnologías de sensores. Rev. Tecnol. ESPOL 33(2), 226–238 (2021)
3. Chóliz Montañés, M.: Psicología de la emoción: el proceso emocional, Valencia: Dpto de Psicología Básica - Universidad de Valencia (2005)
4. Paul, M., Garg, K.: The effect of heart rate variability biofeedback on performance psychology of basketball players. Appl. Psychophysiol. Biofeedback 37, 131–144 (2012). https://doi.org/10.1007/s10484-012-9185-2
5. Hackfort, D., Spielberger, C.: Anxiety in Sports: An International Perspective. Taylor and Francis, New York (1989)
6. Korobeynikov, G., Korobeynikova, L., Potop, V., Nikonorov, D., Semenenko, V.: Heart rate variability system in elite athletes with different levels of stress. J. Phys. Educ. Sport 18(2), 550–554 (2018)
7. Nieto-Jimenez, C., Ruso-Álvarez, J., Pardos-Mainer, E., Naranjo, J.: Heart rate varibility in the training monitoring of an ironman runner. a case study. RETOS. Nuevas tendencias en Educación Física, Deporte y Recreación, n° 37, pp. 339–343 (2020)

8. Nasteski, V.: An overview of the supervised machine learning methods. Horizons **4**, 51–62 (2017)
9. Carlos Amaya, M., Espinosa Sánchez, M.: El análisis de la conducción del balón en el futbol soccer, Estudios de Antropología Biológica - Universidad Nacional Autónoma De México, vol. XIII, pp. 1180–1193 (2007)
10. Pérez Serrano, G.: Investigación cualitativa. Retos, interrogantes y métodos, España: La Muralla (1994)
11. Gil, D., et al.: Validity of average heart rate and energy expenditure in polar OH1 and verity sense while self-paced running. Int. J. Exerc. Sci.: Conf. Proc. **14** (2021)
12. Visual studio code (2022). https://code.visualstudio.com/docs. Accessed 2022
13. Pandas (2022). https://pandas.pydata.org/. Accessed 2022
14. Matplotlib: visualization with python (2021). https://matplotlib.org/. Accessed 2022
15. Scikit-learn (2022). https://scikit-learn.org/stable/. Accessed 2022
16. Watson, D., Tellegen, A.: Toward a consensual structure of mood. Psychol. Bull. **98**, 219–335 (1985)

Optimization Models Used in Water Allocation Problems in River Basin with Reservoirs: A Systematic Review

Berenice Guerrero[iD], Magali Mejía-Pesántez[iD], and Jaime Veintimilla-Reyes[(✉)][iD]

Department of Computer Sciences, Faculty of Engineering, Universidad de Cuenca, Cuenca, Ecuador

{berenice.guerrero,magali.mejia,
jaime.veintimilla}@ucuenca.edu.ec

Abstract. In recent years, several works dedicated to obtaining optimization models have been published. Many of them have been applied in the management of water resources, especially since water is a vital resource that brings economic, social and environmental benefits. The main objective of this article is to review the published literature on optimization models and understand what methods their authors used to solve optimization problems in water allocation in a river basin with reservoirs. A systematic methodology was applied to select research questions, digital databases and search terms to later use practical and methodological filters to carry out this systematic review. This procedure allowed a review and synthesis of the results obtained on the optimization models. It was found that the models resulting from the systematic review vary depending on the objectives set by the diverse authors. However, algorithms based on particle swarm optimization (PSO) have a greater presence compared to the rest of the algorithms present in this systematic review.

Keywords: Systematic review · Water allocation · River basin · Meta-heuristics · Heuristics · Reservoirs

1 Introduction

Water is an important resource that can be represented by a nexus known as the WEF-nexus (water-energy-food nexus). The nexus includes water supply, sewage treatment, and hydro-power generation in a reservoir water system [1]. The optimal design of a water allocation system that meets this nexus has become an urgent research topic [2].

The allocation of water in a river basin with reservoirs can be optimized to meet the demands of different nodes that seek to comply with the WEF-nexus. This optimization problem can be approached with different methods, one of them being heuristic and meta-heuristic methods [3]. These methods have been applied in other problems related to the management of water resources; including, optimization of reservoir operation, distribution of water through pipelines, expansion of the capacity of water infrastructure facilities, water conduction problems/shortest water route, etc. [4]. It should be noted

© The Author(s), under exclusive license to Springer Nature Switzerland AG 2022
K. Abad and S. Berrezueta (Eds.): DSICT 2022, CCIS 1647, pp. 83–93, 2022.
https://doi.org/10.1007/978-3-031-18347-8_7

that in all these studies the objectives to be optimized were exclusive to the study area. The objectives vary as the methods applied. For this reason, it is intended to carry out a systematic literature review on heuristic or meta-heuristic methods applied specifically in water allocation optimization problems in a river system with reservoirs.

As indicated above, systematic reviews focusing on water resources and heuristic methods are found in the literature, but an exclusive systematic review for optimizing water allocation in a river system with reservoirs is not found. The rest of the paper is organized as follows. Section 2 indicates the methodology used to review the optimization models systematically. Section 3 presents the results and discussion. Finally, the conclusion of the document is provided in Sect. 4.

2   Materials and Methods

The systematic review design responded to the purpose of collecting, selecting, evaluating and summarizing the evidence found regarding the heuristic or meta-heuristic methods that have been applied in optimization problems of water allocation in a river system with reservoirs. To carry out this systematic review, the Fink methodology was used, which consists of the following tasks: 1) Select Research Questions, 2) Select Bibliographic Databases and Websites, 3) Choose Search Terms, 4) Apply Practical Screen, 5) Apply Methodological Quality Screen, 6) Do the review and 7) Synthesize the results [5].

The systematic review began with the selection of the research questions. It was established that the main question to be answered was: What heuristic or meta-heuristic methods have been applied in water distribution optimization problems in a river system with reservoirs? Subsequently, the search sub-questions were defined, whose objective was to obtain information to delimit the field of research studied. These questions were: 1) What were the objectives of the water allocation optimization problems in the river basin? 2) What tools or solvers are used to solve optimization models? 3) What parts are involved in the optimization process? And 4) What indicators are used to analyze or validate the results of the optimization model?

Once the field of the research was defined, it was necessary to select the bibliographic databases and the websites. Google Scholar is selected because this search engine allows to incorporate personalized search strings with 'and' and 'or' operators; and also allows access to articles published in various journals and databases. To search for the primary articles to reference this work, a search string was defined, which is detailed in Table 1.The string was made up of the relevant terms and logical connectors, which made it possible to combine different terms and establish logical relationships between them. Articles referenced within the articles resulting from the search are also considered if they meet the criteria indicated in Table 1.

With the structured search string, 178 articles were retrieved. With the results obtained after applying the first filters, the articles that met the inclusion criteria were selected after reviewing titles, abstracts and keywords. Once all the filters were applied, a manual review of the articles was carried out to determine the secondary sources. A total of 43 articles were read to determine their reliability. Next, the articles were selected based on the use of an optimization method and the explanation on how to use

Table 1. Search criteria for the systematic literature review

Search string	("heuristic" or "meta heuristic") and ("optimization" and modeling or simulation) and ("water allocation") and (river "basin" or "river" or river with "reservoirs")
Search dates	2010–2022
Language	English and Spanish
Inclusion criteria	**Exclusion criteria**
Studies that apply heuristic or meta-heuristic methods for optimizing or simulating the allocation of water over a river basin or similar water systems. May or may not contain reservoirs	Studies focused exclusively on reservoir management, since the objective is the entire river system and not just the reservoir
Literature reviews that include heuristic or meta-heuristic methods applied in problems of optimization and/or simulation in a river system or similar	Distribution of water in cropping areas that do not consider the river system as part of the problem
Articles that include heuristics or meta-heuristics in hydro-logical projects that are similar to the allocation of water in a river system	Piped water distribution and groundwater allocation

it, the objective functions, the restrictions and the results obtained with their proposed model. In addition, the articles also had to meet the inclusion criteria detailed in Table 1. Through this selection, a total of 16 articles were obtained for the systematic review. It is worth mentioning that literature review articles related to this topic were also found, which provide an overview of heuristic methods, of which 6 literature reviews stand out.

3   Results and Discussion

This section presents the main findings on this systematic review and summarizes the results obtained after filtering the articles. Considering the inclusion criteria mentioned in the previous section, articles useful for this literature review were classified and can be seen in Table 1.

3.1   Research Questions

In the main research question of this literature review, which is: What heuristic or meta-heuristic methods have been applied in water allocation optimization problems in a river system with reservoirs? To answer this question, the classification of heuristic algorithms mentioned in [6] should be mentioned, which can be seen in Fig. 1.

The classification showed in Fig. 1 plus the histogram (see Fig. 2) allow to observe that there is an emphasis on population-based algorithms, where algorithms of the

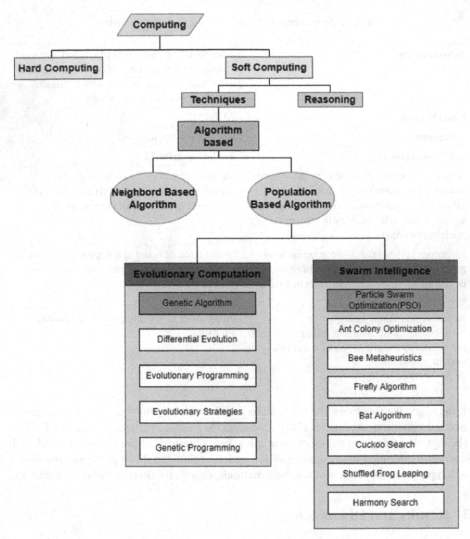

Fig. 1. Part of the classification of the heuristic algorithms by Kumar and Yavar [6].

"swarm intelligence" type have a greater presence with a total of 13 items. Within these articles, specific algorithms such as PSO, ACO, HS, etc., are applied.

In the research sub-question 1: What were the objectives of the water allocation optimization problems in the river basin? The articles reviewed had different objectives, however, the difference is that certain articles had the objective of testing or validating a novel hybrid algorithm, while other studies had the objective of solving the optimization problem without giving priority to the algorithm. Another of the objectives found is the focus on the reservoirs, but it should be emphasized that the study did not focus only on the reservoirs, however, it does present greater interest in these rather than the rest of the variables to be considered within the problem. For example, [7] aims to find optimal

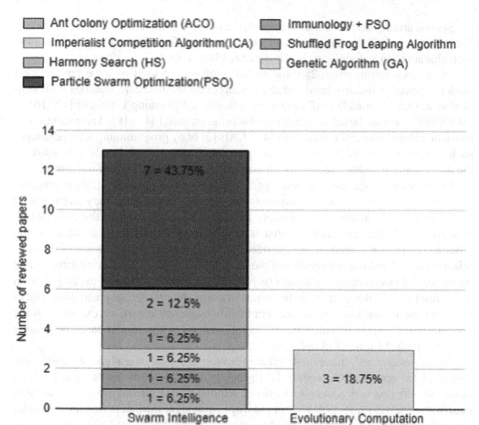

Fig. 2. Histogram of the heuristic methods used in the reviewed articles.

values for a large number of water discharges in the network links (rivers and canals) and nodes (reservoirs and demands) while also looking for the optimal values of reservoir capacities and their storage priorities.

Another objective to highlight is the emphasis on social aspects. This is the case of [8], which proposes a socioeconomic model with two objectives. The first one is to maximize economic profitability and maximize employment. In the second objective the influence of water distribution on social welfare is considered. Other studies [2, 8–11] also have a social approach when considering the allocation of water to meet the population's demand for water without considering whether there is economic benefit or not.

It is also considered an important objective to seek an ecological balance when allocating water. This is the case in studies [9, 11–14]. For example, in [14] the objective is summarized in minimizing water scarcity and the amount of contaminated water, but it also seeks to maximize economic interests including the generation of hydroelectric power. The other articles also presented several objectives, but they considered ecological balance important.

Several articles also mention the importance of agricultural areas [2, 8, 9, 12, 15–17]. For example, in [17] there is a focus on water allocation for irrigation that is compatible with climate change conditions in the Borkhar Plain in Iran.

In research sub-question 2: What tools or solvers are used to solve optimization models? Some of the articles decided to incorporate the heuristic methods with simulation models such as WEAP (water assessment and planning software) [12, 16] or MODSIM (software based on network flow programming) [17, 18]. The execution of heuristic algorithms can be done with MATLAB [2] or by programming with languages such as python. The articles do not specify in detail what software tools were used for the programming and/or execution of the algorithms, they only present the results.

In research sub-question 3: What parts are involved in the optimization process? The steps carried out in [8] encompasses the steps to follow in a study starting with data collection. In addition, it considers the distribution of water in the agricultural, industrial and human consumption area, with the incorporation of social and economic criteria. The parts involved are summarized in: Data collection, preparation of the optimization model and implementation of the model. In the data collection is contemplated the water sources, necessary statistics (economic, population, etc.) and existing data on water resources. When preparing the optimization model, the decision variables, objectives and restrictions must be defined. For the implementation part, the execution of the optimization model is included as well as the analysis of the results based on what is indicated in the objectives of the study.

In the research sub-question 4: What indicators are used to analyze or validate the results of the optimization model? Two general forms of validation of results can be observed. The first way is to compare the developed meta-heuristic model with another heuristic model [2, 11, 19, 20]. The second way is to analyze the Pareto front and consider the different trade-offs between the objectives [2, 9, 10, 12, 14, 16]. Comparisons are also made with the current situation, as is the case of [8], where the PSO algorithm gave results that produced a growth of 38% in economic benefits and profitability in the agricultural sector, a growth of 86% in the industrial sector and overall economic growth of 54% relative to current condition.

The results of the systematic review have revealed the main characteristics of two families of recurrent optimization methods, such as algorithms based on evolution and algorithms based on population intelligence. Furthermore, it is highlighted that these methods could work alone or be combined with other optimization processes, simulation techniques or meta-models to improve model performance.

In addition to minimizing water scarcity in demand areas for human consumption, there is also interest in distributing water in industrial and agricultural areas. These areas not only produce goods such as food but can also be a job generator and produce economic benefit to the region. Another interest is how the allocation of water can affect the environment and also how to comply with the ecological well-being of the region. The area that appears most in the revised bibliography is the socioeconomic part. This area is large and encompasses social aspects such as the right to access to drinking water as well as the reduction of costs (costs in reservoirs, agricultural production that will give more income, industrial production that brings economic income and also a source of job, etc.). These areas can present conflicts. For example, to increase the economic benefit in an area such as the industrial one, the amount of water in the agricultural area can be restricted.

The articles found for this literature review have simulation-optimization approaches, multi-objective optimization, improvements of classical algorithms, or construction of hybrid algorithms. In this study context, simulation-optimization models refer to the process of incorporating a meta-heuristic algorithm into a simulation model. For example, in [16] this approach is used. WEAP is the simulation model, which consists of a water evaluation and planning software that optimizes water distribution decisions using linear programs [12]. But water distribution optimization problems are usually nonlinear on a large scale, so it is possible to integrate this WEAP system with the meta-heuristic algorithm to optimize the problem. In this way, the general framework consists of defining the objective functions, executing the meta-heuristic algorithm and determining if the objective was met using the simulation (WEAP) to evaluate the objective functions with the values found by the meta-heuristic algorithm.

Another term to mention is multi-objective optimization. In order to understand the concept, is necessary to emphasize that there are different approaches for handling constraints in evolutionary algorithms [21], which include: penalty functions, repair operators or local search, modified matching/mutation operators that preserve constraints, and multi-objective formulations where constraints are reformulated as objectives. Multi-objective optimization seeks to approximate Pareto optimal trade-offs between conflicting objectives. These trade-offs are made up of the set of solutions that are better than all other solutions in at least one objective and are called non-dominated or Pareto optimal solutions [22]. A strength of multi-objective optimization is its ability to quickly approximate the true Pareto surface, even if it is not exactly quantified [21].

Starting with the classical PSO algorithm, which is based on the social behavior of flocks of birds to search through multidimensional dimension spaces, it has been widely used in the optimization of water resource systems [16] and it is also one of the most recurrent algorithms within this systematic review (table). This algorithm has been applied in conjunction with the multi-objective and simulation-optimization approach. In [16] both approaches are used generating a MOPSO-WEAP model to analyze the effectiveness of a water distribution project. In this case WEAP is the simulation model while MOPSO is the heuristic goal. Two objective functions were defined which were to minimize the sizes of the project infrastructures and to maximize the reliability of the water supply to the agricultural lands. The results of applying optimization-simulation with PSO (MOPSO-WEAP) indicated that the project can meet these objectives.

Another study that uses the simulation-optimization technique is the one carried out in [17], which in this case uses MODSIM (based on network flow programming) as a simulation model and it is combined with the optimization algorithm lobo gris (GWO – Gray Wolf Optimization) to obtain the optimal amounts of irrigation and crop areas in the plain under two conditions: status quo, and with flows affected by climate change. The studied basin is the Zayandehroud basin, first its network is elaborated in the MODSIM model and the information related to each node is entered based on the data measured in the meteorological and hydrometric stations. The objective function of the model is to maximize profits from crop production and plan the optimal distribution of water.

Continuing with the line of studies where simulation and optimization are applied, is the one carried out in [18]. This study affirms that the simulation system would avoid having variables, functions, relationships, among others, and also achieve a continuous system. But the meta heuristic must evaluate the objective function on this simulation, which becomes computationally intensive. For this they propose the meta-model, which is used to produce computationally efficient substitutes for high-fidelity models. The most common are ANN, SVM, kriqing and polynomial functions, which are evaluated in a water allocation problem based on surrogate optimization in the Atrak river basin in Iran. The simulation model used is MODSIM, which is a tool that allows analyzing the operation of river systems as networks of nodes and segments. While the applied heuristic goal is PSO. As conclusions, they determine that the ANN and SVM metamodels work better than others by saving the cost of evaluating the objective functions on the original model.

Another approach used is algorithm improvement. The study carried out by [23] uses a metaheuristic algorithm based on PSO, the Whale Optimization Algorithm (WOA). And on this algorithm, it uses an improvement (AWOA) to obtain a higher rate of convergence and precision. The aim of this study is to test the improvement versus traditional WOA and PSO algorithms for multi-objective water resource allocation resolution. In this case, the AWOA results indicate that there is higher convergence accuracy.

Hybrid algorithms are also presented, as is the case of [19], which integrates the weed optimization algorithm (WOA) and the particle swarm optimization algorithm (PSO), calling this hybrid WOAPSO. This algorithm is validated on two case studies, the first case study consists of an example of a river basin with 10 reservoirs, while the second is a hydropower optimization problem of three reservoirs in the Karoon river basin in Iran, which maximizes the efficiency index of hydroelectric power production. The results are compared with those obtained by the traditional algorithms of linear programming (LP), non-linear programming (NLP), WOA (in this case it is the weed algorithm - Weed Optimization Algorithm) and PSO; where WOAPSO proved to be more reliable in solving complex multi-reservoir systems in the context of integrated river basin management than classical optimization algorithms.

The next algorithm with the greatest presence is the genetic algorithm and its extensions. In [12] a Multi-Objective Optimization Genetic Algorithm (MOGA) is linked to Water Assessment and Planning (WEAP) software to optimize water allocation decisions over multiple years. The study region is Sistán, which is characterized as an arid zone, where the design variables of the problem consist of the cultivated area, the cultivation pattern and the wetland influx requirements for 30 years. The objective is to maximize the long-term net economic benefit and maximize the flow of water to the wetland. These objectives are incompatible between them, but the approach adopted in this study allows to obtain results that are analyzed by comparing purely economic scenarios versus multi-objective scenarios in the Pareto front. The authors also provide a description of the trade-offs in these scenarios to aid in the decision process for water resource stakeholders.

There is also the use of ant colonies (ACO) as an inspiration algorithm, which is a discrete combinatorial optimization algorithm based on the collective behavior of ants in their search for food. The literature review by [24] mentions that there are different versions of ACO that have proven to be flexible and powerful in solving a series of spatially and temporally complex water resource problems in discrete and continuous domains with unique objectives and/or multiple. One of the articles to highlight within this review is [13], which presents a multi-objective optimization framework with ACO to develop optimal trade-offs between water allocation and ecological benefit over a stretch of the Murray River in the South Australia. The results indicate that limited additional ecological benefit can be obtained as the allocation increases, by relaxing the flow constraints of the system. Additionally, the use of regulators can increase ecological benefits by using less water.

As indicated in the answer to question 4 of this systematic review, the majority of the authors of the reviewed articles include an analysis of the results. The analysis can be a comparison between optimization methods, or Pareto front analysis. It is also considered whether the algorithms can converge to an answer and the time taken. Another recurring analysis is the benefit obtained by optimizing the allocation of water and how much water was allocated to each demand node. Although not all the articles found are mentioned in detail, it can be seen that there is a strong inclination towards multi-objective methods and simulation-optimization. The improvement of classic algorithms or a mixture of algorithms to obtain new heuristics is also highlighted. Water resource management optimization problems in general are complex problems to be solved that depend on the number of variables to be considered, the objectives, the restrictions and the desired approach. Therefore, using improved metaheuristic, multi-objective and simulation-optimization methods turns out to be the best option for these problems. Another aspect to consider is the strong presence of PSO-based algorithms, since it offers a number of variants, as well as the flexibility to incorporate it with decision systems such as WEAP.

4 Conclusions

Although not all the articles found are mentioned in detail, it can be seen that there is a strong inclination towards multi-objective methods and simulation-optimization. The improvement of classic algorithms or the use of hybrid algorithms is also highlighted. Water resource management optimization problems in general are complex problems to be solved that depend on the number of variables to be considered, the objectives, the restrictions and the desired approach. Therefore, using improved meta-heuristic, multi-objective and simulation-optimization methods turns out to be the best option for these problems. In order to answer the main research question about which heuristic or meta-heuristic methods have been applied in water allocation optimization problems in a river system with reservoirs, it has been found that each author decided to use the method that best adapted to their needs. However, it is necessary to mention that there is a strong presence of PSO-based algorithms, since it offers a number of variants, as well as the flexibility to incorporate it with decision systems such as WEAP.

Both PSO and the others algorithms mentioned in this review have their limitations. In the study carried out in [6], the advantages and disadvantages of some meta-heuristic algorithms in water resources problems, including PSO, are summarized. For PSO's family of algorithms, [6] mentions that the advantage of this type of algorithm is that they are simple to code and provide fast convergence, also implying a low computational cost. As a disadvantage, it is necessary to adjust parameters such as inertial weight, social and cognitive parameters. However, if the parameters are set correctly, the algorithm can achieve a global solution.

This systematic review aims to facilitate decision making on optimization models that can be used in water allocation optimization problems in a river system with reservoirs, considering the effectiveness and efficiency that these had when applied in real scenarios.

References

1. Liu, D., et al.: Optimisation of water-energy nexus based on its diagram in cascade reservoir system. J. Hydrol. **569** (2018). https://doi.org/10.1016/j.jhydrol.2018.12.010
2. Yang, Y., Luo, Q., Ye, G.: Optimization of water allocation system at the river basins. In: 2018 14th International Conference on Natural Computation, Fuzzy Systems and Knowledge Discovery (ICNC-FSKD), Huangshan, China, pp. 482–488, July 2018. https://doi.org/10.1109/FSKD.2018.8687202
3. Labadie, J.W.: Optimal operation of multi reservoir systems: state-of-the-art review. J. Water Resour. Plann. Manag. **130**, 93–111 (2004)
4. Janga Reddy, M., Nagesh Kumar, D.: Evolutionary algorithms, swarm intelligence methods, and their applications in water resources engineering: a state-of-the-art review. H2Open J. **3**(1), 135–188 (2020). https://doi.org/10.2166/h2oj.2020.128
5. Fink, A.: Conducting Research Literature Reviews: From the Internet to Paper. Sage, Thousand Oaks (2013)
6. Kumar, V., Yadav, S.M.: A state-of-the-art review of heuristic and metaheuristic optimization techniques for the management of water resources. Water Supply (2022). https://doi.org/10.2166/ws.2022.010
7. Shourian, M., Mousavi, S.J.: Performance assessment of a coupled particle swarm optimization and network flow programming model for optimum water allocation. Water Resour. Manag. **31**(15), 4835–4853 (2017). https://doi.org/10.1007/s11269-017-1781-8
8. Habibi Davijani, M., Banihabib, M.E., Nadjafzadeh Anvar, A., Hashemi, S.R.: Multi-objective optimization model for the allocation of water resources in arid regions based on the maximization of socioeconomic efficiency. Water Resour. Manag. **30**(3), 927–946 (2016). https://doi.org/10.1007/s11269-015-1200-y
9. Babamiri, O., Azari, A., Maro, S.: An integrated fuzzy optimization and simulation method for optimal quality-quantity operation of reservoir-river system, p. 23 (2022)
10. Kazemi, M., Bozorg-Haddad, O., Fallah-Mehdipour, E., Loáiciga, H.A.: Inter-basin hydropolitics for optimal water resources allocation. Environ. Monit. Assess. **192**(7), 478 (2020). https://doi.org/10.1007/s10661-020-08439-3
11. Qu, G., Lou, Z.: Application of particle swarm algorithm in the optimal allocation of regional water resources based on immune evolutionary algorithm. J. Shanghai Jiaotong Univ. (Sci.) **18**(5), 634–640 (2013). https://doi.org/10.1007/s12204-013-1442-x
12. Farrokhzadeh, S., Hashemi Monfared, S., Azizyan, G., Sardar Shahraki, A., Ertsen, M., Abraham, E.: Sustainable water resources management in an arid area using a coupled optimization-simulation modeling. Water **12**(3), 885 (2020). https://doi.org/10.3390/w12030885
13. Szemis, J.M., Dandy, G.C., Maier, H.R.: A multiobjective ant colony optimization approach for scheduling environmental flow management alternatives with application to the River Murray, Australia: multiobjective approach for environmental flow management. Water Resour. Res. **49**(10), 6393–6411 (2013). https://doi.org/10.1002/wrcr.20518

14. Liu, D., et al.: A macro-evolutionary multi-objective immune algorithm with application to optimal allocation of water resources in Dongjiang River basins, South China. Stoch Environ. Res. Risk Assess. **26**(4), 491–507 (2012). https://doi.org/10.1007/s00477-011-0505-5

15. Ashrafi, S.M., Dariane, A.: A novel and effective algorithm for numerical optimization: Melody Search (MS), pp. 109–114, December 2011. https://doi.org/10.1109/HIS.2011.612 2089

16. Jamshid Mousavi, S., Anzab, N.R., Asl-Rousta, B., Kim, J.H.: Multi-objective optimization-simulation for reliability-based inter-basin water allocation. Water Resour. Manag. **31**(11), 3445–3464 (2017). https://doi.org/10.1007/s11269-017-1678-6

17. Jamshidpey, A., Shourian, M.: Crop pattern planning and irrigation water allocation compatible with climate change using a coupled network flow programming-heuristic optimization model. Hydrol. Sci. J. **66**(1), 90–103 (2021). https://doi.org/10.1080/02626667.2020.1844889

18. Mirfenderesgi, G., Mousavi, S.J.: Adaptive meta-modeling-based simulation optimization in basin-scale optimum water allocation: a comparative analysis of meta-models. J. Hydroinf. **18**(3), 446–465 (2016). https://doi.org/10.2166/hydro.2015.157

19. Asgari, H.-R., Bozorg-Haddad, O., Soltani, A., Loáiciga, H.A.: Optimization model for integrated river basin management with the hybrid WOAPSO algorithm. J. Hydro-Environ. Res. **25**, 61–74 (2019). https://doi.org/10.1016/j.jher.2019.07.002

20. Fang, G., et al.: Multi-objective differential evolution-chaos shuffled frog leaping algorithm for water resources system optimization. Water Resour. Manag. **32**(12), 3835–3852 (2018). https://doi.org/10.1007/s11269-018-2021-6

21. Nicklow, J., et al.: State of the art for genetic algorithms and beyond in water resources planning and management. J. Water Resour. Plann. Manag. **136**(4), 412–432 (2010). https://doi.org/10.1061/(ASCE)WR.1943-5452.0000053

22. Pareto, V.: Cours D'Economic Politique. Rouge, Lausanne (1896)

23. Yan, Z., Sha, J., Liu, B., Tian, W., Lu, J.: An ameliorative whale optimization algorithm for multi-objective optimal allocation of water resources in Handan, China. Water **10**(1), 87 (2018). https://doi.org/10.3390/w10010087

24. Afshar, A., Massoumi, F., Afshar, A., Mariño, M.A.: State of the art review of ant colony optimization applications in water resource management. Water Resour. Manag. **29**(11), 3891–3904 (2015). https://doi.org/10.1007/s11269-015-1016-9

Factors that Limit the Achievement of Learning in Telemedicine of Health Professionals in Peru

Augusto Felix Olaza-Maguiña[1]([✉]) [iD], Santiago Angel Cortez-Orellana[2] [iD],
Yuliana Mercedes De La Cruz-Ramirez[1] [iD],
and Nadezhda Tarcila De La Cruz-Ramirez[3] [iD]

[1] Universidad Nacional Santiago Antúnez de Mayolo, Centenario 200, Huaraz 02002, Peru
{aolazam,ydelacruzr}@unasam.edu.pe
[2] Universidad Peruana Los Andes, Giráldez 231, 12000 Huancayo, Peru
d.scortez@upla.edu.pe
[3] Hospital Víctor Ramos Guardia, Luzuriaga 1248, Huaraz 02001, Peru

Abstract. This research was carried out with the main objective of determining the factors that limit the achievement of learning in telemedicine of health professionals in primary healthcare institutions of the North Pacific Health Network of the Ancash region-Peru. A cross-sectional research design was applied, with 171 health professionals who worked during the 2020–2021 period in primary healthcare institutions of the North Pacific Health Network. An online questionnaire was developed and applied in January 2022. The SPSS V24.0 program and the Chi square statistical test were used. Regarding the results, the majority of health professionals considered having achieved unsatisfactory learning regarding the use of telemedicine services during the 2020–2021 period (49.1%). Regarding socio-demographic factors, the majority of professionals with an unsatisfactory learning achievement were women (43.8%), aged 50 years or older (40.9%), married (29.8%), nurses by profession (27.5%) and with a monthly salary of less than 2,500 soles or 638.21 USD (46.2%). Likewise, in relation to institutional factors, the majority of professionals was not beneficiaries of training in digital health education (47.3%), did not receive labor facilities of time to train in the application of telemedicine services (48.5%) and did not count with care protocols (46.2%), adequate equipment (48.5%) or agreements with other institutions for training by specialists (47.9%). All the aforementioned factors presented a statistically significant relationship with the achievement of learning in telemedicine ($p < 0.05$). It was concluded that socio-demographic and institutional factors limit the achievement of learning in telemedicine of health professionals in primary healthcare institutions of the North Pacific Health Network of the Ancash region-Peru, during the 2020–2021 period. The aforementioned should be taken into account by the authorities for the urgent training and improvement of the working conditions of health professionals, in order to promote the increasing implementation of telemedicine services in Peru.

Keywords: Digital health education · Healthcare · e-Learning · Telemedicine

K. Abad and S. Berrezueta (Eds.): DSICT 2022, CCIS 1647, pp. 94–105, 2022.
https://doi.org/10.1007/978-3-031-18347-8_8

1 Introduction

Telemedicine based on virtuality has been applied worldwide in various countries for several decades [1–3], not having had the same development and interest in Peru, due, among other reasons, to the lack of knowledge of most professionals of health about this term, as well as the lack of resources that still exists in health institutions, especially in the most remote and poorest places, where the percentage of digital divide and lack of Internet access exceeds the 50% [4].

However, despite what was stated in the preceding paragraph, a drastic and sudden change has been evidenced in Peru due to the COVID-19 pandemic, a change that has also been evidenced at the international level [5–7]. In this way, various researchers have highlighted the enormous effort that many health workers have developed to adapt to the challenges of health care during the health emergency, including learning new technologies and virtual application digital tools, which are used by telemedicine [8–10].

On the other hand, together with the effort shown by health professionals, the existence of factors that have influenced the telemedicine learning process has also been concluded. Thus, for example, in a study carried out in the United States, it was concluded that the ease of application perceived by professionals and the quality of the training received have had a positive impact on their perception of learning, the opposite happening when there were limitations as the lack of support from the authorities [11].

The North Pacific Health Network comprises a set of primary healthcare institutions dedicated to the care of communities located in the Ancash region-Peru, whose management is totally dependent on the Peruvian government, that is, it has state financing. In this way, as in other public health networks in the country, workers have had to face a difficult situation as a result of the health emergency caused by COVID-19, due to deficiencies in terms of infrastructure and equipment, as well as limited access to technological means and Internet services.

For its part, the level of digital health education of the workers of the North Pacific Health Network has also become a serious limitation, a situation similar to that observed in other countries such as Singapore [12]. In this sense, each health institution, together with its professionals, have had to look for training opportunities that ensure accelerated learning on issues related to telemedicine during the 2020–2021 period, whose self-perception of the level of learning achieved has not yet been studied in sufficient detail, as well as the exact limitations they have presented are unknown, especially in the most remote places of Peru.

Faced with the aforementioned considerations, the present study sought to address the following research questions:

What is the level of achievement perceived by health professionals regarding their learning in telemedicine in primary healthcare institutions of the North Pacific Health Network?

What are the socio-demographic factors that limit the achievement of learning in telemedicine of health professionals in primary healthcare institutions of the North Pacific Health Network?

What are the institutional factors that limit the achievement of learning in telemedicine of health professionals in primary healthcare institutions of the North Pacific Health Network?

In this sense, the present investigation was carried out with the main objective of determining the factors that limit the achievement of learning in telemedicine of health professionals in primary healthcare institutions of the North Pacific Health Network of the Ancash region-Peru, during the 2020–2021 period.

2 Methodology

2.1 Research Design and Population Under Study

It was decided to apply a cross-sectional research design, with a population made up of a total of 214 health professionals who worked during the 2020–2021 period in the primary healthcare institutions of the North Pacific Health Network, Ancash region-Peru.

It was considered as inclusion criterion to have worked during the 2020–2021 period in the North Pacific Health Network, regardless of the profession of the health worker; while the non-acceptance of participation was the only exclusion criterion that was taken into account.

Of the total population of 214 health professionals, 35 of them participated in the pilot test to assess the reliability of the data collection instrument, 8 refused to participate in the study, and 171 answered the final version of the data collection instrument.

2.2 Variables

Socio-demographic Factors. Age (25–49 years, ≥ 50 years), gender (male, female), marital status (single, married, cohabiting), profession (physician, nurse, obstetrician, dentist) and monthly salary (<2500.00 soles, ≥ 2500 soles).

Institutional Factors. Beneficiary of training in digital health education (yes, no), labor facilities of time to be trained in the application of telemedicine services (yes, no), existence of telemedicine care protocols (yes, no), suitable equipment (yes, no) and agreements with other institutions for training by specialists (yes, no).

Achievement of Learning in Telemedicine. Perception about the achievement of learning in telemedicine (unsatisfactory, moderately satisfactory, satisfactory).

2.3 Data Collection Procedure

Taking into account the aforementioned research variables, a questionnaire was prepared in an online format using the free Google Forms application, for which 11 questions were considered (Appendix section).

The validity of the online questionnaire was evaluated using the expert judgment technique, whose results of the 7 judges consulted were analyzed with the Kendall concordance test, demonstrating the validity of the questionnaire with a significance level of 0.001. Likewise, as previously mentioned, the reliability of the questionnaire was evaluated through a pilot test with 35 health professionals, also demonstrating the reliability of said data collection instrument (Cronbach's alpha index of 0.872).

The online application of the final version of the questionnaire was carried out during the month of January 2022, for which the link of the respective online form was sent to the personal emails of the health professionals, emphasizing voluntary participation.

2.4   Statistical Analysis

The information was processed using the statistical package SPSS, with a version of 24.0 for the Windows operating system. Likewise, according to the type of variable, a descriptive statistical analysis was applied, for which the results were presented by means of absolute frequencies and percentages. In the same way, the Chi square statistical test was applied with a significance level of $p < 0.05$, to evaluate the relationship between the research variables.

2.5   Ethical Considerations

The confidentiality of the data and the right to privacy of health professionals were respected throughout the research process, requiring in all cases the virtual registration of the declaration of informed consent, where the voluntary participation in the study was recorded, as part of the current ethical standards of the World Medical Association and the Declaration of Helsinki [13]. It should be noted that the research protocol was evaluated and approved by the Ethics Committee of the most important academic institution in the Ancash region, such as the Santiago Antúnez de Mayolo National University.

3   Results

Table 1 shows the demographic characteristics of the 171 health professionals who answered the final version of the online questionnaire, as detailed below:

Table 1. Demographic characteristics of health professionals.

Characteristic	n	%
Age:		
- 25–49 years	68	39.8
- ≥50 years	103	60.2
Gender:		
- Male	54	31.6
- Female	117	68.4
Marital status:		
- Single	21	12.3
- Married	84	49.1
- Cohabiting	66	38.6

Table 2 shows that the highest percentage of health professionals working in the North Pacific Health Network presented an unsatisfactory learning achievement in telemedicine during the 2020–2021 period (49.1%). Of this group, the majority was women (43.8%), aged 50 or over (40.9%), married (29.8%), nurses by profession (27.5%) and with a monthly salary of less than 2,500 soles, equivalent to 638.21 USD (46.2%). Likewise, a statistically significant relationship was found between all the socio-demographic factors studied and the learning achievement of health professionals in telemedicine (p < 0.05).

Table 2. Socio-demographic factors according to the achievement of learning in telemedicine.

Socio-demographic factors	Achievement of learning in telemedicine						Total		Chi-square results
	Unsatisfactory		Moderately satisfactory		Satisfactory				
	n	%	n	%	n	%	n	%	
Age:									
- 25–49 years	14	8.2	31	18.1	23	13.5	68	39.8	$X^2 =$ 52.554
- ≥ 50 years	70	40.9	32	18.7	1	0.6	103	60.2	p < 0.001
Total	84	49.1	63	36.8	24	14.1	171	100	
Gender:									
- Male	9	5.3	27	15.7	18	10.6	54	31.6	$X^2 =$ 41.576
- Female	75	43.8	36	21.1	6	3.5	117	68.4	p < 0.001
Total	84	49.1	63	36.8	24	14.1	171	100	
Marital status:									
- Single	7	4.1	11	6.4	3	1.8	21	12.3	$X^2 =$ 15.107
- Married	51	29.8	28	16.4	5	2.9	84	49.1	p = 0.005
- Cohabiting	26	15.2	24	14.0	16	9.4	66	38.6	
Total	84	49.1	63	36.8	24	14.1	171	100	
Profession:									
- Physician	3	1.8	15	8.8	8	4.7	26	15.3	
- Nurse	47	27.5	30	17.5	5	2.9	82	47.9	$X^2 =$ 47.969
- Obstetrician	30	17.5	14	8.2	2	1.2	46	26.9	p < 0.001
- Dentist	4	2.3	4	2.3	9	5.3	17	9.9	
Total	84	49.1	63	36.8	24	14.1	171	100	
Monthly salary:									
- <2500.00 soles	79	46.2	14	8.2	3	1.8	96	56.2	$X^2 =$ 97.019
- ≥2500 soles	5	2.9	49	28.6	21	12.3	75	43.8	p < 0.001
Total	84	49.1	63	36.8	24	14.1	171	100	

On the other hand, with respect to institutional factors (Table 3), it is observed that the majority of health professionals with unsatisfactory learning achievement, was not beneficiaries of training in digital health education (47.3%), did not receive labor facilities of time to train in the application of telemedicine services (48.5%) and did not count with care protocols (46.2%), adequate equipment (48.5%) or agreements with other institutions for training by specialists (47.9%). In this case, there was also evidence of a statistically significant relationship between all the institutional factors studied and the learning achievement of health professionals in telemedicine ($p < 0.05$).

Table 3. Institutional factors according to the achievement of learning in telemedicine.

Institutional factors	Achievement of learning in telemedicine						Total		Chi-square results
	Unsatisfactory		Moderately satisfactory		Satisfactory				
	n	%	n	%	n	%	n	%	
Beneficiary of training in digital health education:									
- Yes	3	1.8	37	21.6	18	10.5	58	33.9	$X^2 = 69.889$
- No	81	47.3	26	15.2	6	3.6	113	66.1	$p < 0.001$
Total	84	49.1	63	36.8	24	14.1	171	100	
Labor facilities of time:									
- Yes	1	0.6	21	12.3	20	11.7	42	24.6	$X^2 = 72.119$
- No	83	48.5	42	24.5	4	2.4	129	75.4	$p < 0.001$
Total	84	49.1	63	36.8	24	14.1	171	100	
Existence of telemedicine care protocols:									
- Yes	5	2.9	44	25.7	16	9.4	65	38.0	$X^2 = 72.092$
- No	79	46.2	19	11.1	8	4.7	106	62.0	$p < 0.001$
Total	84	49.1	63	36.8	24	14.1	171	100	
Suitable equipment:									
- Yes	1	0.6	18	10.5	18	10.5	37	21.6	$X^2 = 62.805$
- No	83	48.5	45	26.3	6	3.6	134	78.4	$p < 0.001$
Total	84	49.1	63	36.8	24	14.1	171	100	
Agreements with other institutions:									
- Yes	2	1.2	24	14.0	19	11.2	45	26.4	$X^2 = 63.897$
- No	82	47.9	39	22.8	5	2.9	126	73.6	$p < 0.001$
Total	84	49.1	63	36.8	24	14.1	171	100	

4 Discussion

The results found with respect to the main objective of the study, allowed determining that socio-demographic and institutional factors limit the achievement of learning in telemedicine of health professionals in primary healthcare institutions of the North Pacific Health Network of the Ancash region-Peru, during the period 2020–2021. In this way, similar results are evident in other studies regarding the existence of limitations that restrict and/or make it impossible to implement telemedicine services in many countries, especially those located in geographic regions characterized by a lack of planning and public health policies in primary healthcare institutions [14–17].

In this regard, socio-demographic factors constitute an important aspect to take into account, when evaluating training opportunities for health professionals, since it is a learning model based on adult education. Thus, for example, in a study carried out in South Africa [18], it is highlighted that factors such as the age of the participants influence the fulfillment of educational objectives and goals in postgraduate studies in telemedicine, due to the lack of knowledge of the most current technological tools, based mostly on virtuality [19].

Another important aspect is the gender of health professionals [20], on which it is highlighted that female workers have greater limitations to attend training in general, probably due to family activities, than in countries like Peru, are mostly in charge of women, regardless of their work or position held. This situation of inequity, such as the one disclosed in this article, would be even more marked in married or cohabiting health professionals, due to the multiple responsibilities and activities that they have to fulfill, mainly in the family environment.

In relation to the profession of health workers, it is also an important issue for the achievement of learning in telemedicine, especially for those health careers whose work performance in primary healthcare institutions is more focused on the development of educational tasks and home monitoring. The latter, according to other studies, would not affect medical professionals, since their activities would be of an eminently care nature through health consultations based on diagnosis and treatment [21, 22].

For its part, the monthly salary of health professionals, as found in this research, is a factor that definitely limits training opportunities, especially in courses that require the presence of trained educational institutions such as the telemedicine [19, 23]. In this way, in Peru the salary income of professionals is well below that of other countries, which together with the aforementioned socio-demographic conditions, has caused a gap between the level of specialization of professionals who work in large cities of Peru such as Lima, and those whose work centers are located in distant places, such as the North Pacific Health Network.

On the other hand, not only socio-demographic factors limit the achievement of telemedicine learning by health professionals, but also institutional factors. Thus, the training events that health establishments organize in favor of their workers, has also been a limitation observed in the present investigation, which is probably due to the lack of economic resources to subsidize said events, as well as the lack of interest of the authorities on duty, who in many cases do not provide the time facilities for the training of professionals, a finding also evidenced in other studies [18, 24].

The aforementioned is related to the absence of telemedicine care protocols, a factor that is due, on the one hand, to the non-existence of a health policy in Peru regarding the permanent implementation of telemedicine services in health establishments, as well as the resistance of some authorities to changing the traditional patient care model [23]. This last attitude was even more evident during the COVID-19 pandemic, in which many problems arose in the provision of telemedicine services, mostly due to the lack of knowledge that existed in Peru on this subject. Research such as that carried out in the United States has led to the conclusion that when working in a coordinated manner among the members of health institutions, management documents can be generated that allow the sustainability and permanent strengthening of telemedicine services, avoiding future problems that harm patients [25, 26].

Another situation that unfortunately is very common in poor countries, unlike countries with more resources [27, 28], is the inadequate equipment of health establishments and the lack of agreements with other institutions for training by specialists, a product of the system bureaucratic that unfortunately characterizes public management institutions in Peru. This situation has harmed the intentions to modernize the health sector, whose authorities have also been involved in corruption processes with respect to the use of public funds, a very common circumstance in Latin America.

On the other hand, it is important to clarify the limitations that have arisen during the development of this research, which were mainly referred to the impossibility of academically determining the achievement of learning with respect to telemedicine, due to the non-existence of a formal record on the training courses and evaluations that workers have received on this subject in the North Pacific Network. In this way, it has only been possible to evaluate the self-perception of the workers themselves with respect to their achievement of learning in telemedicine, which, although it could mean a certain bias in their answers, does not detract from the importance of the self-assessment that professionals of health can make of their academic training.

In the same way, the online modality in which the data collection instrument was applied, as well as the lack of background on the subject addressed in a similar context in Peru, are also assumed as limitations. All of the above did not allow the evaluation of other research variables, although it did mean a starting point for other authors who wish to investigate in this regard in primary healthcare contexts in geographical areas distant from large cities, point at which falls the contribution of the present study, whose findings related to telemedicine can be taken into account by other researchers and health authorities committed to their work at the service of society.

5 Conclusions and Future Steps

5.1 Conclusions

Socio-demographic and institutional factors limit the achievement of telemedicine learning by health professionals in primary healthcare institutions of the North Pacific Health Network of the Ancash region-Peru, during the 2020–2021 period. In this way, the achievement of learning regarding the use of Telemedicine services is related to gender, age, marital status, profession, monthly salary, training in digital health education, labor facilities of time to train, existence of care protocols, adequate equipment and agreements with other institutions for the training of specialists .

5.2 Future Steps

The government and health authorities of Peru have the responsibility to implement efficient health policies such as telemedicine that ensure timely attention to people's health problems, especially those who are in a situation of vulnerability and inequity in access to specialized services. In this sense, not only are new studies needed that address the characteristics of the application of telemedicine in Peru by health professionals, but also urgent management, training and equipment actions are required for institutions, in order to improve working conditions of professionals, who despite their personal effort, do not have the tools and labor facilities necessary to improve their professional performance.

Acknowledgements. To the health professionals and authorities of the North Pacific Health Network of the Ancash region-Peru, for their participation and support during the development of this study.

Appendix

See Table 4.

Table 4. Questionnaire applied to health professionals.

Section 1: *Socio-demographic factors*
Q1. Age:
(a) 25–49 years
(b) ≥50 years

(continued)

Table 4. (*continued*)

Section 1: *Socio-demographic factors*
Q2. Gender:
(a) Male
(b) Female
Q3. Marital status:
(a) Single
(b) Married
(c) Cohabiting
Q4. Profession:
(a) Physician
(b) Nurse
(c) Obstetrician
(d) Dentist
Q5. Monthly salary:
(a) <2500.00 soles
(b) ≥2500 soles
Section 2: *Institutional factors*
Q1. Beneficiary of training in digital health education:
(a) Yes
(b) No
Q2. Labor facilities of time to be trained in the application of telemedicine services:
(a) Yes
(b) No
Q3. Existence of telemedicine care protocols:
(a) Yes
(b) No
Q4. Suitable equipment:
(a) Yes
(b) No
Q5. Agreements with other institutions for training by specialists:
(a) Yes
(b) No

(*continued*)

Table 4. (*continued*)

Section 1: *Socio-demographic factors*
Section 3: *Achievement of learning in telemedicine*
Q1. Perception about the achievement of learning in telemedicine:
(a) Unsatisfactory
(b) Moderately satisfactory
(c) Satisfactory

References

1. Scofano, R., Monteiro, A., Motta, L.: Evaluation of the experience with the use of telemedicine in a home dialysis program—a qualitative and quantitative study. BMC Nephrol. **23**, 190 (2022). https://doi.org/10.1186/s12882-022-02824-5

2. Deda, L.C., Goldberg, R.H., Jamerson, T.A., Lee, I., Tejasvi, T.: Dermoscopy practice guidelines for use in telemedicine. NPJ Digit. Med. **5**(1), 55 (2022). https://doi.org/10.1038/s41746-022-00587-9

3. Jahan, F., et al.: Evaluation of community health worker's performance at home-based newborn assessment supported by mHealth in rural Bangladesh. BMC Pediatr. **22**, 218 (2022). https://doi.org/10.1186/s12887-022-03282-6

4. Instituto Nacional de Estadística e Informática: Encuesta Nacional de Hogares. INEI, Lima (2020). https://www.datosabiertos.gob.pe/dataset/encuesta-nacional-de-hogares-enaho-2020-instituto-nacional-de-estad%C3%ADstica-e-inform%C3%A1tica-inei

5. Agbali, R., Balas, A., Beltrame, F., De Leo, G.: A review of audiovisual telemedicine utilization and satisfaction assessment during the COVID-19 pandemic. Int. J. Technol. Assess. Health Care **38**(1), e2 (2022). https://doi.org/10.1017/S026646232100060X

6. Nanda, M., Sharma, R.: A review of patient satisfaction and experience with telemedicine: a virtual solution during and beyond COVID-19 pandemic. Telemed. e-Health **27**(12), 1325–1331 (2021). https://doi.org/10.1089/tmj.2020.0570

7. Andrews, E., Berghofer, K., Long, J., Prescott, A., Caboral-Stevens, M.: Satisfaction with the use of telehealth during COVID-19: an integrative review. Int. J. Nurs. Stud. Adv. **2**, 100008 (2020). https://doi.org/10.1016/j.ijnsa.2020.100008

8. Dopelt, K., Avni, N., Haimov-Sadikov, Y., Golan, I., Davidovitch, N.: Telemedicine and ehealth literacy in the era of COVID-19: a cross-sectional study in a peripheral clinic in Israel. Int. J. Environ. Res. Public Health **18**(18), 9556 (2021). https://doi.org/10.3390/ijerph18189556

9. Huret, L., Stoeklé, H.C., Benmaziane, A., Beuzeboc, P., Hervé, C.: Cancer and COVID-19: ethical issues concerning the use of telemedicine during the pandemic. BMC Health Serv. Res. **22**(1), 703 (2022). https://doi.org/10.1186/s12913-022-08097-w

10. Marques, S., et al.: Patient and family experience with telemedicine and in-person pediatric and obstetric ambulatory encounters throughout 2020, during the COVID-19 epidemic: the distance effect. BMC Health Serv. Res. **22**, 659 (2022). https://doi.org/10.1186/s12913-022-08037-8

11. Ford, J.H., Jolles, S.A., Heller, D., Langenstroer, M., Crnich, C.: There and back again: the shape of telemedicine in U.S. nursing homes following COVID-19. BMC Geriatr. **22**, 337 (2022). https://doi.org/10.1186/s12877-022-03046-y

12. Tan, A.J., Rusli, K.D., McKenna, L., Tan, L.L., Liaw, S.Y.: Telemedicine experiences and perspectives of healthcare providers in long-term care: a scoping review. J. Telemed. Telecare (2021). https://doi.org/10.1177/1357633X211049206

13. World Medical Association. Declaration of Helsinki – Ethical principles for medical research involving human subjects. https://www.wma.net/policies-post/wma-declaration-of-helsinki-ethical-principles-for-medical-research-involving-human-subjects/. Accessed 10 July 2022

14. Driessen, J., Castle, N.G., Handler, S.M.: Perceived benefits, barriers, and drivers of telemedicine from the perspective of skilled nursing facility administrative staff stakeholders. J. Appl. Gerontol. **37**(1), 110–120 (2016). https://doi.org/10.1177/0733464816651884

15. Owolabi, E.O., Mac Quene, T., Louw, J., Davies, J.I., Chu, K.M.: Telemedicine in surgical care in low- and middle-income countries: a scoping review. World J. Surg. **46**(8), 1855–1869 (2022). https://doi.org/10.1007/s00268-022-06549-2

16. Golechha, M., Bohra, T., Patel, M., Khetrapal, S.: Healthcare worker resilience during the COVID-19 pandemic: a qualitative study of primary care providers in India. World Med. Health Policy **14**(1), 6–18 (2022). https://doi.org/10.1002/wmh3.483

17. Guiroy, A., et al.: COVID-19 impact among spine surgeons in Latin America. Glob. Spine J. **11**(6), 859–865 (2022). https://doi.org/10.1177/2192568220928032

18. Akoob, S., Akbar, K., Van Wyk, J.: The use of technology in postgraduate medical education within radiology: a scoping review. Egypt. J. Radiol. Nucl. Med. **53**(1), 94 (2022). https://doi.org/10.1186/s43055-022-00763-7

19. Montoya, M.I., et al.: An international survey examining the impact of the COVID-19 pandemic on telehealth use among mental health professionals. J. Psychiatr. Res. **148**, 188–196 (2022). https://doi.org/10.1016/j.jpsychires.2022.01.050

20. Rosales, K.M., et al.: Mental health of healthcare workers of Latin American countries: a review of studies published during the first year of COVID-19 pandemic. Psychiatry Res. **311**, 114501 (2022). https://doi.org/10.1016/j.psychres.2022.114501

21. McRoy, C., et al.: Radiology education in the time of COVID-19: a novel distance learning workstation experience for residents. Acad. Radiol. **27**(10), 1467–1474 (2020). https://doi.org/10.1016/j.acra.2020.08.001

22. Belfi, L.M., Jordan, S.G.: Web-based radiology learning module design: the author perspective. Acad. Radiol. **29**(4), 584–590 (2022). https://doi.org/10.1016/j.acra.2021.02.017

23. Lipschitz, J.M., Connolly, S.L., Van Boxtel, R., Potter, J.R., Nixon, N., Bidargaddi, N.: Provider perspectives on telemental health implementation: lessons learned during the COVID-19 pandemic and paths forward. Psychol. Serv. (2022). https://doi.org/10.1037/ser0000625

24. Driessen, J., Chang, W., Patel, P., Wright, R.M., Ernst, K., Handler, S.M.: Nursing home provider perceptions of telemedicine for providing specialty consults. Telemed. e-Health **24**(7), 510–516 (2018). https://doi.org/10.1089/tmj.2017.0076

25. Gillespie, S.M., et al.: Standards for the use of telemedicine for evaluation and management of resident change of condition in the nursing home. J. Am. Med. Dir. Assoc. **20**(2), 115–122 (2019). https://doi.org/10.1016/j.jamda.2018.11.022

26. Jen, S.P., Bui, A., Leonard, S.D.: Maximizing efficiency of telemedicine in the skilled nursing facility during the coronavirus disease 2019 Pandemic. J. Am. Med. Dir. Assoc. **22**(6), 1146–1148.e2 (2021). https://doi.org/10.1016/j.jamda.2021.04.009

27. Mateos-Nozal, J., et al.: Proactive geriatric comanagement of nursing home patients by a new hospital-based liaison geriatric unit: a new model for the future. J. Am. Med. Dir. Assoc. **23**(2), 308–310 (2022). https://doi.org/10.1016/j.jamda.2021.12.006

28. Low, J.A., Toh, H.J., Tan, L.L.C., Chia, J.W.K., Soek, A.T.S.: The nuts and bolts of utilizing telemedicine in nursing homes – the GeriCare@North experience. J. Am. Med. Dir. Assoc. **21**(8), 1073–1078 (2020). https://doi.org/10.1016/j.jamda.2020.04.014

Multimodal Deep Learning for Crop Yield Prediction

Luis-Roberto Jácome-Galarza(✉) 🆔

Escuela Superior Politécnica del Litoral, ESPOL, Facultad de Ingeniería en Electricidad y Computación, CIDIS, Gustavo Galindo Km. 30.5 Vía Perimetral, Guayaquil, Ecuador
lrjacome@espol.edu.ec

Abstract. Precision agriculture is a vital practice for improving the production of crops. The present work is aimed to develop a deep learning multimodal model that can predict the crop yield in Ecuadorian corn farms. The model takes multispectral images and field sensor data (humidity, temperature, or soil status) to obtain the yield of a crop. The use of multimodal data is aimed to extract hidden patterns in the status of crops and in this way obtain better results than the use of vegetation indices or other state-of-the-art methods. For the experiments, we utilized multi-spectral satellite images obtained from the google earth engine platform and monthly precipitation and temperature data of the 24 Ecuadorian provinces collected from the Ecuadorian Ministry of agriculture and livestock; likewise, we obtained the area of corn plantation in each province and their corn production for the years 2016 to 2020. Results indicate that the use of multimodal deep learning models (pre-trained CNN for images and LSTM for time series sensor data) gives better prediction accuracy than monomodal prediction models.

Keywords: Precision agriculture · Remote sensing · Convolutional neural networks · Recurrent neural networks · Multimodal deep learning

1 Introduction

The prediction of crop yield is very difficult because multiple factors intervene like the crop genotype, environmental factors, management practices, etc. [1]. Many studies have used machine learning techniques such as regression trees, random forest, multivariate regression, association rule mining, and artificial neural networks for crop yield prediction. Machine learning models treat the crop yield as a function of variables such as weather and soil conditions, which can be complex and nonlinear [1].

In the plant growth process, mineral nutrients play a key role. The macronutrients include calcium, potassium, nitrogen, magnesium, sulfur, and phosphorous; while the micronutrients include boron, iron, manganese, copper, chloride, zinc, and molybdenum. The deficiency of these nutrients affects the growth, yield, and quality of plants [2].

Accurate yield estimation and optimized nitrogen management are essential in agriculture [3]; these two aspects would help to secure food production.

K. Abad and S. Berrezueta (Eds.): DSICT 2022, CCIS 1647, pp. 106–117, 2022.
https://doi.org/10.1007/978-3-031-18347-8_9

1.1 Theoretical Framework

Vegetation Indices

Vegetation Indices (VIs) are mathematical combinations of ratios of red, green, and infrared spectral bands; they are designed to find functional relationships between crop characteristics and remote sensing observations [4]. The work in [5] enumerates the most common vegetation indices and their formulas.

Field Sensor Data

The Internet of things is formed by connected devices and transmits large amounts of data [6]. It is currently being applied in fields like agriculture [7, 8], smart cities [9], smart homes [10, 11], health care [12, 13], and human activity recognition [14, 15]. While more IoT sensors are used, more insights can be obtained from them that may help to predict the behavior of systems which is useful for systems maintenance [16, 17], yield performance [18, 19], resource allocation [20], or business planning [21].

Multimodal Learning

Information in the real world comes through multiple input channels, for example, images are associated with captions and tags, videos contain visual and audio signals, and sensory perception includes simultaneous inputs from the visual, auditory, motor, and haptic pathways [22]. Each modality is characterized by very distinct statistical properties which makes it difficult to disregard the fact that they come from different input channels [22].

Multimodal datasets consist of data from different sensors observing a common phenomenon, and the goal is to use the data in a complementary manner toward learning a complex task. One of the advantages of deep learning is that features can be automatically learned for each modality, instead of manually designing specific features [23].

1.2 Literature Review

Concerning the literature review, we have the following works related to, on the one hand, precision agriculture and on the other hand deep learning architectures:

In [1] authors compare the performance of hand-drawn features versus features drawn from Convolutional Neural Networks. The features obtained from the two different techniques are fed into a multilayer perceptron. The results indicate that features extracted from CNN networks with batch normalization between convolution and activation layers gave the best performance. On the contrary, NDVI is better than CNN without batch normalization, this fact shows that it is beneficial to apply normalization to classify remote sensing images; since they tend to vary in aspects like brightness. The results also indicate that the use of batch normalization strongly influences obtaining better results. On the other hand, it also mentions that the use of vegetation indices is redundant when they are used as a feature in a deep learning model.

The paper in [24] presents a study about the prediction of soybean crop yields using Unmanned Aerial Vehicles and deep learning models. The results indicate that multimodal data fusion gave better results than a single modal of data. The authors utilized multispectral and multi-spectral imaging, spectral, structural, thermal, and texture information from crops. Finally, Intermediate-level feature fusion DNN (DNN-F2) outperformed input-level feature fusion DNN (DNN-F1) in prediction accuracy, spatial adaptivity, and robustness.

In the paper in [25], they utilize a CNN architecture (AlexNet as a pre-trained CNN model) to recognize and classify phenological stages of six types of plants based on visual data. The results suggest that the CNN model gives better results than traditional methods that utilize handcraft features like the gray level co-occurrence matrix or the histogram of oriented gradients.

Among other contributions, the work in [26] presents a summary of general and fine-grained vision datasets with plants like Flowers 102 [27], LeafSnap [28], and Urban Trees datasets [29].

Multimodal Deep Learning Datasets

For its part, the work in [23] presents a survey in which it highlights multimodal learning datasets and challenges, and diverse applications of multimodal deep learning like human action recognition, emotion recognition, medical diagnosis, or semantic segmentation.

The work in [30] presents a list of datasets related to agriculture, these datasets contain leaf species, flowers, crops and diseases, field images, vegetation segmentation maps, weed images, or plant type annotations. Even though some of these datasets are used for crop yield prediction, they do not contain concurrently multimodal data of field sensors and multispectral images.

In contrast, the Ladybird Cobbitty 2017 Brassica dataset [31] is related to agriculture (cauliflower and broccoli plants) and contains RGB image data, multi-spectral data, manual data (SPAD and length of plants), and field sensor data (temperature, humidity, or soil condition data). The disadvantage of this dataset is that there are many null values, and it is not suitable for a deep learning model that requires large quantities of data.

Deep Learning Architectures

The paper in [32] presents a deep learning architecture called GeThR-Net which is a recurring neural network for multimodal learning that can be applied to any type of modality and to a large number of temporal modalities. It is made up of $M + 1$ components where the first component is the LSTM temporal network, the following M components correspond to the timeless patterns of each modality. The temporary component of the architecture is made up of 3 layers. The first layer treats the temporal patterns of each modality with LSTM nodes; the multimodal information is not shared. The second layer uses a linear function followed by a sigmoid function that forms a multimodal representation for each time step. The third layer is an LSTM network that takes the outputs from the second layer. The output of the third layer goes to a softmax function for final classification.

Generative Models, Discriminative Models, Hybrid Models

The work in [33] is a literature review of deep learning applications for multimodal data fusion, in which they mention Deep Belief Nets (DBN), Stacked Autoencoders, Convolutional Neural Networks and Recurrent Neural Networks. It also mentions variants of DBN networks used in multimodal learning like SRBM (Sparse Restricted Boltzmann Machine), FRBM (Fast Restricted Boltzmann Machine), TTRBM (Tensor-Train Restricted Boltzmann Machine). Autoencoder architectures used in multimodal learning are DAE (Denoising Autoencoder), SAE (K-sparse Autoencoder), GAE (Generative Autoencoder), FAE (Fast Autoencoder), BAE (Blind Autoencoder). Regarding CNN networks, the variants utilized in multimodal learning are Alexnet (Alex Convolutional Net), ResNet (Residual Convolutional Net), Inception, SEnet (Squeeze excitation Network), or ECNN (Efficient Convolutional Neural Network). For their part, the RNN variants used for multimodal learning are BiRNN (Bidirectional Recurrent Neural Network), LSTM (Long Short-Term Memory), SRNN (Slight Recurrent Neural Network), VRNN (Variational Recurrent Neural Network).

The work in [34] introduces the UNet model, which is a deep learning architecture, used for semantic segmentation of images. The UNet is formed by an encoder and a decoder: the encoder utilizes multiple convolution layers to obtain different levels of image characteristics. The decoder uses multilayer deconvolution on the top-level feature map and combines different feature levels in the downsampling process to restore the feature map to the original input image size and complete the end-to-end semantic segmentation. The decoder layers use the UpConv operation.

For its part, the intermediate characteristics map generated by the encoder is concatenated with the characteristics map generated by the decoder using Skip Connect (these connections allow the reuse of characteristics and stabilize training and convergence). The architecture of the encoder-decoder scheme, together with the long skip connections, has the shape of a U (UNet). It is used for tasks where the prediction has the same spatial dimension as the input, such as image segmentation, optical flow estimation, or video prediction. This paper could be useful for the present project because the encoder part of the UNet architecture can be used to extract patterns of images of agriculture fields and the decoder part could generate a health map of the crop.

Moreover, the work in [35] explains that in multimodal learning, auto-encoders are used as a first step for processing images and text (sequential models), and then the attention mechanism is applied for the alignment of those multimodal sources. Figure 1 presents the types of attention mechanisms utilized in multimodal learning. These types of architectures might be useful in other domains like agriculture in which, we analyze multispectral image data and field sensor data.

The rest of the paper follows with Sect. 2 which describes Materials and Methods, Sect. 3 presents the results, Sect. 4 presents the discussion and Sect. 5 presents the conclusions.

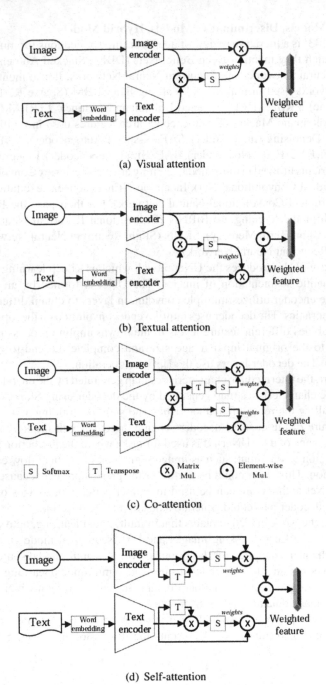

(a) Visual attention

(b) Textual attention

(c) Co-attention

S Softmax   T Transpose   ⊗ Matrix Mul.   ⊙ Element-wise Mul.

(d) Self-attention

Fig. 1. Attention mechanism types utilized in multimodal learning: Visual attention (a), Textual attention (b), Co-attention (c), Self-attention (d) [35].

2 Materials and Methods

2.1 Research Methodology

For conducting this doctorate thesis, we consider the development of a multimodal deep learning model that extracts the patterns of field sensors like temperature and precipitations and it also models the patterns of multi-spectral images. The combination of these processing heads in a neural network would provide an accurate prediction of crop yield. For the accomplishment of this goal we have the following research question:

2.2 Research Question

Can Ecuadorian farmers benefit from multimodal deep learning models to better predict the yield of crops?

2.3 Research Objectives

General Objective

Design and implement a multimodal deep learning model for crop yield prediction utilizing multispectral images and field sensor data.

Specific Objectives

- Evaluate multimodal deep learning architectures for time-series evaluation and image processing.
- Design and implement a multimodal deep learning model with multispectral images and field sensor data.
- Validate the multimodal deep learning predicting model and compare it with the state-of-the-art approaches.

2.4 Justification

The justification of this doctoral proposal is based on the fact that it is aligned with the objectives of the Ecuadorian National Institute of Investigation of Agriculture and Livestock (INIAP) which proposes several goals in the field for the years 2018–2022 [36]. The research proposal is relevant for the improvement of yield production of crops, and its technique and methodology can be applied to many agricultural products. The present research proposal expects it to contribute to the development of the country and improve its production systems.

2.5 Experiments

To prove that multimodal learning can be applied for the prediction of crops yield and since the dataset is not still available, we propose a proof of concept in which we use multispectral satellite images obtained from the Google earth engine platform and, sensor data like temperature, or precipitation, and the agricultural production obtained from the website of the Ecuadorian Ministry of agricultural and livestock. In this dataset, we find the monthly temperature and precipitation data of the 24 provinces of Ecuador from the year 2002 to the year 2020, and the annual production of 56 agricultural products in 23 provinces (the production of Galapagos is not included).

In the experiment, we obtained the coordinates of corn farms in the 5 provinces of larger production in Ecuador (Los Rios, Guayas, Manabi, Loja) utilizing the Geographic Viewer of INIAP (Ecuadorian National Institute of Investigation of Agriculture and Livestock) (See Fig. 2.)

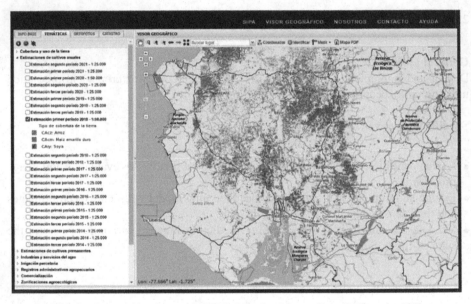

Fig. 2. Geographic viewer of INIAP. Location of corn farms in Ecuador [37]

After getting the coordinates of corn farms, we obtained RGB and NIR images of those farms from 2015 to 2020 using Google Earth Engine and the Copernicus satellite Program, and the subsystem SENTINEL-2 which has 10-60 m image resolution and 5 day of revisit period. The image set provided by Google Earth Engine was filtered by the amount of clouds in the image, giving less than 30% of clouds in the images. Likewise, the SENTINEL-2 possesses 13 multi-spectral bands, Table 1 enumerates the bands that we utilized in this project.

Table 1. SENTINEL-2 multi-spectral bands utilized in the project

Band	Use	Wavelength	Resolution
B2	Blue	490 nm	10 m
B3	Green	560 nm	10 m
B4	Red	665 nm	10 m
B8	NIR	842 nm	10 m

In the Fig. 3 and Fig. 4 we can see a sample of the images utilized in the project, we can observe a RGB and a NIR image of a corn farm located in the "Los Rios" province in the year 2018.

Fig. 3. Satellite RGB image of a corn farm in Los Rios province in Ecuador from the Sentinel-2 dataset in Google Earth Engine [38]

Fig. 4. Satellite NIR image of a corn farm in Los Rios province in Ecuador from the Sentinel-2 dataset in Google Earth Engine [38]

After this pre-processing step, both groups of images RGB and NIR were resized to 175 × 175 pixels. For each province and year period, the RGB and NIR images were concatenated to feed a pre-trained CNN part of the model (VGG + ImageNet). For its part, the sensor data of temperature and precipitation is fed to a LSTM model. We utilize a late fusion approach to join the CNN and LSTM parts and a FCNN gives the final prediction.

The experiments were conducted with Google Colab, python programming language, TensorFlow and Keras libraries.

3   Results

We considered many approaches for developing multimodal deep learning models for crop yield prediction and most of them gave unsatisfying results. Finally, the proposed multimodal model obtained Mean Squared Error of 0.0454 and Mean Absolute Error of 0.1958 loss values which consists of an improvement of the yield prediction obtained by a mono modal LSTM model that got Mean Squared Error of 0.0480 and Mean Absolute Error of 0.1996 loss values.

4   Discussion

Even though the improvement in the performance of the multi-modal deep leaning network is not large, it demonstrates that the use of the different sources of information can be complementary and could help to obtain more robust prediction models.

The limitation of this project is that we had to utilize the average values of temperature and precipitation of each Ecuadorian province which lessen the precision of the model.

As a future work and considering the limitation, we plan to improve the experiment by the use of field sensor data and Unmanned Aerial Vehicles for capturing the multi-spectral data.

5 Conclusions

For conducting this doctorate thesis we have done experiments with multimodal deep learning models applied to the prediction of crop yield in Ecuadorian corn farms. The results demonstrate that using distinct sources of information like multi-spectral images and field sensor data can help to build more robust prediction models that take advantage of the complementary information of the two modalities.

For its part, it is important to highlight that the use of satellite imagery is inexpensive and is useful for studying large extensions of land like provinces or states.

It is very important to utilize machine learning models in precision agriculture in developing and agricultural countries like Ecuador, to improve the quality of crops, increment their yield while decreasing expenses, and as a consequence increase the profits of farmers.

As further work, and for the continuity of the theses, we intend to experiment with multi-spectral images obtained from unmanned aerial vehicles and sensor field data. Those images have better resolution and can add more insights to our analysis. Likewise, we plan to experiment with different deep learning architectures in order to identify the models that give the best predictions of crop yield.

References

1. Ramanath, A., Muthusrinivasan, S., Xie, Y., Shekhar, S., Ramachandra, B.: NDVI versus CNN features in deep learning for land cover classification of aerial images. In: IGARSS 2019–2019 IEEE International Geoscience and Remote Sensing Symposium, pp. 6483–6486. IEEE (2019)
2. Tran, T., Choi, J., Le, T., Kim, J.: A comparative study of deep CNN in forecasting and classifying the macronutrient deficiencies on development of tomato plant. Appl. Sci. **9**(8), 1601 (2019)
3. Chlingaryan, A., Sukkarieh, S., Whelan, B.: Machine learning approaches for crop yield prediction and nitrogen status estimation in precision agriculture: a review. Comput. Electron. Agric. **151**, 61–69 (2018)
4. Wiegand, C., Richardson, A., Escobar, D., Gerbermann, A.: Vegetation indices in crop assessments. Remote Sens. Environ. **35**(2–3), 105–119 (1991)
5. Basso, B., Cammarano, D., Carfagna, E.: Review of crop yield forecasting methods and early warning systems. In: Proceedings of the First Meeting of the Scientific Advisory Committee of the Global Strategy to Improve Agricultural and Rural Statistics, FAO Headquarters, Rome, Italy, pp. 18–19 (2013)
6. Mahdavinejad, M., Rezvan, M., Barekatain, M., Adibi, P., Barnaghi, P., Sheth, A.: Machine learning for Internet of Things data analysis: a survey. Digit. Commun. Netw. **4**(3), 161–175 (2018)
7. Gondchawar, N., Kawitkar, R.: IoT based smart agriculture. Int. J. Adv. Res. Comput. Commun. Eng. **5**(6), 838–842 (2016)

8. Muangprathub, J., Boonnam, N., Kajornkasirat, S., Lekbangpong, N., Wanichsombat, A., Nillaor, P.: IoT and agriculture data analysis for smart farm. Comput. Electron. Agric. **156**, 467–474 (2019)
9. Kim, T., Ramos, C., Mohammed, S.: Smart city and IoT (2017)
10. Samuel, S.: A review of connectivity challenges in IoT-smart home. In: 2016 3rd MEC International Conference on Big Data and Smart City (ICBDSC), pp. 1–4. IEEE (2016)
11. Kim, Y., Park, Y., Choi, J.: A study on the adoption of IoT smart home service: using value-based adoption model. Total Qual. Manag. Bus. Excell. **28**(9–10), 1149–1165 (2017)
12. Ukil, A., Bandyoapdhyay, S., Puri, C., Pal, A.: IoT healthcare analytics: the importance of anomaly detection. In: 2016 IEEE 30th International Conference on Advanced Information Networking and Applications (AINA), pp. 994–997. IEEE (2016)
13. Tyagi, S., Agarwal, A., Maheshwari, P.: A conceptual framework for IoT-based healthcare system using cloud computing. In: 2016 6th International Conference-Cloud System and Big Data Engineering (Confluence), pp. 503–507. IEEE (2016)
14. Rghioui, A., Sendra, S., Lloret, J., Oumnad, A.: Internet of Things for measuring human activities in ambient assisted living and e-health. Netw. Protoc. Algorithms **8**(3), 15–28 (2016)
15. Shi, C., Liu, J., Liu, H., Chen, Y.: Smart user authentication through actuation of daily activities leveraging WiFi-enabled IoT. In: Proceedings of the 18th ACM International Symposium on Mobile Ad Hoc Networking and Computing, pp. 1–10 (2017)
16. Al-Douri, Y.K., Hamodi, H., Lundberg, J.: Time series forecasting using a two-level multi-objective genetic algorithm: a case study of maintenance cost data for tunnel fans. Algorithms **11**(8), 123 (2018)
17. Baptista, M., Sankararaman, S., de Medeiros, I., Nascimento, C., Jr., Prendinger, H., Henriques, E.: Forecasting fault events for predictive maintenance using data-driven techniques and ARMA modeling. Comput. Ind. Eng. **115**, 41–53 (2018)
18. Kamir, E., Waldner, F., Hochman, Z.: Estimating wheat yields in Australia using climate records, satellite image time series and machine learning methods. ISPRS J. Photogramm. Remote. Sens. **160**, 124–135 (2020)
19. Adeniyi, O.D., Szabo, A., Tamás, J., Nagy, A.: Wheat Yield Forecasting Based on Landsat NDVI and SAVI Time Series (2020)
20. Kadri, F., Harrou, F., Chaabane, S., Tahon, C.: Time series modelling and forecasting of emergency department overcrowding. J. Med. Syst. **38**(9), 1–20 (2014). https://doi.org/10.1007/s10916-014-0107-0
21. Demir, E., Dincer, S.: Place and solution proposals of data mining in production planning and control processes: a business application. Press Academia Procedia **11**(1), 189–193 (2020)
22. Srivastava, N., Salakhutdinov, R.: Multimodal learning with deep Boltzmann machines. In: Advances in Neural Information Processing Systems, vol. 25 (2012)
23. Ramachandram, D., Taylor, G.: Deep multimodal learning: a survey on recent advances and trends. IEEE Sig. Process. Mag. **34**(6), 96–108 (2017)
24. Maimaitijiang, M., Sagan, V., Sidike, P., Hartling, S., Esposito, F., Fritschi, F.: Soybean yield prediction from UAV using multimodal data fusion and deep learning. Remote Sens. Environ. **237**, 111599 (2020)
25. Yalcin, H.: Plant phenology recognition using deep learning: Deep-Pheno. In: 2017 6th International Conference on Agro-Geoinformatics, pp. 1–5. IEEE (2017)
26. Zheng, Y.Y., Kong, J.L., Jin, X.B., Wang, X.Y., Su, T.L., Zuo, M.: CropDeep: the crop vision dataset for deep-learning-based classification and detection in precision agriculture. Sensors **19**(5), 1058 (2019)
27. Nilsback, M., Zisserman, A.: A visual vocabulary for flower classification. In: Proceedings of the 2006 IEEE Computer Society Conference on Computer Vision and Pattern Recognition (CVPR 2006), New York, NY, USA, pp. 1447–1454 (2006)

28. Kumar, N., et al.: Leafsnap: a computer vision system for automatic plant species identification. In: Fitzgibbon, A., Lazebnik, S., Perona, P., Sato, Y., Schmid, C. (eds.) Computer Vision, vol. 7573, pp. 502–516. Springer, Heidelberg (2012). https://doi.org/10.1007/978-3-642-33709-3_36

29. Wegner, J., Branson, S., Hall, D., Schindler, K., Perona, P.: Cataloging public objects using aerial and street-level images-urban trees. In: Proceedings of the IEEE Conference on Computer Vision and Pattern Recognition, Las Vegas Valley, NV, USA, pp. 6014–6023 (2016)

30. Kamilaris, A., Prenafeta-Boldú, F.: Deep learning in agriculture: a survey. Comput. Electron. Agric. **147**, 70–90 (2018)

31. Bender, A., Whelan, B., Sukkarieh, S.: Ladybird Cobbitty 2017 Brassica dataset (2019)

32. Gandhi, A., Sharma, A., Biswas, A., Deshmukh, O.: GeThR-Net: a generalized temporally hybrid recurrent neural network for multimodal information fusion. In: Hua, G., Jégou, H. (eds.) Computer Vision, vol. 9914, pp. 883–899. Springer, Cham (2016). https://doi.org/10.1007/978-3-319-48881-3_58

33. Gao, J., Li, P., Chen, Z., Zhang, J.: A survey on deep learning for multimodal data fusion. Neural Comput. **32**(5), 829–864 (2020)

34. Zhao, X., et al.: Use of unmanned aerial vehicle imagery and deep learning UNet to extract rice lodging. Sensors **19**(18), 3859 (2019)

35. Chen, W., Wang, W., Liu, L., Lew, M.: New ideas and trends in deep multimodal content understanding: a review. arXiv preprint https://arxiv.org/abs/2010.08189 (2020)

36. Iniap. http://www.iniap.gob.ec/pruebav3/wp-content/uploads/2018/03/281-iniap-OK-baja.pdf

37. Sistema de Información Pública Agropecuaria. http://sipa.agricultura.gob.ec/index.php/maiz

38. Google Earth Engine data catalog, Sentinel-2 MSI. https://developers.google.com/earth-engine/datasets/catalog/COPERNICUS_S2

Augmented Reality for Real-Time Control of a Robotic Arm with IoT Connection

Gabriel Montenegro🆔, Johanna Salvador🆔, and Gustavo Caiza$^{(\boxtimes)}$🆔

Universidad Politécnica Salesiana, UPS, 170146 Quito, Ecuador
{gmontenegroa,jsalvador}@est.ups.edu.ec, gcaiza@ups.edu.ec

Abstract. Augmented Reality (AR) is one of the most important technologies that takes part in the Fourth Industrial Revolution, and for this reason, this document presents the development of an AR application for real-time control of a Robotic Arm with IoT communication. The application provides AR visualization of the state of the process in real-time, as well as an interface for controlling the position of the robotic arm. The document presents a detailed description of the hardware architecture that includes the AR device, the AR marker, and the infrastructure used for interacting with the robot. In addition, it is presented the architecture of the software for communication of the AR application with the process, to establish remote and real-time control of the position of the robotic arm using IoT. The AR application has been tested with a robotic arm used in the field of medicine, participating in the analysis process of blood chemistry in biological tests carried out in clinical laboratories. The development of this application has various advantages, highlighting the use of low-cost technological devices, easy acquisition, and the remote connection that improves the control efficiency of the robot, improving the security for user integrity because he/she is not exposed to dangerous environments.

Keywords: Augmented Reality (AR) · Internet of Things (IoT) · Robotic arm

1 Introduction

Augmented reality is a technology that enables users to place virtual elements that contain visual information about the real environment that surrounds them, with the assistance of a technological device [1]. It is a technology currently booming since it is the foundation for the continuous improvement, industrial innovation, and economic development of companies around the world [1, 2, 4]. Many companies are incorporating this new technology, since it is a fundamental pillar within the Fourth Industrial Revolution, also known as Industry 4.0 [3, 5, 6], which combines technologies such as Artificial Intelligence (AI), Internet of Things (IoT), Computing, Robotics, Industrial Automation, among others [1]. Industry 4.0 will set a big trend, not only in the industrial sector but also in the health and educational sectors, and thus it is very important to adapt to these new technologies since they will begin to be incorporated into the daily routine of human beings, as well as in their work, and for this reason, it is convenient to investigate about this topic with greater depth [3–5, 7].

K. Abad and S. Berrezueta (Eds.): DSICT 2022, CCIS 1647, pp. 118–131, 2022.
https://doi.org/10.1007/978-3-031-18347-8_10

At present, various immersive environment applications have been developed, such as Virtual Reality (VR) and Augmented Reality (AR), with different approaches that are applied in the industry. The use of Augmented Reality is varied and may be potentially applied in most of the activities performed in companies. The main uses are detailed below:

Production. Any production line that follows a process, may benefit from the application of AR. A clear example is the use of AR applications for assisting in mounting and assembly tasks in factories, to eliminate possible failures due to the lack of staff experience [8].

Industrial Maintenance. Any machine with a preventive maintenance plan may implement the use of AR to assist maintenance tasks, to reduce execution time and human mistakes caused by a lack of process knowledge [9].

Training. AR may be effectively used in companies in which the staff training processes involve many technicians that are geographically dispersed. Similarly, AR may be used in factories as induction for technicians without work experience when they join the company, to train them appropriately in the execution of mounting, assembly, and industrial safety processes [3].

Based on the above, the main objective of this research is to develop an AR application for real-time control of a robotic arm with an IoT connection, which is used in the health sector. It is intended to generate an intuitive and easy-to-operate control for the robotic arm. The AR will enable real-time interaction, combining the real and digital worlds to offer a more detailed experience of the process being performed; in addition, AR makes it possible to leverage the use of low-cost technologies, such as smartphones. The IoT communication will enable remote control so that users may interact with the robotic arm through the internet, without requiring to be physically present at the place.

The document is designed as follows. Section 2 presents the State of the Art. Section 3 details the features of the hardware and software tools used during the execution of the work. Section 4 contains a detailed description of the proposed solution and its implementation to fulfill the objective previously posed. The operation of the system is detailed in Sect. 5. Section 6 presents the results obtained from such an operation. At last, Sect. 7 presents the conclusions of the research work, describing its contributions and the limitations found, as well as the statement of potential future works.

2 State of the Art

Sotiris Makris et al. [8] implemented an AR tool in the automotive sector that consists in assisting operators in a collaborative hybrid, robotic and human, industrial environment. The objective of the application is to provide information to operators about the production process and the status of task execution. With the development of this application, it may be improved the immersion of operators in the safety mechanisms and mounting processes within the industry.

Moreover, Riccardo Masoni et al. [4] conducted similar research focused on the area of mechanical maintenance, which consists of an AR application that enables the remote connection of an expert operator with a non-specialized operator located at the place where the maintenance task should be carried out, to provide remote assistance to fix particular machinery. The development of this application has wide advantages; the main one is that it enables the reduction of very long dead production times, caused by the unavailability of a specialized technician capable of performing the maintenance of a machine in a specific production process. In the area of manipulator robots, it is possible to find works such as the one by Elena Peña et al. [10], who developed an interface that uses Virtual Reality for controlling a manipulator robot. This interface enables the introduction of the operator to the working environment and thus improves his/her visual perception, to facilitate robot control and increase safety conditions, avoiding subjecting the operator to high-risk environments. Similarly, to maintain the operator in a safe environment, Sunao Hashimoto et al. [7] developed a tactile AR application for remote control of a robot from the point of view of a third person. This interface is very intuitive, since it enables the user to manipulate each part of the robot by touching it directly, and thus it does not require previous training to be used.

One of the advantages of generating intuitive and friendly AR applications is that they may be used by any person without requiring prior training. This is the case of the work by Rodrigo Cañadillas et al. [10], who implemented an AR application for the control of a robot anchored to a wheelchair. This application helps disabled people to perform different daily tasks of great difficulty, such as lifting a cup, opening or closing a valve, etc. The commands executed by the robotic arm are sent through the AR application to which the disabled user has access using immersive reality glasses.

In some cases, acquiring immersive reality glasses may involve a high investment, and thus Miguel Romero et al. developed an AR application for mobile devices, such as tablets and smartphones, for the control of a mobile robot through teleoperation. With the use of mobile devices, it is intended to reduce the investment cost and to have available a tool of easy acquisition, to introduce the operator in an immersive environment in which it may be simulated different scenarios that may result in a hazard for the physical integrity of the operator.

3   Technological Framework

This section describes the specifications of all devices and tools, both hardware and software, used during the development of this research work.

3.1   Hardware Used

The system developed consists of different hardware components to implement the control functions of the robotic arm. The physical components of the system are detailed below:

Mobile Devices. A 6.57 in. Honor 50 smartphone with Android version 11.0 and a 5.5 in. Sony Xperia L1 smartphone with Android version 7.0, were used for the development of this research work. Table 1 details the hardware features of the equipment used.

Table 1. Features of the mobile devices.

Device	Model	Operating system	Processor	RAM	Camera
Honor 50	NTH-NX9	Android	SNAPDRAGON 778G	8 GB	108 MP
Sony L1	G3313	Android	Cortex – A53	2 GB	13 MP

AR Marker. An AR marker is a unique pattern, generally printed on a sheet, which is used as an activation key to position the model in Augmented Reality. In general, a marker may be any 2D image that may be recognized by the camera of the mobile device [12].

Raspberry Pi. It is a low-cost, compact size, and open hardware microcomputer, which uses the Raspbian operating system. It is capable of performing most of the typical tasks of a computer and it is mainly used for the development of prototypes. It has 40 GPIO pins that enable contact with the external world through the connection of sensors and actuators. In addition, it has I2C, SPI, and UART communication ports.

Robotic Arm. It is a SCARA robot used in the analysis processes of blood chemistry in clinical laboratories. It has three actuators corresponding to bipolar stepper motors with a resolution of 0. 9° per step; each motor has its Pololu A4988 driver, which is in charge of regulating the current and protecting the motor. In addition, each actuator has its position switch to limit the travel or establish the positioning. The model has two degrees of freedom and a turning drum that contains the analysis samples.

3.2 Software Used

The system developed consists of different hardware components to implement the control functions of the robotic arm. The physical components of the system are detailed below:

Autodesk Inventor. It is software developed by Autodesk for the 3D modeling of solids. It has available specific tools with functions such as parametric design, modeling of parts and joints, simulation, and documentation for mechanical design and prototyping [13]. (see in "Fig. 1").

Unity 3D. It is software created by Unity Technologies for developing multiplatform videogames. It has an integrated development environment for generating simple mobile applications compatible with operating systems such as Windows, Linux, iOs, Android, and more. It also enables creating, managing, and setting features to 3D models. The programming language is C# Sharp [6].

Blynk. It is an Internet of Things (IoT) platform that enables controlling electronic devices remotely connected to the cloud. It has a board on which the user may generate the graphical interface using different widgets. Blynk has various libraries to use the most important platforms such as Raspberry Pi, Arduino, ESP8266, and more [14].

Thonny IDE. It is a development and programming environment integrated into the Raspberry Pi microcomputer, that enables the creation of folders of code that are then run by the interpreter, Python in this case. It also has a debugger that enables running the lines of code step by step, to diagnose and detect programming bugs [2].

Fig. 1. The robotic arm used in this research work

4   Implementation of the Proposed Solution

This section presents the architecture of the system. Figure 2 shows the general scheme of the interaction between the components that constitute the control of the robotic arm, both at the hardware and software levels.

4.1   Hardware Architecture

The hardware architecture is based on the development of physical communication between the hardware components that constitute the control system of the robotic arm. Figure 3 displays a Unified Modeling Language (UML) diagram that details the interaction between the components, to establish the proposed control scheme.

The user interacts with the system using a mobile device with an Android operating system, which uses the AR application to scan the AR Marker and obtain the 3D visualization of the robotic arm, as well as an interface that enables changing the position of the robotic arm. The Raspberry Pi microcomputer communicates with the virtual environment through the ethernet or Wi-Fi communication ports, using a communication protocol based on Web APIs that receives all signals coming from the mobile device. The RPI interacts with the robotic arm using the signals sent to the controllers of each of the stepper motors to move the links; similarly. (see "Fig. 4").

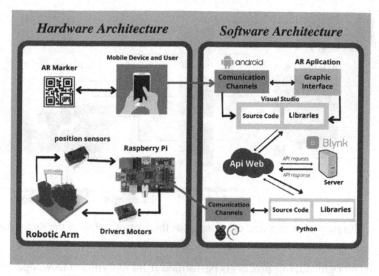

Fig. 2. The robotic arm used in this research work

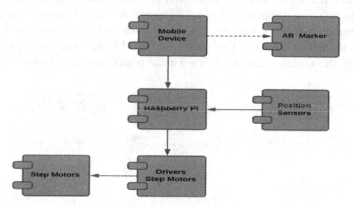

Fig. 3. Diagram of the physical components of the control system of the Robotic Arm

4.2 Software Architecture

The software architecture details the 3D modeling process, the development of the augmented reality application, the communication protocol, and the robotic arm control.

3D Modeling of the Robotic Arm. To obtain a visualization close to the reality of the model, the Autodesk Inventor Software was used for modeling all the elements that constitute the robot, such as structure, actuators, final effector, etc.

Development of the AR Interface. Once the virtual model of the robot has been obtained, it is exported to the Unity 3D software, where the interface of the application is developed. The recognition of the AR marker starts with the generation of a package that contains the license for the AR camera and a database that includes the

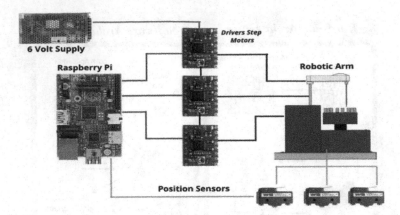

Fig. 4. Diagram of the physical components of the control system of the Robotic Arm

image to be recognized; this process is performed from the Vuforia Developer platform. The package is imported into the Unity development environment so that, with the aid of the Vuforia SDK complement, the application generated can recognize the AR Marker and position the virtual robot in the real environment. A series of buttons is implemented for the virtual movement, which executes the angular and linear movement actions of each link with Scripts written in C# Sharp language. Figure 5 presents a class diagram that specifies the actions necessary for the virtual positioning of the robot.

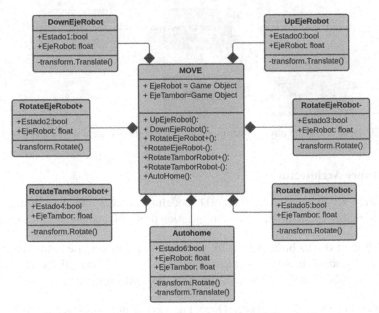

Fig. 5. Class diagram for virtual movement of the robotic arm

Implementation of the Communication. The communication method is using a Web API, a web service residing in a server, Blynk in this case; the AR application of the mobile device and the Raspberry Pi communicates with this Web API. It is used a representational state transfer (REST) architecture designed to use the HTTP protocol as a communication path to access the data. The communications are represented as GET, POST, PUT, and DELETE requests to URLs. An interface was initially developed in the Blynk server, which contains all the commands to control the robot. The server also generates a Token that contains user information and is employed to have access to the server data as identification. For this case, the generated Token is the following:

$$AuthToken : 5ucWwK - czl6kzDw - 7jN4SgYL4C\_qLa **$$

where the last two digits are omitted for security purposes. A button was generated in the AR application for every control action of the robotic arm; each button is responsible for moving a particular link and also for generating a GET request to access the destination URL. Using the AR application, the user presses any button of the interface and a request is generated according to the control action desired to be executed. The Token is entered in the authorization header in the requests, as indicated in Fig. 6. In the development of the AR application, Scripts were created in Unity in C# Sharp language so that each button sends the request for the action required.

Control of the Robotic Arm. The control of the robotic arm is developed in the Raspbian Thonny IDE, which enables coding the instructions necessary to receive the requests sent from the AR application and the instructions for the activation of the robotic arm

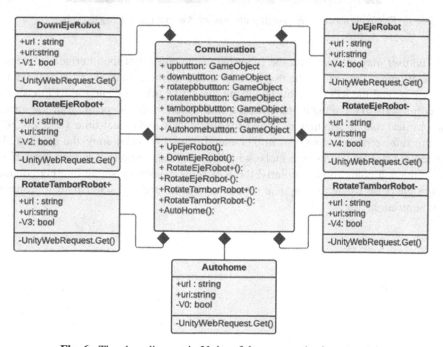

Fig. 6. The class diagram in Unity of the communication protocol.

actuators. When the user sends a move request, the RPI receives the token, verifies that it is correct, and performs the necessary actions. (see "Fig. 7").

5   Operation of the System

The user should have a mobile device, either a smartphone or tablet, with the Android operating system, and it should also have installed the AR application developed in this research work. In addition, it must have the AR marker for recognition and positioning of the 3D model in the real environment. For the operation of the system, the user should run the application and scan the AR marker to position the virtual robotic arm in the real environment. If the marker is the appropriate one, the robot will position itself on the image. (see in "Fig. 8").

Fig. 7. Process of recognizing the AR marker and positioning the robot.

The user may interact with the robot using the buttons of the interface to execute the positioning. Every time the user presses a button, the communication between the application and the RPI is established using the HTTP protocol, and the RPI generates the commands to drive the motors of each link. In this way, the position of the virtual and physical robotic arm may be varied simultaneously and in real-time. (see "Fig. 9").

Since the remote control was implemented using IoT technology, the user may be located at any place across the globe with the only requirement of having available a stable internet connection. Similarly, the RPI must maintain a stable internet connection in the place where the physical robotic arm is located, to establish an appropriate communication.

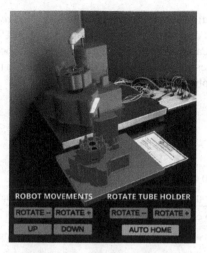

Fig. 8. Real and virtual robotic arm.

6 Results

Operation tests were carried out involving various participants, to analyze the performance of the application. It was requested to the participants perform positioning of the robotic arm using the AR application installed on their mobile devices, giving them the chance to interact with it; afterward, a survey was conducted. First, the analysis of the time it takes for each participant to locate in a specific position was carried out, as shown in Fig. 9.

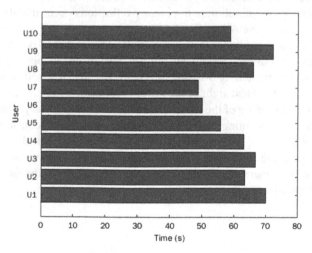

Fig. 9. Analysis of the time

Figure 9 presents the time that each user takes to locate the robot in a specific position through the use of the AR application in order to observe the performance and difficulties that the use of this application presents. The average time it took users is 61,506 s.

Table 2 shows the questions included in the survey made to the participants, to know the limitations of the application.

Table 2. Questions

Item	Question
Q1	Was the app easily installed on your mobile device?
Q2	Is it easy to position the virtual Robot with the AR marker?
Q3	Is it easy to control the robot with the AR app?
Q4	Do you consider necessary extensive training for using this app?
Q5	Do you consider reliable the remote control of the robot using this app?

The results of the survey are shown in Fig. 10. For item Q1, 30% of the participants had problems with the installation of the application, because their mobile devices had a security configuration that did not allow the installation of applications of unknown origin; for this reason, the users had to momentarily disable this security configuration to be able to install the application in their devices and this increased the difficulty of the installation.

Item Q2 was the one with the lowest result since 60% of the participants had problems when performing the recognition of the AR marker because if the user does not steadily point the camera to the marker, the visualization of the virtual robot is lost. Similarly, if there is not an appropriate illumination, many reflections occur that do not allow the application to recognize the AR marker.

In item Q3 it may be evidenced that the application interface is very intuitive and easy to use since 70% of the participants did not have problems placing the robot in a specific position. The remaining 30% had problems because it was difficult to scan the AR marker, and thus they lost sight of the virtual robot.

Regarding item Q4, 80% of the users agree that it is not necessary a prior training to use the application. Concerning item Q5, 40% of the users do not consider it reliable to remotely control the robot, since they consider it an open-loop control because there are no sensors that generate feedback on the position of the physical robot concerning the virtual one; moreover, there may be disturbances in the real world that are not perceived in the virtual environment.

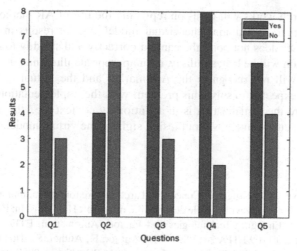

Fig. 10. Results of the survey conducted.

7 Conclusions

This document presented the development of an application based on Augmented Reality (AR), which is executed in an Android mobile device for the remote and real-time control of a robotic arm with IoT communication. This research work has focused on generating a control system with an easy-to-use interface, for the implementation of user-robot interaction mechanisms. Through an analysis of the literature, different types of technological devices and AR interfaces have been found that are being currently implemented, such as the Microsoft HoloLens glasses or the Google Glasses, whose cost is between 3,000 and 5,000 US dollars; this represents a high acquisition value for students or small companies that would like to work in the implementation of AR technologies. Based on the above, it was decided to generate this AR application compatible with tablets and smartphones with the Android operating system, which are low-cost and easy to acquire devices.

The robot used in this research work has applications in the field of medicine, mainly in clinical laboratories where tests of biological samples are carried out. As it is known, the risks of infection by viruses, bacteria, and fungi have currently increased, and this represents a very high risk to the health of the operator or of the robot calibration technician. For this reason, it was implemented the IoT communication between the application and the robot, represents a higher efficiency for remote control of the system because the user may be located at any place on earth and position the robot with high precision. In addition, the remote control offers safety, since the operator is not exposed to environments that put at risk his/her physical integrity.

Future research works will focus on replacing the use of AR markers with a more advanced system for positioning the virtual model since it results in uncomfortable because if the user does not point the camera correctly and steadily to the marker, the robot visualization will be lost; similarly, if an appropriate illumination is not available, the application will not recognize the AR marker and the virtual robot will not be visualized. It is expected to solve this problem with the implementation of projection-based AR, where the visualization is in a stationary context, i.e., the user may move freely within the environment without losing sight of the virtual model.

References

1. Guhl, J., Nguyen, S.T., Krüger, J.: Concept and architecture for programming industrial robots using augmented reality with mobile devices like microsoft HoloLens. In: IEEE International Conference on Emerging Technologies and Factory Automation, ETFA, pp. 1–4 (2017). https://doi.org/10.1109/ETFA.2017.8247749. Author, F., Author, S.: Title of a proceedings paper. In: Editor, F., Editor, S. (eds.) Conference 2016, LNCS, vol. 9999, pp. 1–13. Springer, Heidelberg (2016)
2. Caiza, G., Bonilla-Vasconez, P., Garcia, C.A., Garcia, M.V.: Augmented reality for robot control in low-cost automation context and IoT. IEEE International Conference on Emerging Technologies and Factory Automation, ETFA, vol. 2020-Septe, no. i, pp. 1461–1464 (2020). https://doi.org/10.1109/ETFA46521.2020.9212056. Author, F.: Contribution title. In: 9th International Proceedings on Proceedings, pp. 1–2. Publisher, Location (2010)
3. Bravo, D.C.: Aplicación de asistencia basada en realidad aumentada para la industria (2019)
4. Masoni, R., et al.: Supporting remote maintenance in industry 4.0 through augmented reality. Procedia Manufact. 11(June), 1296–1302 (2017). https://doi.org/10.1016/j.promfg.2017.07.257
5. Maly, I., Sedlacek, D., Leitao, P.: Augmented reality experiments with industrial robot in industry 4.0 environment. In: IEEE International Conference on Industrial Informatics (INDIN), vol. 0, pp. 176–181 (2016).https://doi.org/10.1109/INDIN.2016.7819154
6. Pierdicca, R., Frontoni, E., Pollini, R., Trani, M., Verdini, L.: The use of augmented reality glasses for the application in industry 4.0. In: De Paolis, L.T., Bourdot, P., Mongelli, A. (eds.) AVR 2017. LNCS, vol. 10324, pp. 389–401. Springer, Cham (2017). https://doi.org/10.1007/978-3-319-60922-5_30
7. Hashimoto, S., Ishida, A., Inami, M., Igarash, T.: TouchMe: an augmented reality based remote robot manipulation. In: The 21st International Conference on Artificial Reality and Telexistence (ICAT), pp. 1–6 (2011)
8. Mourtzis, D., Zogopoulos, V., Vlachou, E.: Augmented reality application to support remote maintenance as a service in the robotics industry. Procedia CIRP 63, 46–51 (2017). https://doi.org/10.1016/j.procir.2017.03.154
9. Peña-Tapia, E., Roldán, J.J., Garzón, M., Martín-Barrio, A., Barrientos, A.: Interfaz de control para un robot manipulador mediante realidad virtual, pp. 829–835 (2020). https://doi.org/10.17979/spudc.9788497497749.0829
10. Cañadillas, F., Jardón, J., Balaguer, C.: Diseño preliminar de interfaces de realidad aumentada para el robot asistencial ASIBOT (2013)
11. Romero, M.A., Hernández, W., Abreu, D.P.: NxtAR : un sistema de control para robots móviles basado en realidad aumentada, pp. 147–159
12. Reina, M., González, M., Francisco, C., Galicia, A., Flores, P., Manuel, J., Marcadores para la realidad aumentada para fines educativos. http://www.redalyc.org/articulo.oa?id=512251564004

13. Alvarez-Marin, A., Castillo-Vergara, M., Pizarro-Guerrero, J., Espinoza-Vera, E.: Realidad aumentada como apoyo a la formación de ingenieros industriales. Formacion Universitaria **10**(2), 31–42 (2017). https://doi.org/10.4067/S0718-50062017000200005
14. Durani, H., Sheth, M., Vaghasia, M., Kotech, S.: Smart automated home application using IoT with Blynk app. In: Proceedings of the International Conference on Inventive Communication and Computational Technologies, ICICCT 2018, pp. 393–397, September 2018. https://doi.org/10.1109/ICICCT.2018.8473224

Development of an IoT-Based Precision Agriculture System for Strawberry Plantations in Guamote Ecuador

Carlos M. Molina[1]([⊠]) , Héctor F. Chinchero[2] , and Néstor Caral[1]

[1] Universidad Intercultural de las Nacionalidades y Pueblos Amawtay Wasi, Quito, Ecuador
carlos.molina@uaw.edu.ec
[2] Electrical Engineering Department, University of Oviedo, Campus de Viesques, 33204 Gijón, Asturias, Spain

Abstract. In this paper a research on Precision Agriculture (PA) for Strawberrys Plantations is presented. The proposed PA System is based on the integration of Internet of Things (IoT) elements using LoRa Communication. Thus, by using a temperature, humidity and CO_2 wireless sensor network (WSN), the PA Parameters can be monitored in order to determine the correct ambient for strawberry plantation. This work demonstrates how the IoT based PA System improve the analysis of PA Parameters in real time. An experimental prototype has been built to test the wireless communication method and PA parameters monitoring, and to verify its feasibility and possibilities.

Keywords: Precision Agriculture (PA) · Information and Communication Technology (ICT) · Internet of Things (IoT) · Wireless Sensor Network (WSN) · Ancestral sciences

1 Introduction

The world population will exceed nine billion inhabitants in 2050, so the demand for agricultural products will increase between 60 and 70% according to the Food and Agriculture Organization (FAO) of the United Nations [1].

In Ecuador, the agricultural sector represents 0.1% of GDP. Additionally, together with cattle raising, forestry and fishing, they represent the fourth economic sector and contribute 9.63% to the GDP with approximately 10 million dollars [2].

The Ecuadorian Institute of Statistics and Census (INEC) in the Survey of Surface and Continuous Agricultural Production (ESPAC), for the years 2014 and 2018, has determined that 46.4% of the Ecuadorian land used is occupied by mountains and forests, on 19.3% for cultivated pastures, 11.6% for permanent crops, 7% for transitory crops and fallow, 6% natural pastures, 5.4% other uses, 3.1% paramo and 1% for rest [3].

The surface of agricultural work in the year 2020 was 5.2 million hectares, where 39.7% were destined to the cultivation of pastures. On the other hand, permanent crops represent 27.7% of the agricultural work surface, the crops with the highest production

K. Abad and S. Berrezueta (Eds.): DSICT 2022, CCIS 1647, pp. 132–147, 2022.
https://doi.org/10.1007/978-3-031-18347-8_11

volume (from highest to lowest) are: sugar cane, banana and African palm, others such as floriculture and fruits [3].

Every time it is necessary to develop new techniques and methodologies for food production to satisfy a rapidly growing market. In this development it is also important to consider the care of the environment to guarantee the availability of agricultural spaces with an optimal yield for the cultivation of products. This line of research is very extensive, so it is convenient to delimit the studies in areas of work such as the use of technologies, cultivation techniques, care for the environment and, above all, the development of towns and communities in a sustainable and healthy environment.

In the case of technologies, the implementation of innovative solutions based on Information and Communication Technology (ICT) are increasingly in demand in the agricultural sector, both for the production and trade of products. However, there is little development of solutions for the case of the cultivation process and the optimization of care for the environment, for which there is a wide range of research possibilities in this area. On the other hand, the Internet of Things (IoT) currently allows obtaining information, using sensor elements installed in the processes or in the field, such as temperature, humidity, air quality, among others. This information can be used for decision making in the optimization of crops, through monitoring, storage and data processing, which is defined as Precision Agriculture (PA) or Smart Farming (SF).

Precision Agriculture based on IoT, can be used in all practices of the production cycle, so the areas of work where greater optimization of the crop can be carried out should be studied. One of the most important areas of work for analysis is the study of soils before and after planting, to determine the suitability of the environment for a given agricultural product. It is also essential to study the soil and the environment closest to the plantations, in the growth of the plant to optimize the crops. The information obtained in PA applications is obtained by implementing sensors embedded in the soil or in non-invasive infrastructures conditioned in accordance with criteria and standards of care for the environment.

In addition, PA is a discipline of study framed in the field of ICTs that is currently being used in the cultivation of agricultural products such as sugar cane [4], coffee [5], potato [6], barley [7], strawberries, roses, among others.

There are ancestral techniques used very frequently in Andean communities, such as those developed by the Aymara, Quechua, Quitus, Nazca, and Inca civilizations, among others. These peoples developed techniques for agriculture, keeping the Earth and its relationship with the cosmos as the central factor. They also considered environmental factors governed by natural cycles, the Aynoqas and Sayañas, which are traditional agricultural systems of Andean communities framed in sustainability. Additionally, the diversity of environmental conditions in the Andean region has allowed the development of ancestral agriculture based on wisdom and orally transmitted to new generations, allowing better use of natural resources for food and nutrition [9].

2 Information and Communication Technologies Applied to Precision Agriculture

The use of technological tools in agriculture has helped to improve agricultural production, contributing to the food security of the people [10, 13]. ICTs, integrated with electronic systems, software, telecommunications networks, automation and control systems, contribute to the improvement of agricultural processes. This allows optimizing the capture, treatment, storage and dissemination of data for decision-making in the cultivation process. ICTs have initially penetrated the agricultural sector in the field of Business-to-Business (BtB), Business-to-Consumer (BtC), Smart Farming, among others [10]. However, ICTs have not been fully developed into integral solutions, such as those achieved using the IoT, which is why there is a wide range of opportunities to develop research in the use of sensors that analyze the soil, environment, color of the plants, water pollution, etc. for the optimization and improvement of the agricultural sector.

In the communication infrastructures used in AP, data networks contribute to the management of production in the agricultural process. Wireless Sensor Networks (WSN) based on the IEEE 802.15.4 standard can be used to obtain information on temperature, humidity, solar radiation and photosynthetic flow on crops. The WSN usually implements a star topology, with a coordinator node and field sensor nodes, communicating wirelessly using protocols such as Xbee, LoRa, ZigFox, Wings, among others [5]. On the other hand, the TCP/IP protocol is the most used standard in the transport layer of a WSN, it allows information to be transmitted to a Concentrator Gateway [11] or to the cloud. In some IoT applications, infrared (Irda) technology is also used for point-to-point communications in short-range know as Wireless Personal Area Networ (WPAN). In addition, multipoint communications use protocols such as Bluetooth (IEEE 802.15.1) or ZigBee multi-hop medium-range networks (IEEE 802.15.4).

Solutions are also integrated with technologies such as WiFi (IEEE 802.11g) for Wireless Local Networks (WLAN), Wimax technology (IEEE 802.16) for Wireless Metropolitan Networks (WMAN), or long-range cellular technology (GSM/GPRS/LTE) to implement Machine to Machine (M2M) communications [12].

In the case of the Andean region, Precision Agriculture has been used ancestrally for more than four thousand years in the communities of the Ecuadorian coast and highlands, such as the Albarradas technique, which are artificial wetlands, complex structures that have allowed ancestral communities obtaining and using the water resource for many centuries, in an equitable and sustainable way [14].

There is also the technique to burn the residues of the previous harvest, so that the ash acts as a fertilizer and disinfectant for the soil where the new planting is going to be carried out, this is still done by burning the trunk and weeds combined with medicinal plants such as mint, rue, marco, rosemary, etc. in cold weather seasons to prevent the impact of low temperatures on crops such as potatoes, carrots, broad beans, strawberries, among others [15].

Another of the ancestrally used techniques is the soilless cultivation technique known as Hydroponics, it is a set of techniques that allows the cultivation of plants in a free medium without the use of soils to obtain vegetables of excellent quality, allowing a more efficient use of the water and the maximum use of light and nutrients [16]. Many of these techniques have been transmitted from generation to generation in the Andean peoples, although there is not much documentation of these methodologies, they can be used as a reference framework to implement PA projects that comply with the ancestral premises of caring for the environment, the soil, crops and communities.

On the other hand, the care, protection and preservation of the environment applies the ISO 14000 standards, in relation to the use of air, water and soil. In addition, the ISO 14001 standard includes the necessary criteria to carry out an Environmental Management System [17]. These standards provide a guide for the implementation of sustainable PA projects that, combined with criteria of ancestral techniques, will allow us to address case studies in Andean communities with solvency.

Until now there has not been a study of Precision Agriculture using IoT that meets the technical criteria and premises of ancient sciences, so this line of research is an opportunity to present novelties in the use of ICTs applied in agricultural processes that use ancient sciences. This paper presents the development of a precision agriculture system based on IoT for strawberry plantations in the TAL community of Guamote, Ecuador.

3 Development of Precision Agriculture System for Strawberry Plantations

3.1 Analyzed Parameters for Strawberry Plantations

The use of technological tools in agriculture has helped to improve agricultural production, contributing to the food security of the people [10, 13, 18]. ICTs, integrated with electronic systems, software, telecommunications networks, automation and control systems, contribute to the improvement of agricultural processes. This allows optimizing the capture, treatment, storage and dissemination of data for decision-making in the cultivation process. ICTs have initially penetrated the agricultural sector in the field of Business-to-Business (BtB), Business-to-Consumer (BtC), Smart Farming, among others [10]. However, ICTs have not been fully developed into integral solutions, such as those achieved using the IoT, which is why there is a wide range of opportunities to develop research in the use of sensors that analyze the soil, environment, color of the plants, water pollution, etc. for the optimization and improvement of the agricultural sector.

Carbon dioxide (CO_2) is an odorless, colorless, non-flammable greenhouse gas (GHG), which is present in the environment. This gas is 1.5 times heavier than air. In high concentrations, that is, more than 30,000 ppm, CO_2 can cause various health problems in people, such as dizziness, drowsiness, respiratory problems, among others. However, in plants, CO_2 fulfills a fundamental factor for their optimal growth. On the other hand, an ideal concentration of CO_2 around 1000 ppm is required for plants to carry out photosynthesis [B] [18, 22].

Finally, it is necessary to analyze the ambient temperature values. The optimal temperatures that strawberries require for their correct growth are between 15 °C and 25 °C. If plantations exceed or fall below these temperatures for a short period of time, the plants are not damaged [19, 22].

3.2 PAS Requirements for Strawberry Plantations in Guamote Ecuador

This work has been developed to meet the needs derived from the losses obtained annually in the strawberry plantations of the producers of the Andean communities of Guamote.

Location: Gozoy Comunity, Cebadas Parish, Guamote Canton, Province of Chiimborazo, Ecuador.

Area of Strawberry Plantation: 1100 m^2
First Harvest Time: 6 months
Harvest Cycle: biweekly
Production: 25 buckets of strawberries/40 lb
Average Cost: Average 13 dollars per 40 lb bucket
Weight of Bucket: 40 lb
Cost per pound: 3,1 USD
Number of producers: 150 (Table 1)
Harvest Losses: When the life of plants is less than one year, there is a loss of approximately 5,000 dollars per plantation.
Environmental factors for losses: excess rain, pests and freezing weather.
Type of Pistests: powdery mildew, fungus on the stem of the plant.

Table 1. Cost estimation of strawberry plantation production.

Production	Amount bucket	Total weight [Pound]	Total USD
One week	50	2000	6200
One month	200	8000	24800
Six months	1200	48000	148800
One year	2400	96000	297600

Figure 1 shows the location of the impact zone of this research work.

3.3 Architecture of Precision Agriculture System Using IoT

The implemented prototype is composed of electronic elements, sensors, actuators and network interfaces for wireless communications, in an IoT platform for Precision Agriculture Applications [19, 20]. Figure 2 shows a schematic with the main components of Precision Agriculture System (PAS). In this architecture, the field IoT Node and the IoT

Fig. 1. Location of strawberry plantations in Cebadas Community, Guamote Ecuador.

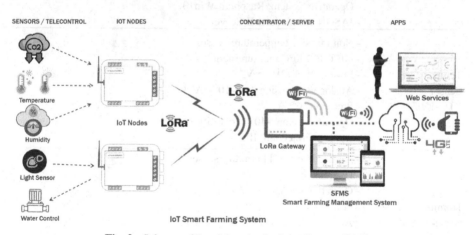

Fig. 2. Schema of Precision Agriculture System (PAS).

Server Node stand out, the same ones that are arranged in a mesh-type communications network topology, using LoRa protocol.

Technical Specifications of Precision Agriculture System Using IoT
See Table 2.

Table 2. Minimum technical specifications of PAS using IoT [19–22].

Device Name	Function	Form
PAP Measurement IoT Node 4ANI-SFS	- PAP remote measurement - LoRa Communication - 4 Analog channels conditioned by ADC - BUS 12Vdc - Solar panel powered - Consume: 40 mA (BUS). - WaspMote Pro V1.5 Development Board - ATMEGA4081 Microcontroller - LoRa SX1272 Transceiver - Installation: embedded in protection box IP67	
LoRa Gateway Server WSBD-100	- Web Server and MySQL BDD - Processor: AMD 400MHz - RAM: 32MB - Ports: 10M/100M RJ45 Ports x 2 - WiFi : 802.11 b/g/n - IoT: LoRa Wireless SX1272 - Power: 110VAC/12V DC - USB Port: USB 2.0 host x 2 - Operative System: Raspbian/Win10 - JASON and NodeRED Server	
Temperature Sensor STC-150ADC	- Non-invasive temperature sensor - -40°C to 150°C measurement - Power: BUS 12V / 5 V. - Analog voltage signal / 0-10 V ADC. - Precision: 1-2% - Operation Temp: -40°C to 175°C. - Outdoor Protection: IP65.	
Humidity Sensor SHM-50ADC	- Anticorrosive soil humidity sensor - Hygrometer - Operation voltage: 3.3V - 12V - Power: BUS 12V / 5 V. - Analog voltage signal / 0-10 V ADC. - Precision: 1-2% - Operation Temp: -25°C to 85°C. - Outdoor Protection: IP67.	
CO2 Gas Sensor SCO2-10ADC	- CO_2 Gas sensor for Agriculture - Measurement range: 0-30%/0-100 - Working humidity: <0-100%RH - Power: BUS 12V / 24 V. - Output signal: 4-20 mA. - Precision: 1-2% - Operation Temp: -30°C to 50°C. - Outdoor Protection: IP67.	

(*continued*)

Table 2. (*continued*)

LoRa Gateway Server Development Tools	- Node-RED - JASON - MQTT - MySQL, MS SQL Server - Win10, Visual Studio, Java Script	

3.4 Precision Agriculture Parameter Measurement IoT Node

The measurement of the Precision Agriculture Parameters (PAP) is carried out using the 4ANI-SFS IoT Node [19]. This node is a reader for up to 4 different physical analog channels.

The measurements are achieved by implementing sensors associated with each PAP in the inputs of the node. To measure humidity, the SHM-50ADC sensor [19, 22] is used. The temperature is obtained using the STC-150ADC sensor [19, 22]. To measure CO2 levels, the SCO2-10ADC sensor [19, 22] has been used.

The PAP information read on each analog channel is sent via LoRa communication to the WSBD100 Web Server Concentrator Node [19, 22]. The 4ANI-SFS IoT Node has a measurement capacity of up to 4 analog sensors from 0 to 10 V conditioned by ADC conversion. There is the option of using current sensors, in this case the system admits signals from 0 to 20 mA.

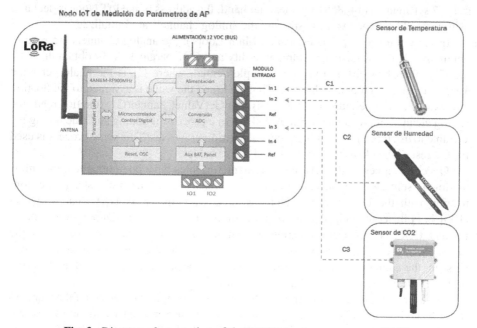

Fig. 3. Diagram of connection of the IoT Node of measurement of PAP.

Communication from the 4ANI-SFS IoT Node to the WSBD100 Server depends on the implemented Wireless Transceiver, in this case there is an SX1272 type interface for LoRa protocol [19, 22].

The configuration and programming of the IoT Node, SX1272 Transceiver and WSBD100 LoRa Gateway is done using WaspMote IDE tool, with the help of direct connection via USB port. Figure 3 shows the connection diagram of the elements used to measure PAP on the field IoT Node [19, 22].

3.5   Precision Agriculture Parameters Measurement Algorithm – Field IoT Node

The measurement of PAP in each field IoT Node is performed according to the algorithm shown in Fig. 4. The implemented process is described below.

First the libraries are defined, in this case it is necessary to specify the library for LoRa communication using the SX1272 module as transceiver. For this process, the library is included through the declaration: #include <WaspSX1272.h>. Next, the address of the concentrator web server node to which the information is transmitted is defined by: uint8_t rx_address = 1. In addition, in this initial process the address of the IoT Node is defined, in this case it has been specified by: int src = 2, this value will change depending on the node that will be used. In an extended wireless sensor network (WSN) it is possible to have from 0 to 255. The analog channels to be used are also declared and initialized for the conversion process.

In the following process called Setup(), the specific channel to perform LoRa communication is activated and established through the sx1272.ON() function. Channel 14 is established, which allows the use of the 900 MHz frequency through: sx1272.setChannel (14_868). On the other hand, the address of the IoT Node is declared using: sx1272.setNodeAddress(src) and the analog channels are initialized.

In the foremost loop process called Main Loop(), the analog channels are read to obtain the values of the temperature, humidity and CO2 parameters. To obtain the data, the GetValueChannel(C1) function is implemented, where C1 is the analog channel assigned to a given input, in this case Channel1, and the value is assigned to the floating point variable Temperature_C1. Internally, the GetValueChannel(C1) function reads the analog channel implemented in CHANNEL1 in a process of adding and calculating the variable to use this value in subsequent calculation processes. This same process is used for the rest of the channels to get all the PAP variables.

Once the values of the PAP measurement variables have been obtained, the information is sent to the Concentrator Node by means of sendVariables(). If the connection with the Lora Gateway Node is successful, the array type Char Variables [100] is built, containing the information of the node number, temperature, humidity and CO2. Next, the information is sent through the transceiver port using the sx1272.sendPacketTimeout(rx_address, (char *) messageVariables) function. As can be seen, the address of the Concentrator Node has been specified, as well as the array with the information of the PAP measurement node.

Once the sending of the information has been completed, it is verified if the Concentrator Node has received it correctly by means of an ACK response and the values sent are printed through the USB serial output. Printing the PAP values to the field IoT Node

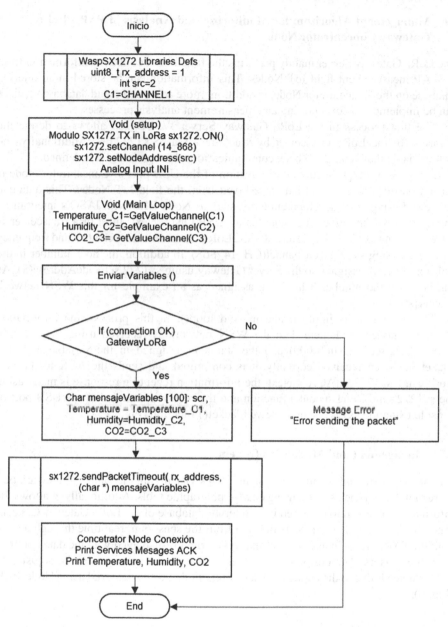

Fig. 4. Precision Agriculture Parameters (PAP) measurement algorithm.

USB port is used to verify communications in the prototype development process. It is recommended to have a serial console to display the IoT Node messages.

3.6   Management Algorithm for Monitoring and Analysis of PAP - LoRa Gateway Concentrator Node

The LoRa Gateway Server mainly performs the function of collecting information from the PAP measurement field IoT Nodes. This information can be stored in an internal database on the Concentrator Node, in addition, more advanced cloud database services can be implemented for reporting and measurement analysis processes.

The first process in the LoRa Gateway Server WSBD-100 allows to define the libraries for the LoRa transceiver by #include <WaspSX1272.h>. Additionally, the state variable that is used to check communications through int8_t e is defined.

In the Void setup() section, the activation of the USB port of Concentrator Node is carried out to send the information received from the field IoT Nodes. This data can be viewed using HMI development tools, such as Node-RED with JASON integration, among others. This process is done using USB.ON(). Next, the LoRa transceiver is activated using sx1272.ON(). Here also the LoRa communication channel and frequency is selected using sx1272.setChannel(CH_14_868). In addition, the node number in the LoRa network is assigned to the Server Gateway using sx1272.setNodeAddress(8). As can be seen, the number 8 has been assigned as an example for this WSN network prototype.

The main loop is implemented in void loop(). In this process, the information of all the nodes implemented in the WSN network is received using the function e = sx1272.receiveAll(10000) and the status is assigned in the variable e. If the packet has been received correctly, it is configured and sends the ACK to the network using sx1272.setACK(). Next, the information reception response is made using the sx1272.sendWithTimeout() function and the received data is sent via USB port or console using the sx1272.showReceivedPacket() function (Fig. 5).

3.7   Management and Monitoring System

The management and monitoring system allows visualizing the values of the variables corresponding to each sensor, using chart-type graphic tools. Additionally, it allows the information obtained to be stored in an internal database of the LoRa Gateway Concentrator Node. The system presents the data from the sensors in real time through a table with the PAP values. In addition, a Chart type graph is displayed with the data obtained from the sensors. The customization of the management software can be adjusted to different needs due to the application development flexibility achieved using Node-RED (Fig. 6).

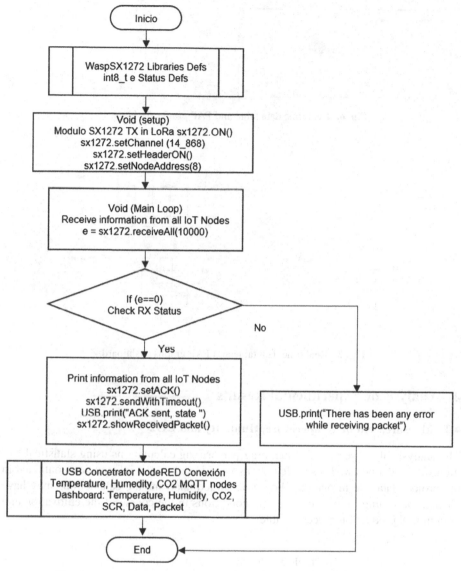

Fig. 5. Precision Agriculture Parameters (PAP) measurement algorithm.

The management system also allows you to view the data from each sensor in an individual graph for each one, as shown in Fig. 7. On the abscissa axis is the reading time of the data, and on the ordinate axis is the value of measured temperature, air humidity, soil humidity and CO2.

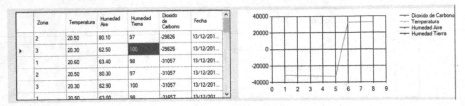

Fig. 6. Real time data table and PAP graphs dashboard.

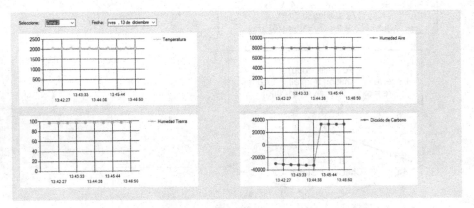

Fig. 7. Real time data table and PAP graphs dashboard.

4 Analysis of Experimental Results

4.1 Measurement of Temperature, Humidity and CO2

The analysis of the results obtained after performing calculations using statistical formulas is shown below. These calculations were based on the information contained in the project database in one day. For an extended analysis, the calculations may have changes according to the daily weather conditions in the course of the cultivation and agricultural production process (Table 3).

Table 3. Measurement PAP results.

Parameter	Ambient temperature	Ambient humidity	Soil humidity	CO2
Median	19,40 °C	78,95%	93,00%	483,00 ppm
Arithmetic average	19,39 °C	80,10%	93,22%	478,43 ppm
Standard deviation	0,39	5,51	0,58	16,87
Interval	1,50 °C	27,40%	4,00%	120,00 ppm
Variance	0,154 °C	30,407%	0,332%	284,60 ppm
Coeff. variation	0,020	0,069	0,036	0,035

Regarding temperature, the result of the arithmetic mean is 19.39 °C, a very acceptable value since it is within the recommended ranges for the correct growth and development of strawberry plantations. The most repeated temperature value is 19.4 °C. In addition, a standard deviation of 0.39 was obtained, which indicates how much dispersion there is in the measured data set. The variance is 0.154 °C, a low and acceptable value together with the coefficient of variation that is barely 2%. This indicates that there is a homogeneity of the data, which is good because there is not much dispersion in the information.

For soil humidity, the average is 80.10%, a suitable value for strawberries to absorb the necessary amount of water for their growth process. On the other hand, the humidity value that is repeated the most is 93%. In addition, a standard deviation of 0.58 was obtained. The variance is 0.332%, a low and acceptable value together with the coefficient of variation of 0.6% indicating homogeneity in the data.

In the case of CO_2, the arithmetic mean is 483 ppm, an acceptable value for the fruit to develop correctly. On the other hand, the value of parts per million that was most obtained was 484. Additionally, a standard deviation of 16.87 and a variance of 284.60 ppm were obtained, a low and acceptable value together with the coefficient of variation of 3.5%.

4.2 Optimization Alternatives for IoT-Based Precision Agricultural System

For future work in this line of research, complementary control devices can be developed, or the system developed in this work can be integrated with traditional automation systems used in smart farming applications to implement automation services.

When temperatures are too low, the agricultural process, greenhouse or plantation area can be sealed to prevent heat loss. Another alternative is the use of thermal screens made of polyethylene. In addition, automated heating systems based on hot water or hot air can be used.

When temperatures are too high, shading systems can be used, which can be static or dynamic. Static systems are installed and shade the greenhouse continuously, dynamic systems allow the amount of shade to be regulated according to climatic needs.

Another alternative is natural or mechanical ventilation to achieve cooling air circulation. In addition, cooling can be done by evaporation of water using diffusers that spray water to the plantation to cool the environment.

To control the levels of carbon dioxide present in the greenhouse or strawberry plantation, direct CO_2 supply systems can be used. This is achieved when the sensors detect low CO_2 values, the valves that allow the passage of this gas are activated to have the necessary conditions in the plantation for the correct development of the strawberry.

Finally, when the soil moisture is below the required percentage, an automatic irrigation system can be implemented that allows the passage of water to each of the strawberry plants.

Finally, a cost analysis has been carried out for the implemented prototype. Since the PAS has IoT electronics elements and integrated circuits (ICs), a low cost of 1200 USD has been found for all materials and accessories.

5 Conclusions

This document has presented the development of a precision agriculture system based on the internet of things for strawberry plantations in COMUNA TAL. It has also been shown that it is possible to use the values of ambient temperature, soil humidity and the CO2 gas present in the plantations as analysis parameters in the PAS. LoRa communication in mesh topology has been used to implement the WSN. The implemented network model allows addressing distances of up to 1,5 km between IoT devices.

The values obtained in the measurements of temperature, humidity and CO2 are within the recommended ranges for the correct growth and development of the strawberry plant. On the other hand, in each case the calculated values of the standard deviation indicate the existing dispersion in the data set, as well as the variance has low and acceptable values together with the coefficient of variation, indicating that there is a large amount of homogeneous data.

Because the field IoT Node uses the SX1272 transceiver with LoRa protocol, a 900 Hz channel has been used, which allows communications without interference from other wireless networks in the impact zone. These work frequency levels do not affect the environment, nor do they affect the growth of strawberry plants. On the other hand, the sensor elements do not generate technological waste in the environment since they are sealed and have degrees of protection for their implementation on floors and outdoors. So it is shown that the system is not invasive and is aligned with the ancestral criteria of respect for the land, care for the environment and soil renewal.

References

1. Collado, A.D.: Tema Discusión: 2050 y la agricultura del futuro. Red de Planificación para el Desarrollo en América Latina y el Caribe ILPES/AECID, 2 (2018)
2. INEC: Boletín Técnico: Encuesta de Superficie y Producción Agropecuaria Continua 2020, Quito (2021)
3. Sánchez, A.M.: Sector Agrícola en Ecuador, Ambato (2020)
4. Orozco, L.R.: Sistemas de información enfocados en tecnologías de agricultura de precisión y aplicables a la caña de azúcar, una revisión. Revista Ingenierías Universidad de Medellín, 1 (2015)
5. Molano, F.A.: Redes de Sensores Inalámbricos Aplicadas a Optimización en Agricultura de Precisión para Cultivos de café en Colombia. Journal de Ciencia e Ingeniería 5(1), 46–52 (2013)
6. Hernández, P.H.: Determinación de normas de fertilización diferenciada para el cultivo de la papa empleando técnicas de agricultura de precisión. Revista Ciencias Técnicas Agropecuarias 15(1) (2006)
7. Peralta, N.B.: Agricultura de Precisión: Dósis variable de nitrógeno en cebada. Ciencia del suelo (2015)
8. Langscape Magazine: Obtenido de (2018). https://swed.bio/wp-content/uploads/2018/07/Mal mer-LS7.1-SUMMER-2018-WEB.pdf
9. Andrade, P.: Tecnología de congelo - deshidratación y condicionantes en la producción familiar del chuño de la comunidad de Taipi - Ayka de la provincia Camacho del departamento de La Paz. (Tesis de Licenciatura). Universidad Mayor de San Andrés, La Paz, Bolivia (2018)
10. Recio Aguado, B.: Las tecnologías de la información en la agricultura: asignatura pendiente. Vida Rural (2009)

11. Pérez, M., Mendoza, M., Suarez. M.: Paradigma IoT: desde su conceptualización hacia su aplicación en la agricultura. Revista Espacios **40**(18) (2019)
12. Jurado, L.V.: Estado del Arte de las Arquitecturas del Internet de las Cosas (IoT). Springer, Heidelberg (2014)
13. Santos, L.K.: El uso de la tecnología en la agricultura. Pro-Sciences: Revista De Producción, Ciencias e Investigación (2018)
14. Vallejo, M.: Albarradas: pertinencia de los saberes. Revista de Ciencias Sociais. Fortaleza 227 (2020)
15. Manosalvas, L.: Análisis de la aplicación de conocimientos ancestrales en el manejo del cultivo de papa (Solanum tuberosum), en la Comunidad de Jesús del Gran Poder, Parroquia La Libertad, Cantón Espejo, Provincia del Carchi 2019. Universidad Técnica de Babahoyo (2019)
16. Beltrano, J., Giménez, D.: Cultivo en hidroponía. Universidad de la Plata (2015)
17. ISO TOOLS Exellence: Software ISO M. Ambiente y Energía. Obtenido de SO TOOLS Exellence (2022). https://www.isotools.org/normas/medio-ambiente/iso-14001/
18. Chinchero, H.F, Alonso, J.M.: Development of an IoT-based electrical consumption measurement and analysis system for smart homes and buildings. In: IEEE International Conference on Environmental and Electrical Engineering 2020 (2020)
19. Chinchero, H.F., Guevara, A.M.: "IoT Smart Metering System" Cintelam Campos Inteligentes de América Cia. Ltda., Technical Manual. (2020)
20. Libelium: Waspmote Tecnical Guide. Libelium Comunicaciones Distribuidas S.L. (2019)
21. Libelium: Waspmote Programing Guide. Libelium Comunicaciones Distribuidas S.L. (2019)
22. Ingenium: Manual Técnico. Ingnium Ingeniería y Domótica S.L. (2021)

Cancer Detection Based on Electrical Properties of Tissues

Anthony Crespo[1] (ID), Nataly López[2] (ID), Nicole Paz[2] (ID), Adriana Estrella[2] (ID),
Diego Almeida-Galárraga[2] (ID), and Andrés Tirado-Espín[1(✉)] (ID)

[1] School of Mathematical and Computational Sciences, Yachay Tech University, Hacienda San
José s/n, San Miguel de Urcuquí 100119, Ecuador
{brian.crespo,ctirado}@yachaytech.edu.ec
[2] School of Biological Sciences and Engineering, Yachay Tech University, Hacienda San José
s/n, San Miguel de Urcuquí 100119, Ecuador
{nataly.lopez,nicole.paz,adriana.estrella,
dalmeida}@yachaytech.edu.ec

Abstract. Cancer is one of the leading causes of death worldwide. Therefore,
early detection is essential since it can prevent its spread and increase the chances
of treating and curing it. The present work focuses on analyzing cancer detection techniques based on the dielectric properties of tissues. Examples of these
techniques are dielectric characterization, bioimpedance spectroscopy, microwave
spectroscopy, and microwave tomography, which can replace other methods that
can cause complications in patients, such as X-ray images, tomography, and biop-
sies. For this purpose, a descriptive method was used by searching for scientific
articles published in a time interval between 2016 and 2021. This search was
made in different databases such as Google Scholar, Scopus, and PubMed. A
Boolean algorithm was defined, with which a total of 32 different combinations
were obtained—finally reaching a selection of 30 articles. All these articles were
studied thoroughly and separated into categories to analyze them properly.

Keywords: Cancer · Biological tissues · Dielectric properties · Bioimpedance ·
Detection

1 Introduction

It is estimated that in 2020 there were about 20 million cancer detections and 10 million
cancer deaths worldwide, causing the death of one in eight men and one in eleven women
diagnosed with some type of cancer [1]. According to Al Ahmad et al. [2], normal cells
exhibit higher dielectric constants than cancer cells from the same tissue. Furthermore, it
was observed that the addition of cancer cells to normal cells increased the capacitance
of normal cells and that cancer cells of different cellular origins possess their own
characteristic electrical parameters. Because cancer is capable of causing alterations in
the biological structure of cells, which produce changes in the electromagnetic properties
of tissues, new detection techniques can be developed to take advantage of this [3]. Some
examples of these techniques are dielectric characterization, bioimpedance spectroscopy,

K. Abad and S. Berrezueta (Eds.): DSICT 2022, CCIS 1647, pp. 148–160, 2022.
https://doi.org/10.1007/978-3-031-18347-8_12

or microwave tomography, which can replace other methods, such as X-ray images that can cause certain complications to patients [4].

Fahmy et al. [5] explain that the dielectric phenomenon consists of making dielectric measurements of tissue using an open-ended coaxial system. After making a dielectric analysis of the biophysical properties of normal and malignant tissues, it was obtained that biophysical changes in tissues are produced by differences in tissue composition, blood flow, and architecture between normal and cancer cells. Furthermore, using the dielectric spectroscopy technique, it was suggested that dielectric parameters, especially conductivity and permittivity, were biomarkers for the densification of cancer patients. Consequently, it is obtained that dielectric spectroscopy rapidly provides the biophysical status of normal and cancerous tissues and can therefore be effectively applied for early diagnosis.

On the other hand, bioimpedance is a term used to describe the response of living organisms when an external current is applied to them. It is a measure of opposition to the flow of the applied current through the tissues, which is non-invasive and evaluates the composition of the living organism [6]. Taking this as a principle, there is a method known as bioimpedance spectroscopy that can be used to differentiate healthy tissues from diseased ones based on the variation of electrical properties of biological material when it is subjected to electric fields of variable frequency [7]. Zou and Guo [8] propose the application of this method in breast cancer detection using noninvasive impedance imaging techniques, such as electrical impedance tomography (EIT) and electrical impedance mapping (EIM).

Lately, the microwave tomography technique for the detection of tumors is attracting a lot of attention from scientists [4]. Using this method as a principle, methods such as the Finite Difference Time Domain (FDTD) were developed, which is used as a computational tool for the development, validation, and optimization of emerging techniques for the detection and treatment of breast cancer by microwave [9]. In another study, a hypothetical assumption based on the variations of complex dielectric permittivity of the water content of cells at different stages of cancer was implemented, obtaining a quite satisfactory result with a low margin of error. Therefore, it is proposed that the microwave imaging technique is one of the best methods for detecting the presence of cancer cells inside the human body [4]. These methods are the key to cancer detection at an early stage since it implies a higher probability of survival and also a decrease in the treatment cost.

This article provides knowledge about how these methods work with the electromagnetic properties of cancerous tissues and explains how easily accessible techniques have advantages in cancer detection. In this way, its use can be encouraged in sectors where they do not have more sophisticated technology and increase the detection of the disease. The method employed is a review of scientific articles. The search was carried out in databases such as Google Scholar, Scopus, and PubMed, choosing the articles published between 2016 and 2021. The whole process was performed to achieve the search objective: compare and contrast the literature of authors to find agreements or discrepancies on the effectiveness of techniques that use the dielectric properties of tissues in cancer detection. In this way, this research work focuses on answering the following research question:

RQ: What techniques efficiently employ the electrical properties of tissues in cancer detection?

2 Materials and Methods

This study is categorized as descriptive. To carry it out, a search method was first defined for the scientific articles on which this work would be based. Thus, the Boolean search [10, 11] was chosen. For this purpose, eight descriptors were defined, three fixed and five variables. The fixed descriptors were «cancer», «biological tissues» and «dielectric properties», and were present in all searches. On the other hand, «bioimpedance», «cell membrane», «electric field», «detection» and «applications» were chosen as variable descriptors and were used in the searches according to the combinations obtained with the Boolean method.

As a next step, in order to establish the number of total searches to be performed, the mathematical formula 2^N was used, N being the number of variable descriptors, 5 in this case. From this, $2^5 = 32$ different combinations were obtained. Likewise, Google Scholar, PubMed, and Scopus were selected as the databases in which to carry out the previously defined number of searches. A highly relevant feature is that the articles must have been published in an interval from 2016 to 2021, that is, the last 5 years at the date

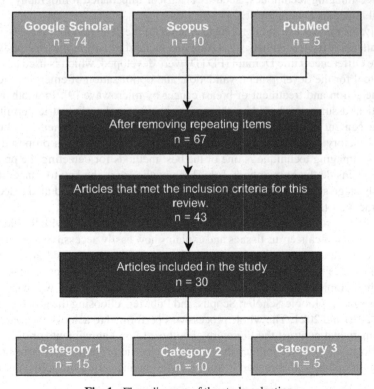

Fig. 1. Flow diagram of the study selection

of elaboration of this study. Thus, a total of 30 scientific articles focused on the use of the dielectric properties of tissues as a means for cancer detection were obtained and selected for the study. Finally, 3 categories were defined and each of the articles was assigned to one of them (see Fig. 1).

3   Results

Regarding the production of articles related to the use of the electrical properties of tissues for cancer detection, the publications made in 2016 correspond to 10.00% (n = 3) of the total. For 2017, there is a slight increase and a 13.33% (n = 4) is reached. For the year 2018, it is observed that the number of published articles is much higher than in the previous two years; this results in a percentage of 26.67% (n = 8). On the other hand, in 2019, scientific production related to the subject in question presents 20.00% (n = 6). For 2020, the number of articles presents a light increase and represents 26.67% (n = 8), matching the number obtained in 2018. Finally, in 2021, 3.33% (n = 1) of the total percentage was reached. The statistics show that the years both 2018 and 2020 correspond to those with the highest number of scientific publications within the analyzed period, while 2021 represents the year with the fewest found items (see Fig. 2).

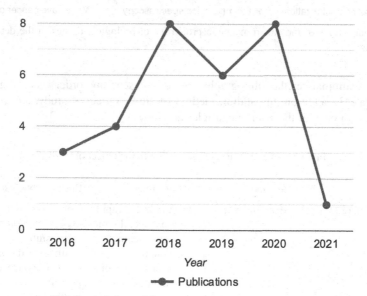

Fig. 2. Articles published per year between 2016–2021

In this study, three categories were identified, and each category allowed for further analysis of the items selected for the sample. Normal cells exhibit higher dielectric constants than cancer cells of the same tissue due to changes in the cells' physiological, biochemical, and morphological properties. Based on this idea, the possible applications of electromagnetic properties of biological tissues in the detection of cancer cells were investigated. After analyzing the scientific articles reviewed, it was possible to identify that 50% (n = 15) addressed the use of dielectric characterization to compare healthy cells with cancer cells. Additionally, 33% (n = 10) of the articles analyzed the use of bioimpedance-based devices for the early detection of cancer. Finally, the remaining 17% (n = 5) focused their ideas on microwave-based diagnostics (see Fig. 3).

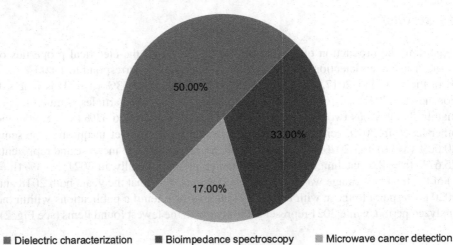

Fig. 3. Applications of the electromagnetic properties of biological tissues in the detection of cancer cells

Table 1 summarizes the bibliography sorted in descending order according to publication date. In addition, the author, method of study, object of study, and results or conclusions of each of the scientific articles are shown.

Table 1. Scientific articles according to the object of study.

Author	Method	Object of Study	Results/Conclusions
Huang et al. (2021) [12]	Experimental	Find a simple and rapid method to detect thyroid diseases at different stages, from the dielectric properties of thyroid nodules	Normal, benign, and malignant nodules were successfully distinguished from each other. The dielectric properties have application prospects for cancer detection and diagnosis

(continued)

Table 1. (*continued*)

Author	Method	Object of Study	Results/Conclusions
Denkçeken and Ayşegü (2020) [13]	Experimental	Distinguish low metastatic human breast cells from normal human breast cells using the bioimpedance spectroscopy	Distinguish breast cancer cells in cell culture using the FOBIS system
Cheng et al. (2020) [14]	Experimental	This study presents SmartProbe, an electrical bioimpedance (EBI) sensing system based on a concentric needle electrode (CNE)	There was a great potential for SmartProbe to be used in various cancer detection tasks
Hossain (2020) [15]	Descriptive	Provide the framework for future innovation that can be considered to diagnose cancer cells. Using electrical impedance measurements	There is a significant difference in electrical properties between malignant and healthy cells, allowing active and early diagnosis of a patient
Mansouri et al. (2020) [16]	Experimental	Use of a bioimpedance device designed for early detection of breast cancer	The difference between resistances in each breast allows early detection of cancer
Pathiraja et al. (2020) [17]	Descriptive	Application of electrical impedance in the detection of malignant neoplasms	Electrical impedance is feasible to differentiate between normal, premalignant, and malignant lesions
Jahangiri et al. (2020) [18]	Experimental	Study of the dielectric and electric cell membrane characteristics for the separation of cancerous cells from normal cells	A cytological slide chip (CSC) is designed and fabricated based on AC electric field stimulation of breast cell lines and blood cells at low frequencies

(*continued*)

Table 1. (*continued*)

Author	Method	Object of Study	Results/Conclusions
Nasir and Al Ahmad (2020) [19]	Descriptive	Cell dielectric properties and electrical-based cell detection techniques	Phase-shifting laser microscopy (PLM), Atomic force microscopy (AFM), Gas chromatography, Mass spectrometry, (GCMS), Capacitive-voltage and capacitive frequency method, and Electrical impedance spectroscopy are electrical-based cancer cells detection techniques
Fahmy et al. (2020) [5]	Descriptive	Study the applications of dielectric spectrometry in the clinical diagnosis of cancer and distinguish between normal and tumor tissues	Dielectric spectrometry provides the biophysical status of normal and cancerous tissues and can be applied for the early detection of cancers
Fornés Leal (2019) [3]	Experimental	Propose applications for CRC detection that aid in colonoscopy procedures using differences in electromagnetic properties	The electromagnetic properties of the suspect tissues of a patient should be compared with their healthy tissues
Uncu and Avşar Aydin (2019) [20]	Experimental	Investigate the effects of each factor and their interactions on cancer cell detection using factor analysis with microwaves	Factors such as the permittivity of fat and skin, tumor size, and breast size are effective in detecting breast tumors

(*continued*)

Table 1. (*continued*)

Author	Method	Object of Study	Results/Conclusions
Basu and Purkait (2019) [4]	Experimental	To implement a hypothetical assumption based on the variations of complex dielectric permittivity of the water content of cells	It is proposed that the microwave imaging technique is one of the best methods for detecting the presence of cancer cells
Gupta and Jogi (2019) [21]	Experimental	Fabrication of biodevice to distinguish normal cells from malignant, based on cell electrical characteristics	Relative cellular impedance measurement could be employed for the diagnosis of cancer and its stage
Yao et al. (2019) [22]	Experimental	Characteristics of biological tissue by establishing an electrical equivalent circuit with electrical impedance spectroscopy	The extracted equivalent electrical parameters can clearly characterize the variation of the internal change of components of biological tissues
Hussein et al. (2019) [23]	Experimental	Show that microwave characterization of breast cancer cell lines is reliable with potential in biomedical applications	Microwave characterization has potential in biomedical applications such as cancer detection and the design of electromagnetic models
Ruvio et al. (2018) [24]	Experimental	Compare two methods of measuring the dielectric properties of aqueous samples	The well-calibrated Stuchly and Stuchly method is valid for the measurement of dielectric properties
Di Meo et al. (2018) [25]	Experimental	Present the correlation between the dielectric properties at 30 GHz of healthy and tumor tissues	There is a large contrast in dielectric properties between healthy and tumor tissues
Al Ahmad et al. (2018) [2]	Experimental	Characterize and discriminate between normal and cancerous cells from three different tissue	Normal cells exhibited higher dielectric constants compared to cancer cells from the same tissue

(*continued*)

Table 1. (*continued*)

Author	Method	Object of Study	Results/Conclusions
Teixeira et al. (2018) [7]	Experimental	Apply the technique to measure the impedance of five different tissues from healthy and cancerous mice arranged with two tumor lines	Both cancerous tumors have the highest conductivity values or, equivalently, the lowest impedance values
Gavazzi et al. (2018) [26]	Experimental	Investigate whether there are differences in electromagnetic properties between normal and diseased human thyroid tissues	There are significant differences between the dielectric properties of normal and malignant thyroids, at frequencies below 2.45 GHz
Cheng and Fu (2018) [27]	Experimental	Investigate microwave parameters as a non-invasive method of detecting breast cancer	Microwave-measured effective dielectric permittivity and conductivity could distinguish breast cancer
Guardiola et al. (2018) [28]	Experimental	Measure the complex permittivity of colon polyps, cancer, and normal mucosa to see if the dielectric properties are suitable for classification	The contrast in complex permittivity between normal and abnormal colon tissues demonstrates the potential for tissue classification
Zubair et al. (2018) [29]	Experimental	Dielectric spectroscopy in the terahertz frequency range to differentiate normal human tissues from cancerous ones	The proposed terahertz dielectric spectroscopy may be used to identify the cancer tissues
Farina et al. (2017) [30]	Experimental	Propose a portable setup suitable for in vivo measurements of tissue dielectric properties	The designed system enables reliable and accurate dielectric measurements while ensuring portability
Du et al. (2017) [31]	Experimental	Identify breast tumors using bioimpedance spectroscopy (BIS)	Regression factor (RF') derived from BIS can discriminate between benign tumors and cancers

(*continued*)

Table 1. (*continued*)

Author	Method	Object of Study	Results/Conclusions
Wang et al. (2017) [32]	Descriptive	Comprehensive descriptions of the most important MI approaches for early breast cancer detection	Summary of MI approaches with particular focus on implementations of microwave breast imaging theory
Hesabgar et al. (2017) [33]	Experimental	Measure the dielectric properties of normal and cancerous tissue corresponding to low frequencies, using a recently developed technique	Electrical permittivity at low frequencies can potentially be used as a powerful biomarker for the detection of breast malignancies
Sarode et al. (2016) [6]	Descriptive	Report on the deliberate role of bioimpedance in various malignancies of the body	There are significant differences in electrical impedance between normal and cancerous tissues. Being important in the early detection of oral cancer
Solanki et al. (2016) [34]	Experimental	Develop and characterize oil-in-gelatin dispersions that approximate the dielectric properties of human tissues	The development of different means of mimicking human tissue can be used for cancer detection
Martellosio et al. (2016) [35]	Experimental	Characterize the dielectric properties of normal and tumorous breast tissues for the frequency range from 0.5 to 50 GHz	Normal tissues had more variability in their dielectric properties than tumorous tissues

Table 1 shows that the majority of the articles, 80.00% (n = 24) of the total, used an experimental method in their studies. These articles aimed to evaluate the use of different techniques for cancer detection based on the electrical properties of tissues. On the other hand, descriptive studies or review articles accounted for 20.00% (n = 6) of the total. These articles compiled information from previous work focused on the use of differences between the electrical properties of tissues as a differentiator between healthy and cancerous cells.

The following analysis identified that experimental studies could be carried out using different data collection methods or techniques. After analyzing the information provided by each of the selected articles, a new division was made according to the method used. Thus, four new groups or categories were defined. The simulation corresponds to the first one. This consists of using algorithms, modelling programs, or simulating the conditions necessary for a phenomenon (Articles 5, 11, 12, 13, 14, 15, 19, 27). On the other hand, the ex-vivo represents the second category and refers to the extraction of a sample of an organ with the help of a medical procedure, cells or tissues from a living body, which is subsequently used to obtain data (Articles 2, 3, 7, 10, 16, 17, 20, 21, 22, 23, 24, 26, 30). Finally, the third category corresponds to in vivo experimentation performed inside a living organism, usually mice or pigs (Articles 1, 18, 29).

4 Discussion and Conclusion

Regarding dielectric characterization, Fahmy et al. [5] mention that dielectric parameters, such as conductivity and permittivity, were biomarkers of densification in cancer patients. Strengthening this idea, Guardiola et al. [29] and Hesabgar et al. [34] mention that the contrast between the permittivity of healthy and tumour tissues allows a classification of them, functioning as a biomarker for the early detection of abnormal tissues. Furthermore, Fahmy et al. [5] concluded that dielectric spectroscopy provides the biophysical status of normal and cancerous tissues. In this way, it can be effectively applied for early diagnosis. Similarly, [13, 19, 20, 23, 35] emphasize the effectiveness of electrical spectroscopy in detecting cancer cells based on the dielectric properties of tissues. Therefore, measuring the dielectric parameters of cells allows differentiation between normal and tumour tissues, enabling the detection and diagnosis of cancer.

Bioimpedance describes the response of living organisms when an external current is applied to them, allowing the characterization of tissues and the evaluation of their composition. Basing their conclusions on differences in impedance values shown by cancerous and healthy tissues, several authors agree on its potential use for early detection of breast, cervical, prostate cancer, among others. Teixeira et al. [7], in their study of healthy and cancerous mouse tissues, showed that impedance values vary according to tissue type. Specifically, cancerous tissues have lower impedance values. These results are in agreement between authors, although each adds their own findings or techniques.

Denkçeken and Ayşegül [14] used the fiber optic bioimpedance spectroscopy system (FOBIS) to study mammary epithelial cells, finding that the impedance value decreases in metastatic cancer cells. Mansouri et al. [17] also focused their study on breast cancer. However, unlike Denkçeken and Ayşegül, they compared the resistances between the right and left breast, obtaining that the difference between the resistances is a pertinent parameter to detect the presence of cancer early. Lastly, Du et al. [32] propose using bioimpedance spectroscopy since it can discriminate between benign tumours and cancers and obtain the results in just minutes.

There are several methods for studying the microwave technique, such as in a simulated phantom tissue by oil-in-gelatin dispersions [10] or on the water content of cells in different stages of cancer [4]. From these studies and in agreement with [28], dielectric properties such as permittivity and conductivity are vitally important parameters in breast cancer detection. Furthermore, Hussein et al. [24], who agree with several of the authors mentioned, put on record that microwave characterization is a reliable method for breast cancer cell detection.

Finally, this descriptive study can be used as a reference source on issues related to early cancer detection techniques, dielectric properties of tissues, and methods such as bioimpedance spectroscopy, the use of microwaves for cancer detection, and the dielectric phenomenon.

References

1. World Health Organization: Cancer (2022)
2. Al Ahmad, M., Al Natour, Z., Mustafa, F., Rizvi, T.A.: Electrical characterization of normal and cancer cells. IEEE Access **6**, 25979–25986 (2018)
3. Fornés Leal, A.: Dielectric characterization of biological tissues for medical applications (2019)
4. Basu, D., Purkait, K.: A hypothetical analysis to study the variations of complex dielectric permittivity for detection of various stages of cancer of a biological target using microwave tomography. In: 2019 Devices for Integrated Circuit (DevIC), pp. 433–440 (2019)
5. Fahmy, H.M., et al.: Dielectric spectroscopy signature for cancer diagnosis: a review. Microw. Opt. Technol. Lett. **62**, 3739–3753 (2020)
6. Sarode, G.S., Sarode, S.C., Kulkarni, M., Karmarkar, S., Patil, S.: Role of bioimpedance in cancer detection: a brief review. Int. J. Dent. Sci. Res. **3**, 15–21 (2016)
7. Teixeira, V.S., Krautschneider, W., Montero-Rodríguez, J.J.: Bioimpedance spectroscopy for characterization of healthy and cancerous tissues. In: 2018 IEEE International Conference on Electrical Engineering and Photonics (EExPolytech), pp. 147–151 (2018)
8. Zou, Y., Guo, Z.: A review of electrical impedance techniques for breast cancer detection. Med. Eng. Phys. **25**, 79–90 (2003)
9. Lazebnik, M., Okoniewski, M., Booske, J.H., Hagness, S.C.: Highly accurate Debye models for normal and malignant breast tissue dielectric properties at microwave frequencies. IEEE Microwave Wirel. Compon. Lett. **17**, 822–824 (2007)
10. Tirado-Espín, A., Cuesta, U., Martínez-Martínez, L., Almeida-Galárraga, D.: Framing and immigration: new frames in media and social networks. In: Rocha, Á., Barredo, D., López-López, P.C., Puentes-Rivera, I. (eds.) ICOMTA 2021. SIST, vol. 259, pp. 140–152. Springer, Singapore (2022). https://doi.org/10.1007/978-981-16-5792-4_15
11. Tirado-Espín, A., Cuesta, U., Martínez-Martínez, L., Almeida-Galárraga, D.: Agenda-setting e inmigración: análisis crítico del discurso y frecuencia en los medios: Estudio descriptivo de investigaciones en revistas científicas desde 2015 a 2020. Rev. Ibérica Sist. Tecnol. Inf. 289–301 (2020)
12. Huang, P., Xu, L., Xie, Y.: Biomedical applications of electromagnetic detection: a brief review. Biosens. (Basel) **11**, 225 (2021)
13. Denkçeken, T., Çört, A.: Determination of cancer progression in breast cells by fiber optic bioimpedance spectroscopy system. J. Surg. Med. (2020). https://doi.org/10.28982/josam. 671514
14. Cheng, Z., et al.: SmartProbe: a bioimpedance sensing system for head and neck cancer tissue detection. Physiol. Meas. **41**, 54003 (2020). https://doi.org/10.1088/1361-6579/ab8cb4
15. Hossain, S.: Biodielectric phenomenon for actively differentiating malignant and normal cells: an overview. Electromagn. Biol. Med. **39**, 89–96 (2020)
16. Mansouri, S., Alhadidi, T., Azouz, M.B.: Breast cancer detection using low-frequency bioimpedance device. Breast Cancer: Targets Therapy **12**, 109 (2020)
17. Pathiraja, A.A., Weerakkody, R.A., von Roon, A.C., Ziprin, P., Bayford, R.: The clinical application of electrical impedance technology in the detection of malignant neoplasms: a systematic review. J. Transl. Med. **18**, 1–11 (2020)

18. Jahangiri, M., et al.: Low frequency stimulation induces polarization-based capturing of normal, cancerous and white blood cells: a new separation method for circulating tumor cell enrichment or phenotypic cell sorting. Analyst **145**, 7636–7645 (2020). https://doi.org/10.1039/D0AN01033B

19. Nasir, N., Al Ahmad, M.: Cells electrical characterization: dielectric properties, mixture, and modeling theories. J. Eng. **2020** (2020)

20. Uncu, N., Aydin, E.A.: The effects of dielectric values, breast and tumor size on the detection of breast tumor. Tehn. Glasnik **13**, 197–203 (2019)

21. Gupta, S., Jogi, V.: Segregation of normal and cancer cells based on impedance characteristics of single cell (2019)

22. Yao, J., et al.: Evaluation of electrical characteristics of biological tissue with electrical impedance spectroscopy. Electrophoresis **41**, 1425–1432 (2019)

23. Hussein, M., Awwad, F., Jithin, D., El Hasasna, H., Athamneh, K., Iratni, R.: Breast cancer cells exhibits specific dielectric signature in vitro using the open-ended coaxial probe technique from 200 MHz to 13.6 GHz. Sci. Rep. **9**, 1–8 (2019)

24. Ruvio, G., Vaselli, M., Lopresto, V., Pinto, R., Farina, L., Cavagnaro, M.: Comparison of different methods for dielectric properties measurements in liquid sample media. Int. J. RF Microwave Comput.-Aided Eng. **28**, e21215 (2018)

25. di Meo, S., et al.: Correlation between dielectric properties and women age for breast cancer detection at 30 GHz. In: 2018 IEEE International Microwave Biomedical Conference (IMBioC), pp. 190–192 (2018)

26. Gavazzi, S., Limone, P., de Rosa, G., Molinari, F., Vecchi, G.: Comparison of microwave dielectric properties of human normal, benign and malignant thyroid tissues obtained from surgeries: a preliminary study. Biomed. Phys. Eng. Express **4**, 47003 (2018). https://doi.org/10.1088/2057-1976/aa9f77

27. Cheng, Y., Fu, M.: Dielectric properties for non-invasive detection of normal, benign, and malignant breast tissues using microwave theories. Thorac Cancer **9**, 459–465 (2018)

28. Guardiola, M., et al.: Dielectric properties of colon polyps, cancer, and normal mucosa: ex vivo measurements from 0.5 to 20 GHz. Med. Phys. **45**, 3768–3782 (2018)

29. Zubair, K.S., et al.: Investigation of dielectric spectroscopy response in normal and cancerous biological tissues using S-parameter measurements. J. Electromagn. Waves Appl. **32**, 956–971 (2018). https://doi.org/10.1080/09205071.2017.1411835

30. Farina, L., Ruvio, G., Pinto, R., Vannucci, L., Cavagnaro, M., Lopresto, V.: Development of a portable setup suitable for in vivo measurement of the dielectric properties of biological tissues. In: 2017 11th European Conference on Antennas and Propagation (EUCAP), pp. 2732–2736 (2017)

31. Du, Z., Wan, H., Chen, Y., Pu, Y., Wang, X.: Bioimpedance spectroscopy can precisely discriminate human breast carcinoma from benign tumors. Medicine **96** (2017)

32. Wang, L., Peng, H., Ma, J.: Microwave breast imaging techniques and measurement systems. Breast Imaging New Perspect. **73** (2017)

33. Hesabgar, S.M., Sadeghi-Naini, A., Czarnota, G., Samani, A.: Dielectric properties of the normal and malignant breast tissues in xenograft mice at low frequencies (100 Hz–1 MHz). Measurement **105**, 56–65 (2017)

34. Solanki, L.S., Singh, S., Singh, D.: Development and modelling of the dielectric properties of tissue-mimicking phantom materials for ultra-wideband microwave breast cancer detection. Opt. (Stuttg) **127**, 2217–2225 (2016)

35. Martellosio, A., et al.: Dielectric properties characterization from 0.5 to 50 GHz of breast cancer tissues. IEEE Trans. Microwave Theory Tech. **65**, 998–1011 (2016)

Artificial Intelligence Applied to Video Game for Detection of Mild Cognitive Impairment

Andres Ortega$^{(\boxtimes)}$ ⓘ, Gustavo Lemos, and Julio Martínez

Universidad ECOTEC, Via Samborondon Km 13.5, Guayaquil, Ecuador
aortegao@ecotec.edu.ec, {glemos,jmartinez}@est.ecotec.edu.ec

Abstract. Mild Cognitive Impairment (MCI) is considered the fisrt stage of dementia, where the scientific community has a great interest in providing the solution from multidiscplinary areas. Biological, psychological and environmental variables are the cause of MCI and they can be monitored without invasive processes.

Abnormal brain aging is a natural cause of MCI which can trigger a complex senile dementia. The computer-aided systems will become in the new technologies for diagnosis and prevention of dementia diseases. Our approach is develop a tool for detection of Mild Cognitive impairment using virtual video games. With the aim of diagnosing MCI, we developed a video game based on missions through Montreal Cognitive Assessment (MoCa) and Mini-Mental State Examination (MMSE) standardized tests.

45 samples were realized between both genders of productive age group. Executive and episodic memory was evaluated through spatial orientation, object recognition, numerical calculation and multi-tasks skills to solve activities of daily life.

The AI is an agent player that is used to obtain the time threshold for each mission. The time threshold represents the performance time to be reached by each player in his different age range. The results indicated that female gender spent more time with respect to the AI algorithm for overall missions. In addition, impairments in concentration and executive memory tasks have been determined with increasing age from 35 years onwards.

Keywords: MoCA · MMSE · ML-Agents · Pathfinding · Unity

1 Introduction

For years, the brain's physiological aging has been a top research theme, given its linkage to cognitive impairment related pathologies. While clinical cases are on the rise, one main goal of such research has been the characterization of cognitive impairment triggers and associated negative impacts, finding that patient

Supported by Universidad ECOTEC.

age is the main risk factor in the development of different types of dementia. Poor performance in functional or daily tasks, such as work memory, recognition and learning, are also indicators of early detection in cognitive impairment [10]. Cognitive impairment also shares factors with dementia such as age, sex, educational degree, genetic load and the preexistence of depressive disorders [6]. However, physiological age-dependant decline and pathological genetic load are considered the most important biomarkers [8] for abnormal brain aging. In this context, neurophysiological techniques in [17] are used as an important *low-cost non-invasive* evaluation method.

Computer-aided systems offer opportunities to improve mood and cognitive abilities, but their efficacy has not yet been proven to replace traditional medice drugs. However, video games have been used to evaluation and improvement of processing speed and attention span [1,15]; in fact, they proved valid in stages of the recovery from depression [3]. Cognitive training using biosensors and neuronal stimulation optimized cognitive performance [4,13]. Likewise, Machine Learning (ML) [11], Augmented Reality (AR) and Virtual Reality (VR) [16] are being tested in illnesses associated with cognitive impairment but their full benefit has not yet been demonstrated. Engine graphical tools like Unity ML-Agents uses Artificial Intelligence (IA) techniques where an agent is needed to mimic the tasks using deep reinforcement learning [19].

Mild cognitive impairment (MCI) is the first degree of cognitive impairment, which is usually accompanied by problems with language, thoughts, poor decision-making and memory. The neurological problems can be develop in silence for some years and imperceptible to the naked eyes. For this reason is important to develop a tool which allows to diagnose MCI from an early age [18].

1.1   Principal Contributions

[2] is one of the leading authors in the contributions of neuroscience using video game called Neuro-Racer techniques for enhancing cognitive control (a set of neural process) in older adults to improve attention and working memory. Neuro Racer propose single and multi task of daily living and can be used as a therapeutic tool for older adults with attention deficit, depression and dementia. Years later, the same author, in [3] demonstrates an improvement in late life depression (LLD) and cognitive control with randomized clinical of 22 older adults over the age of 65 suffering from major depression.

Episodix [18] is a video game designed for detecting cognitive impairment in older adults where episodic, semantic and procedural memory is assessed. Psychometric validity study of the game was done through 4 performance metrics based on cognitive status of participants. At the end, ML algorithms were used to statistically classify between DCL, Alzheimer's and healthy patients. In [5] Virtual reality (VR) is used for mental health problems such as ansiety [15], depression, schizophrenia [12], psychosis, eating and compulsive disorders, increasing feelings of self-compassion. VR alleviates some methodological limitations of traditional studies.

1.2 Our Contribution

This article is based on the "Montreal Cognitive Assessment" (MoCa) and "Mini-Mental State Examination" (MMSE) standardized medical tests [9,14], which allows the evaluation of orientation, short-term memory, executive function, language skills, abstraction, animal naming and attention in order to diagnose the cognitive decline in older adults. These test are adapted on the video game over Unity plataform as is shown in Fig. 1. The virtual city design evaluates the quickly response time for object recognition, the rate errors in simple calculus and spatial recognition for 3D video game. The main objective is evaluate the tests score in comparison with the Artificial Intelligence algorithm as base time of reference.

The data collected from the video game was analyzed to compare the time per completed mission from every player. In this context, an Artificial Intelligence (AI) environment has been created to determine the optimal time of the missions. The AI and Machine Learning algorithms allows us to establish the different thresholds values, which are based on automatic learning, imitating the actions of each participant. The best result is the optimal time of every sample executed by the participants.

The other relevant fact is that the female gender takes more time adaptation to solve the missions video game with respect to male gender. In addition, the cognitive decline is marked from 50 years of age because the time to solve daily life tasks increases due to anxiety.

Finally, for the numerical calculation questions, the female gender has 80% error over the threshold level respecto to male gender.

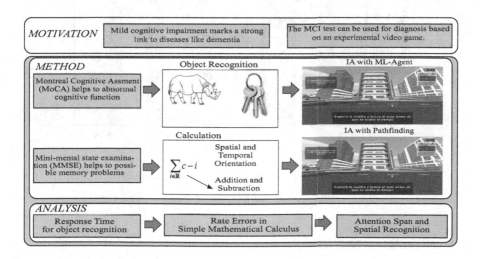

Fig. 1. Summary project.

2 Methodology

2.1 Sampling Description

The study was carried out from a sample with the productive age group of 41 persons between 24 and 50 years of age, of which 27 (65.85%) are the female group and 14 (34.14%) are the male group. From this generalized sample, they have been classified by age range from 24 to 30 years old (26.83%), 31 to 35 years old (29.26%), 36 to 40 years old (12.2%), 41 to 45 years old (14.63%) and 46 to 50 years old (21.95%) as is shown in Fig. 2. All patients who performed the test voluntarily belongs to city of Guayaquil in Ecuador. In addition the profile participants are from the administrative and academic staff of private university. The criteria for the evaluation of mild cognitive impairment are through MoCa and MMSE tests [7].

The usual age of appearance of dementia appears at 65 years. In this study we set the population of productive age with the highest number of concentration from 30 to 50 years; with the aim of evaluating the mild cognitive impairment (MCI) in early age through episodic and executive memory.

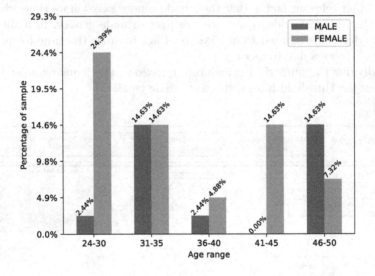

Fig. 2. Productive age group for MCI analysis

2.2 Strategies: Neurocity

Neurocity is the video game design based on city environments where the player uses First-Person shooter (FPS). The main role of the video game is to assess the capacity for abstraction and comprehension of each of the missions that are described inside the game. The activities are evaluated for the amount of time it takes to solve each mission in the video game. In this context, the hippocampus area is related to spatial orientation that comes into operation due to the frontal lobe transforming spatial knowledge into actions.

The object recognition allows us to assess episodic memory using the MoCa test. The main objective are the spatial perception on 3D view and and the understanding of missions o activities of daily living.

Finally, the reasoning through reading comprehension and mathematical skills are used to evaluate the working memory, which normally is known as short-term memory. Finally, it is possible to evaluate multi-tasks such as calculation abilities while another action is being executed. The missions are specified as follows:

Spatial Orientation. Exploration of digital city on 3D view with FPS as is shown in Fig. 3. It is necessary to find the location of a parked vehicle following the arrow indications. The time of recognition and environment adaptability (α), is the most important measurement in order to activate the first mission.

Object Recognition. For the next analysis, the player must reason to the following question to solve the mission: What does it take to start a vehicle and drive in the city? The logical response is obtained the keys and driver's license to start the vehicle. In this context, these objects should be identified by player in order to drive on the road. The time it takes to recognize the objects and return to the vehicle is called β.

Association of elements. For this analysis, object recognition and numerical calculation have been combined in order to associate objects with answers to each question while at the same time the player drives the vehicle. We generated a total of 5 questions of simple numerical calculus. The aim is to evaluate the necessary time, δ, that it takes the player to recognize the association.

Numerical calculation. The total time for responding to mathematical questions is measured by σ, where the number of errors are also accounted. This variable is very important to obtaining the average score for logical thinking.

2.3 Machine Learning Algorithms

The creation of an artificial intelligence (AI) in unity is based on the training dataset, which is able to mimic the best performance of each player. This brain contains the optimal time to be achieved to solve a mission which are shown in the Table 1. The time variables are assigned by each optimal time average calculated by the brain and each memory type to be evaluated.

Pathfinding is achieved based on state of machine where the Agent finds the smallest path from source to destination as is shown in the Fig. 4 for each strategy in the missions. The brain could incorporate the physics of motion such as velocity, revolutions per second and the braking distance of the vehicle.

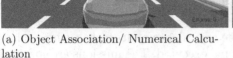

(a) Object Association/ Numerical Calculation

(b) Spatial Orientation

Fig. 3. Neurocity strategies for Cognitive Impairment Detection

Table 1. Optimal time to be achieved.

Time	Description	Memory	Time average
α	Spatial orientation	Episodic memory	30 s
β	Object recognition	Episodic memory	75 s
δ	Associative capacity	Working memory	300 s
σ	Arithmetic calculation	Working memory	400 s

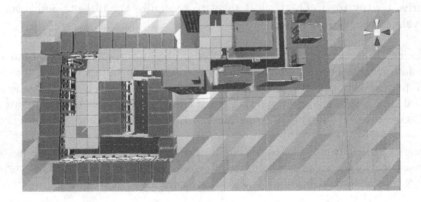

Fig. 4. Pathfinding's coordinates

The pathfinding Agent code is specified in Algorithm 1. The variables are declared in **GameObject** which allows the player's collision with each object mission. The **NavMeshAgent** set the parameters of physical motion for a real scenario. The agent enables the missions once it has collided with the first objective. Each objective is validated to specify the order. The properties that allow identification of the collisions are configured from **Obstacle Avoidance**. After the collision, the agent will search for the following object until all missions are completed.

Algorithm 1

Step 1	Initialize the structure: *Agent, Objective, Time*;
	Initialize set of variables: *Trigger, n*;
Step 2	**Allocate in random mode the Object.position;**
Step 3	**Asign the Agent Properties**

> **while** *trigger* = 1&*time.count* → ∞
> **for** *n* = 1 to *n*
> **if** *Agent.position* = *Objective.position* **then**
>   save time.data;
>   time.count = 0;
> **if** *Objective.n* = *n* **then**
>   trigger = 0;
> **endif**
> **endif**
> **endfor**
> **endwhile**

ML-Agents. Consists of an artificial intelligence learning algorithm, which is programmed to complete certain actions and is complemented with reinforcement learning cycles as is show in Fig. 6 (a). Their purpose is to receive instructions and execute them. If the execution is correct, rewards are granted, otherwise the ML-Agent starts the cycle again until it has favorable results with zero-error and fast convergence as is show in Fig. 5 .

The ML-Agent achieves rewards based on positive or negative rewards, where the configuration of the hyperparameters are given in Table 2. The agent will learn by making mistakes until the objectives achieves an optimal performance.

- **Batch size:** This parameter refers to the number of training examples used in an iteration.
- **Learning rate:** This is the percentage of change that updates the weights of each iteration.
- **Epoch:** Epochs are the trainings that are applied to the agent based on a set of data.

Table 2. ML-Agents parameters.

Variable	Values	Variable	Values
Batch size	120	learning rate	0.0003
Num epoch	20	hidden units	256
Strength	1.0	steps	2000000

– **Hidden units:** These are the feedback that the agent makes while learning in each training.
– **Behavioral cloning:** These are the human parameters such as running, strength and acceleration incorporated in the Artificial Agent.

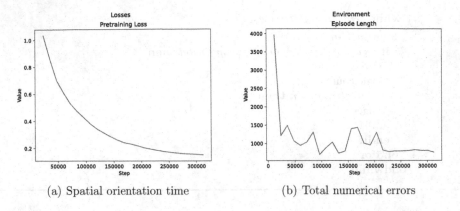

(a) Spatial orientation time   (b) Total numerical errors

Fig. 5. Episodic and Operative Memory measurement

The ML-Agent can take a minimum of 2 h to train depending on the complexity of the environment, but can take up to several weeks if overlearning is generated.

For system simulation, the **tensorflow** library of Python is used. The training process has been evaluated based on the hyperparameters described above. The performance system indicates that 100000 steps more than established are necessary to achieve the minimum error learning for both the pretraining and episode length. These graphs indicate a correct degree of learning of the system and the evaluation of the agent learning. In Fig. 6(b) we have used three different ways to evaluate the optimal times of the automatic algorithms for each mission to compare with the results obtained by the participants. In this context, ML-Agent, Pathfinding are automatic learning algorithms, and Best Player is the time taken by the creators of the video game.

For comparison with the participants, we have taken the most critical time corresponding to the pathfinding algorithm. The results are shown in the following section.

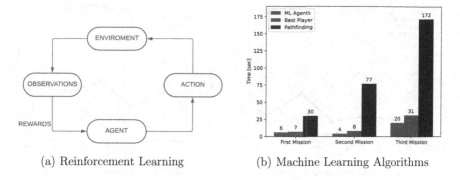

(a) Reinforcement Learning   (b) Machine Learning Algorithms

Fig. 6. Evaluation of Machine Learning.

3   Numerical Results

For the analysis of the different cognitive activities, the time it takes to develop or complete each one of the activities has been taken into consideration; and these are contrasted with two Artificial Intelligence systems that were previously described (the pathfinding model and ML Agent).

In the missions of the video game, one exploration on 3D view of the environment must be carried out in order to evaluate a spatial orientation that allows the user to identify the arrow pointing (Fig. 3(b)) to the vehicle and it allows to activate the first mission to be seen by the player. The search space was delimited with invisible glass in order to reduce the search time of the fisrt mission. This search is the most important since it represents the activation for all missions. The Fig. 7(a), shows that men invested less time to enable missions than women. This implies that they have much greater adaptability to a video game environment and faster spatial orientation, since the linear regression graph serves to compare the threshold generated by pathfinding algorithm. We can see that the female gender doubles its time (from 30 s to 60 s) when increases its age at the highest peaks in 27 years and 45 years respectively.

The object recognition time is shown in Fig. 7(b). Once the first mission is understood, the next step was to pick up the driver's license and the keys. This problem was associated with the time it takes for the players to recognize the objects. This result is the most important in our video game design, due to the curve for women is exactly the same as the prevalence of Alzheimer's disease at 60 years of age, when the signs of mild cognitive impairment occur. The exponential increase from the age of 35 onwards is evident, as a difficulty in solving the task of object recognition is visualized. The average threshold (β) measured by the pathfinding algorithm is 75 years. On another hand, the male gender curve is below the mean of the algorithm, indicating that they have no problem recognizing objects task, even when their age increases.

Figures 7(c) and (d) involve the ability to develop multiple tasks such as driving car with distractors δ and total driving time σ_1 for complete the mission. In this context, the players should be able to associate the objects with numerical calculation responses when driving the car. In the same way, the exponential

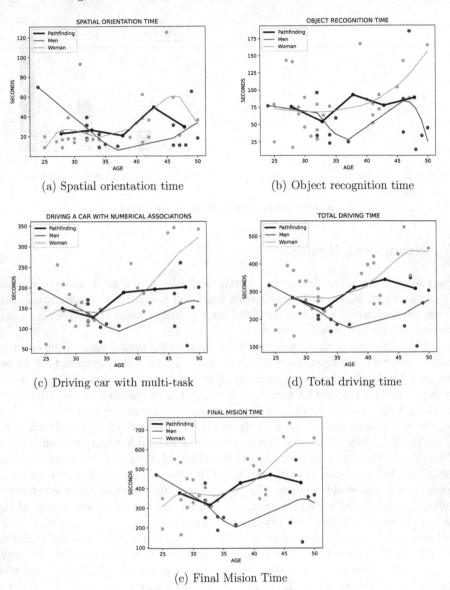

(a) Spatial orientation time

(b) Object recognition time

(c) Driving car with multi-task

(d) Total driving time

(e) Final Mision Time

Fig. 7. Episodic and Operative Memory measurement

increase for the female gender curve tells us the prevalence of MCI as a function of age. Again the focal point is at 35 years of age since it starts to complicate to solve the logical activities of MCI tests.

In this way, the final mission time is referenced by σ_2 where there is a crossover point at approximately 35 years for the two genders with respect to the automatic pathfinding algorithm as is shown in Fig. 7(e). From this point on, the curve for women is an exponential curve that grows with increasing age. This activity, according to the MMSE test, is related to the evaluation of working or executive memory to perform multiple tasks.

4   Conclusions

In this paper we achieve the implementation of both the MoCa and Mini-Mental test, which are tools for Cognitive Impairment detection. These tools were implemented over video game with a First-Person Perspective in a 3D view.

The graphs obtained showed that the prevalence curve of Alzheimer's disease has the same exponentially increasing effect with respect to adult working age. This means that the development of the missions into the video game can evaluate the MCI but above all, we should take into consideration having a larger population to improve the performance results and to avoid bias.

The results evaluated were the counted time, which showed that the female gender is affected from the age of 35, taking into account that all participants are considered non-gamer persons.

In addition, machine learning algorithms were incorporated in order to obtain the time thresholds which we generated a reference curve in the time scale needed to compare the optimal time value for completing the overall missions.

This video game could be implemented in VR and used to assess levels of anxiety in older adults. Even this video game can serve as a preventive and ameliorating mechanism for older adults with already detected dementia.

Acknowledgments. Thanks to all the participants who were part of the data collection sample. This work is dedicated to all people suffering from dementia and all people who accompany this pain. When you forget the simple things in life, you risk losing them, for this reason, I want to be your love forever. Do you accept it Ana?

References

1. Allaire, J.C., McLaughlin, A.C., Trujillo, A., Whitlock, L.A., LaPorte, L., Gandy, M.: Successful aging through digital games: socioemotional differences between older adult gamers and non-gamers. Comput. Hum. Behav. **29**, 1302–1306 (2013). https://doi.org/10.1016/j.chb.2013.01.014. http://dx.doi.org/10.1016/j.chb.2013.01.014

2. Anguera, J.A., et al.: Video game training enhances cognitive control in older adults. Nature **501**, 97–101 (2013). https://doi.org/10.1038/nature12486. http://dx.doi.org/10.1038/nature12486

3. Anguera, J.A., Gunning, F.M., Areán, P.A.: Improving late life depression and cognitive control through the use of therapeutic video game technology: a proof-of-concept randomized trial. Depress. Anxiety **34**, 508–517 (2017). https://doi.org/10.1002/da.22588

4. Bach, D.: Juegos mentales: Cómo los videojuegos pueden desempeñar un papel positivo en la salud mental (2021). https://news.microsoft.com/es-xl/features/juegos-mentales-como-los-videojuegos-pueden-desempenar-un-papel-positivo-en-la-salud-mental/

5. Brito, H., Vicente, B.: Realidad virtual y sus aplicaciones en trastornos mentales: una revisión. Revista chilena de neuro-psiquiatría **56**, 127–135 (2018). https://doi.org/10.4067/s0717-92272018000200127

6. Campbell, N.L., Unverzagt, F., LaMantia, M.A., Khan, B.A., Boustani, M.A.: Risk factors for the progression of mild cognitive impairment to dementia. Clin. Geriatr. Med. **29**, 873–893 (2013). https://doi.org/10.1016/j.cger.2013.07.009

7. Carcavilla, N.: Moca: Test de evaluación cognitiva montreal (2020). https://comunicacionydemencias.com/test-moca-demencia/

8. Crespo Cuevas, A.M.: Marcadores ultrasonográficos asociados a deterioro cognitivo leve y demencia. TDX (Tesis Doctorals en Xarxa) (2021). http://www.tdx.cat/handle/10803/671722

9. Folstein, M.F., Folstein, S.E., McHugh, P.R.: Mini-mental state. A practical method for grading the cognitive state of patients for the clinician. J. Psychiatr. Res. **12**(3), 189–198 (1975). https://doi.org/10.1016/0022-3956(75)90026-6. https://pubmed.ncbi.nlm.nih.gov/1202204/

10. Ángel G. López, Calero, M.D.: Predictores del deterioro cognitivo en ancianos. Revista Espanola de Geriatria y Gerontologia **44**, 220–224 (2009). https://doi.org/10.1016/j.regg.2009.03.006

11. Johansen, M., Pichlmair, M., Risi, S.: Video game description language environment for unity machine learning agents. In: IEEE Conference on Computatonal Intelligence and Games, CIG 2019-Augus, pp. 1–8 (2019). https://doi.org/10.1109/CIG.2019.8848072

12. Macedo, M., Marques, A., Queirós, C.: Realidade virtual na avaliação e no tratamento da esquizofrenia: Uma revisão sistemática. J. Bras. Psiquiatr. **64**, 70–81 (2015). https://doi.org/10.1590/0047-2085000000059

13. Mishra, J., Anguera, J.A., Gazzaley, A.: Video games for neuro-cognitive optimization. Neuron **90**, 214–218 (2016). https://doi.org/10.1016/j.neuron.2016.04.010. http://dx.doi.org/10.1016/j.neuron.2016.04.010

14. Nasreddine, Z.S., et al.: The montreal cognitive assessment, MoCA: a brief screening tool for mild cognitive impairment. J. Am. Geriatr. Soc. **53**(4), 695–699 (2005). https://doi.org/10.1111/J.1532-5415.2005.53221.X. https://pubmed.ncbi.nlm.nih.gov/15817019/

15. Repetto, C., Riva, G.: From virtual reality to interreality in the treatment of anxiety disorders. Neuropsychiatry **1**, 31–43 (2011). https://doi.org/10.2217/npy.11.5

16. Rose, F.D., Brooks, B.M., Rizzo, A.A.: Virtual reality in brain damage rehabilitation: review. Cyberpsychol. Behav. **8**, 241–262 (2005). https://doi.org/10.1089/cpb.2005.8.241

17. Rossini, P.M., Rossi, S., Babiloni, C., Polich, J.: Clinical neurophysiology of aging brain: from normal aging to neurodegeneration. Prog. Neurobiol. **83**, 375–400 (2007). https://doi.org/10.1016/j.pneurobio.2007.07.010

18. Valladares-rodríguez, S., Fernández-iglesias, M.J., Anido-rifón, L., Facal, D.: Episodix : un juego serio para detectar deterioro cognitivo en adultos mayores. un estudio psicomérico, pp. 1–27 (2018)

19. Youssef, A.E., Missiry, S.E., El-Gaafary, I.N., Elmosalami, J.S., Awad, K.M., Yasser, K.: Building your kingdom imitation learning for a custom gameplay using unity ml-agents. In: 2019 IEEE 10th Annual Information Technology, Electronics and Mobile Communication Conference, IEMCON 2019, pp. 509–514 (2019). https://doi.org/10.1109/IEMCON.2019.8936134

YouTube and Instagram Applied to e-Learning

M. Iriarte-Solano(✉) , J. M. Juca-Aulestia , L. D. Andrade-Vargas ,
and V. Riofrío-Leiva

Universidad Técnica Particular de Loja, Loja, Ecuador
{miriarte,jmjuca,ldandrade}@utpl.edu.ec

Abstract. Currently, in social media, there are countless educative resources that support learning, through valid content generated by teachers. Our work is trying to know the frequency for content elaboration, motivation and content transmission, the use of resources and benefits classroom brings through YouTube and Instagram; This investigation is based on an exhausting survey about frequency, use, and transmission of educative resources based on YouTube and Instagram, the same that was applied to 407 teachers from different educative institutions from Ecuador, the instrument was validated by different international experts, secondly, the instrument was analyzed and then proceeded to measure reliability with the Alfa by Cronbach considering it as acceptable. As a result, we have that most recourses are designed frequently for education and health, through video tutorials, forums, and manuals, to promote discussion on subjects of academic interest. In conclusion, this kind of social media develops the creative skill of the teacher for resource design and creation which causes visual impact to students through audio, video, and illustrations and be share between them to form a thoughtful and spontaneous dialogue.

Keywords: "Social network" · "Educational innovation" · "Social media" · YouTube

1 Introduction

Technological advance, especially mobile phones and the internet, have generated new spaces and environments for the interaction and transmission of content through channels that are now not only occupied for leisure, but have also gained a large space in the educational field [1].

Online teaching has configured new scenarios and learning environments from Web 2.0, an aspect that challenges the teacher to have Information and Communication Technologies (TIC) knowledge to generate greater interaction on the web with students and content, which must be easily accessible inside and outside the classroom [20]. It is important to mention that these new environments imply a notorious variety in the behavior and use of skills by teachers and students, and this lies a lot in the management of information since they use the resources and services that exist on the web [2].

In the teaching-learning process, technological resources have been used according to the educational needs of each institution. Currently, online platforms are of great help, which support learning through the exchange of content [33]; Likewise, social networks play an important role since they intensify the trend and social participation [3], these have been growing rapidly in recent years allowing the dissemination and transmission of content [4].

Social networks play an important role in the lives of thousands of people, especially it has a high impact on academic activities using students for self-learning, so teachers must evaluate the material, audio, video, images so that have a greater impact on students [5], what actually becomes a big problem in online teaching lies in the selection or creation of content that are sources of learning for students and that can be accessible as reinforcement inside and outside of class, the teacher must design content that does not are only with scientific content, but also pedagogical aspects and values [6], if it is necessary to develop an educational concept with the intervention of social networks where technologies intervene and use the creation of video and images as a method [7], that cause visual impact on students so that content becomes meaningful learning [8].

It is true that social networks have potential risks regarding the privacy of information, which is why it is a great challenge and intervention of parents, governments and educational institutions that make use of these tools with different digital devices [9], so that they know and implement different aspects of security and privacy. On the other hand, it is necessary to mention that currently students are feeding on contents that are on the network for queries and carrying out tasks, especially on social networks such as YouTube and Instagram, which are asynchronous, transmissive and interactive means of communication that allow sharing. Videos and generate learning communities through the sharing of resources to promote and develop skills [10].

In this sense, the research seeks to publicize the frequency with which teachers create content, the desire to transmit content, how often they use it in the classroom and how it helped to strengthen their classes through YouTube and Instagram.

2 Literature Review

2.1 Teaching Resources

The resources today are turned in to an important tool in learning, especially online where students make use of this for their learning in a self-regulated dorm, these resources get stronger to support knowledge building, where students can learn with educative resources free/open in social media ad online communities, through collaborative activities like videos and podcast [11].

Most students access to the resources for class research, in addition to teacher communication through this media [12], that it is especially important that resources are labeled correctly to be available and accessible on the web, especially when opting for remote mode studies [13], or when they are worked with a set of learning resources such as (audios, videos, texts) known also like repositories where they host a variety of metadata. In the case of accessibility, the teaching resources must be for public consumption without excluding students [14].

That is where the need comes from, teachers being trained to handle new tools for the design and resource creation for YouTube and Instagram and develop new skills such as creativity, curiosity, and constant learning, divergent and future thinking.

2.2 Social Media

The incorporation of social media in the teaching-learning process has increased in recent years that is why it is important to have qualified teachers with TIC management skills, having as the main purpose facilitate social learning in addition to fostering collaboration and interaction between teacher-student and students with each other, improving the learning especially for people who opt for distance or online studies [15].

Social media have transformed people"s daily life and especially the students who together with mobile devices, are a great tool for education, creating individual and group virtual spaces for information sharing. With the arrival of social networks, students have a positive attitude which they use for critical thinking skills [16], the social media, it becomes a way to reach more places by expanding communication with bigger and bigger people [17], this also introduces a myriad of elements such as tools, resources, people and material that help to free the routine to teachers and students [18], it is worth to mention that some studies show that teenagers and higher education students are the ones who attend social media most [19].

Social media becomes a physical space where people share common interests and opinions that have been of great help and support for teaching especially in distance education, because it could be a bridge between formal and informal learning generating new opportunities online, achieving interactions between student-student, student - content in curricular and extracurricular topics [20]; then proposes a category of social media [21]:

1. Podcast.
2. Professional profiles.
3. Short texts.
4. Videos.
5. Long texts.
6. Images (Instagram).
7. Synchronous tools for discussions.

In the case of social media, for the videos, it is more use frequently the platform YouTube, the same that as videos with different qualities, motives, kinds of the ones which cover all aspects of information and knowledge, also allow you to create YouTube channels to share videos by providing profile images [21], and that can be managed by many teachers and students [13].

Then it is shown the Fig. 1. Regarding the design of educative resources in the platforms or YouTube and Instagram repository, having in mind the interaction that exist between each of the designs that exist for the consume, taking into consideration, the abilities for creating and the availability of them through the licenses that provide each one (Standard and Copyright) for the Web.

It is important to mention that social media as YouTube or Instagram play a key role in the teaching-learning process. This article demonstrates the use of these social media for teaching work.

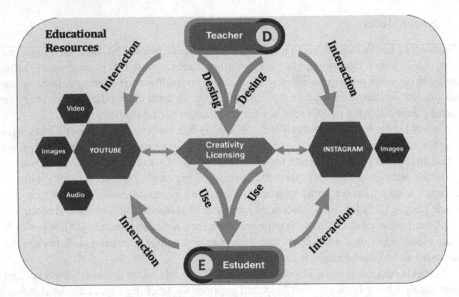

Fig. 1. Educational resources on YouTube and Instagram.

3 Methodology

This study is based on an exhausting survey about frequency, use, and transmission of educative resources based on YouTube and Instagram, with close questions and a nominal and ordinal measurement, the survey was applied to 407 teachers from different educational institutions of Ecuador distributed in the 9 Educational planning zones, both in the public and particular sector, in addition to the type of institution (Fiscal, Fiscomisional and Particular). To apply the survey to teachers from many institutions, their participation was optional and anonymous.

As a first part, the instrument was validated with different international experts including teachers and investigators from Spain, Portugal, Brazil, and Peru. In the second instance, the instrument was analyzed and then it was procced to measure the reliability of it, having, as a result, an index of 0.791 which is considered acceptable.

4 Findings/Results

This section shows the results of the proposed questions regarding educational resources used in YouTube and Instagram social media.

4.1 Create Content for YouTube and Instagram

How often teachers prepare content for YouTube and Instagram is shows **Fig. 2**. It is observed that, for the most part, teachers never prepare content for these two social networks and only sometimes do they prepare content for YouTube; while a single person, out of 407 teachers, always creates content for the two social networks.

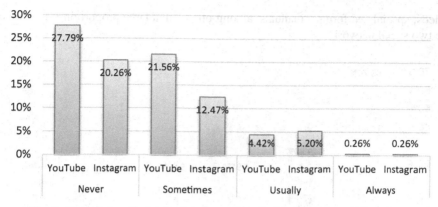

Fig. 2. Frequency with the development of content for YouTube and Instagram.

4.2 Motivation for Stream Content in YouTube e Instagram

The motivation that teachers have to transmit content on YouTube and Instagram shows **Fig. 3**, with the result that most are motivated to disseminate content in different areas (education, health, etc.) through the two social networks, and transmit values such as (respect, love, freedom, responsibility, etc.).

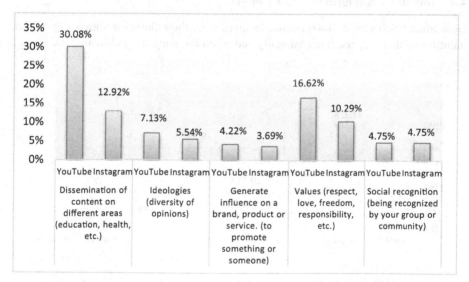

Fig. 3. Motivation to transmit the content you create on YouTube and Instagram

4.3 Resource Use in the Classroom

How the resources on YouTube and Instagram are frequently used in the classroom, is shows Fig. 4, which mostly indicates that it is used for self-learning through tutorial videos, specialized forums, manuals, among others, in a large proportion it is done for the two social networks.

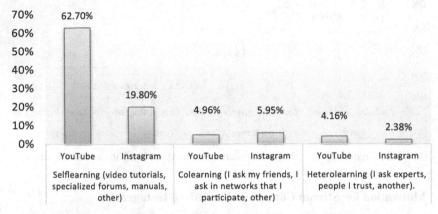

Fig. 4. Resources from YouTube and Instagram most used in the classroom

4.4 YouTube e Instagram Use for Classes

How often teachers use YouTube and Instagram for their classes is shows Fig. 5, most mentioning that they use it occasionally and often for YouTube and Instagram.

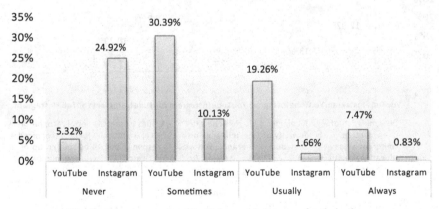

Fig. 5. Frequency using YouTube and Instagram for their classes

4.5 Strengths When Using YouTube e Instagram in Classes

How YouTube and Instagram help teachers strengthen their classes, having in mind the institution kind is shows Fig. 6 and 7. Results show, in the first place, that the

Fiscomisional and Fiscal institutions helped to promote discussion on both social media. In the second instance, Fiscal, Fiscomisional and Particular educative institution realize it for following investigator or referent teachers, last, Fiscal, Fiscomisional and Particular educative institutions have helped to strengthen the class to elaborate articles in YouTube and Instagram.

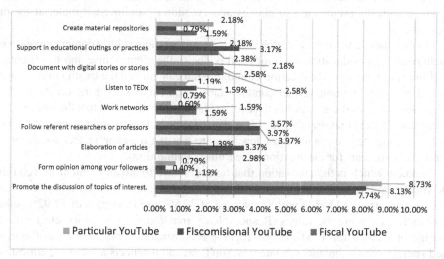

Fig. 6. Strengths when using YouTube in classes

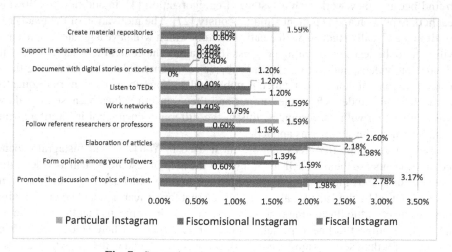

Fig. 7. Strengths when using Instagram in classes

5 Discussion

The investigation results indicated with significant percentages that never or sometimes teachers have developed content for YouTube or Instagram social media, which may be due to the lack of preparation and training in technology use, pedagogical and academic elements, values, and attitudes of teachers for their creation [6], some authors mention that it could be for the lack of training and preparation of the older teachers in the social media use and integration [22]; also, a lot of them do not understand which kind of activities can perform in these media, nor the wealth they can live on [23], in some cases this could be due to lack of time to have to combine their academic and administrative activities with the preparation of classes and creation of audiovisual material for the social media.

On the other hand, in the research it can be seen that there is little content creation by teachers in higher education institutions, this due to the compromise and the attention level they have to pay to the creation of audiovisual content and the treatment of images [24], it is worth mentioning that content elaboration implies working on the student objectives, in which the teacher has to develop resources to the extent that the information is relevant [25] and that way the student adjust his time in function of his learning habits [26]. Knowing this we can tell those teachers are wasting the benefits that social media bring in the students for the creation of learning communities.

To know which is the motivation that teachers have to stream content in YouTube and Instagram results shown at a general level that they are mainly based on YouTube case for education and health with an average of 30,8% and Instagram of 12,92%, other motives to stream are the values (Respect, love, freedom, responsibility, etc.) with an average of 16,92% for YouTube and 10,29% for Instagram; this means that the most used social media to broadcast content is YouTube and it reflects a lot in the educative, where students have an interaction between classmates and resources, which are easy to find because they work with a system of categorization [4], in addition to allowing teachers to publish and comment simultaneously [27]. The motivation of the teacher is to stimulate visually students with creative content which will have a greater impact and will help to the learning-teaching progress [8], making the content teachable in base to illustration, videos, audios to make the subject comprehensible [28]. Analyzing these results, we can tell that content which is published on YouTube is used more frequently by teachers and students from the campus and they transmit values because they allow more interaction with the resources, this in the different educational institutions from Ecuador where the survey was applied.

Talking about the resources that are most used in YouTube and Instagram social media, students use them for self-learning with the help of resources such as video tutorials, manuals, and others having a preference in YouTube with 62,70% unlike Instagram that is just used by the 19,80%; also, we can see that for co-learning and hetero learning they use it very little fluctuating in a percentage of 4%. This means that these resources have a great impact in line, especially in academic activities where students use them frequently for their self-learning. These results are corroborated with [10], who mentions that this kind of digital products which are published on YouTube has the possibility of being shared on the Internet, which after been studied create a reflexive and spontaneous dialogue between the students, these resources and strategies are used to learn without depending on the teachers or books [29]. Although, this kind of platform and resource also has the function of delivering messages from the teacher in the learning process to approach different topics which can be due to lack of time in the classroom, place, or installation educative [30]. In base on these results, we can say that YouTube is the favorite social media of teachers to share resources, generating self-learning in students.

The frequency with which teachers use YouTube and Instagram in the classroom results reflected that there is little use with a large percentage with a 30,39% that sometimes use YouTube and they never use Instagram with a 24,92%; the same way it can be seen that in little percentage teachers always use the social media in their classes both for YouTube and Instagram with a 7,47% and 0,83% respectively, this mean that there exist little frequency of use of YouTube and Instagram social media in classes. These results are supported by [31] who mention that integrating this kind of technology in classes it is required effort from the teachers for the creation of resources and to support the teaching-learning process. Even though it can be said that the low frequency of use by the teachers can be because of the youngest teenagers because they pay more attention to the games in the social media and prefer the e-mail for academic activities [2]. Analyzing these results, we can see that exist little use of social media in classes so it would be important to implement them with academic purposes to innovate education to strengthen the classes using YouTube and Instagram which allow discussing topics of interest, with this, teachers and students can express themselves, share their videos and images, collaborate and study [32]. Many students use these kinds of webs to follow their teachers and investigators who are referents on the web or that make content according to the interest of their subjects.

6 Conclusion

Social media as YouTube and Instagram are a great repository of resources of learning where the internet plays an especially important role in the Web sharing of teachers and colleagues always being availed and easily searchable. In this way, in Ecuador, in the 9 planning areas, both in the public and particular sectors teachers prepare content motivated by the discussion regarding education and health through video tutorials, specialized forums, and manuals, it is important to mention that teachers use the resources for the discussion of topics of interest and use these social media to follow referent researchers or teachers.

According to this study, it is important to use and leverage this kind of social media in the process of learning-teaching through resources to innovate education. In this kind of network, creativity takes an important role in design, and elaboration of content that causes visual impact to students through audio, video and illustrations and being teachable and understandable, as well as having the possibility of sharing them among students to create a reflexive and spontaneous dialogue. Therefore, it is important to use educational content from YouTube and Instagram in the teaching-learning process.

References

1. Arellano, P.R., Pérez, V.G., Fernández, I.B.: YouTube and influencers in childhood. Content analysis and educational proposals. Icono14 **18**(2), 269–295 (2020). https://doi.org/10.7195/RI14.V18I2.1455

2. Núñez, P., García, M., Hermida, L.: Tendencias de las relaciones sociales e interpersonales de los nativos digitales y jóvenes en la web 2.0. Rev. Lat. Comun. Soc. **67**(945–966), 179–206 (2012). https://doi.org/10.4185/RLCS-067-952-179-206

3. García-Galera, M.C., Del-Hoyo-Hurtado, M., Fernández-Muñoz, C.: Engaged youth in the internet. the role of social networks in social active participation. Comunicar **22**(43), 35–43 (2014). https://doi.org/10.3916/C43-2014-03

4. Vintimilla-León, D.E., Torres-Toukoumidis, A.: Covid-19 y TikTok. Análisis de la Folksonomía social. Revista Ibérica de Sistemas e Tecnologias de Informação **40**, 15–26 (2021)

5. Parabhoi, L., Pareek, N., Priya.: Examination of YouTube videos related to DSpace. Library Philosophy and Practice, vol. 2019 (2019)

6. Giraud, F., Saulpic, O.: Research-based teaching or teaching-based research: analysis of a teaching content elaboration process. Qual. Res. Account. Manag. **16**(4), 563–588 (2019). https://doi.org/10.1108/QRAM-10-2017-0097

7. Zahn, C., et al.: Video clips for YouTube: collaborative video creation as an educational concept for knowledge acquisition and attitude change related to obesity stigmatization. Educ. Inf. Technol. **19**(3), 603–621 (2013). https://doi.org/10.1007/s10639-013-9277-5

8. Suárez-Ramos, J.C.: Importancia del uso de recursos didácticos en el proceso de enseñanza y aprendizaje de las ciencias biológicas para la estimulación visual del estudiantado, Revista Electronica Educare, vol. 21(2) (2017). https://doi.org/10.15359/ree.21-2.22

9. Sánchez-Teruel, D., Robles-Bello, M.A.: Riesgos y potencialidades de la era digital para la infancia y la adolescencia. Educ. y Hum. **18**(31), 186–204 (2016). https://doi.org/10.17081/eduhum.18.31.1374

10. Ramírez, M.I.: Posibilidades del uso educativo de youtube. Ra Ximhai **12**(6), 537–546 (2016)

11. Song, D., Bonk, C.J.: Motivational factors in self-directed informal learning from online learning resources. Cogent Educ. **3**(1), 1205838 (2016). https://doi.org/10.1080/2331186X.2016.1205838

12. Azonobi, I.N.M.C., Uwaifo, S.O.P.: User behaviour and self-efficacy as elements on postgraduates use of electronic information resources in federal universities in southern Nigeria. Libr. Philos. Pract. **2020**, 1–23 (2020)

13. García-Floriano, A., Ferreira-Santiago, A., Yáñez-Márquez, C., Camacho-Nieto, O., Aldape-Pérez, M., Villuendas-Rey, Y.: Social web content enhancement in a distance learning environment: Intelligent metadata generation for resources. Int. Rev. Res. Open Dist. Learn. **18**(1), 161–176 (2017). https://doi.org/10.19173/irrodl.v18i1.2646

14. Chib, A., Bentley, C., Wardoyo, R.-J.: Distributed digital contexts and learning: Personal empowerment and social transformation in marginalized populations [entornos digitales distribuidos y aprendizaje: empoderamiento personal y transformación social en colectivos discriminados]. Comunicar. **27**(58), 51–60 (2019). https://doi.org/10.3916/C58-2019-05

15. Mnkandla, E., Minnaar, A.: The use of social media in E-Learning: a metasynthesis. Int. Rev. Res. Open Dist. Learn. **18**(5), 227–248 (2017). https://doi.org/10.19173/irrodl.v18i5.3014

16. Barfi, K.A., Bervell, B., Arkorful, V.: Integration of social media for smart pedagogy: initial perceptions of senior high school students in Ghana. Educ. Inf. Technol. **26**(3), 3033–3055 (2021). https://doi.org/10.1007/s10639-020-10405-y

17. Livingstone, S.: Taking risky opportunities in youthful content creation: teenagers" use of social networking sites for intimacy, privacy and self-expression. New Media Soc. **10**(3), 393–411 (2008). https://doi.org/10.1177/1461444808089415

18. Bransford, J., Brown, A., Cocking, R.: How People Learn - Barin, Mind, Experience and School, in National Academy Press, pp. 57–86. D.C, Washington (1999)

19. Adnan, W.H., Bahar, N.: The use of using social networking sites in teaching and learning among educators and learners. Int. J. Learn. Technol. **14**(3), 236–250 (2019). https://doi.org/10.1504/IJLT.2019.105709

20. Greenhow, C., Askari, E.: Learning and teaching with social network sites: a decade of research in K-12 related education. Educ. Inf. Technol. **22**(2), 623–645 (2015). https://doi.org/10.1007/s10639-015-9446-9
21. Robbins, S.P., Singer, J.B.: From the editor-the medium is the message: integrating social media and social work education. J. Soc. Work Educ. **50**(3), 387–390 (2014). https://doi.org/10.1080/10437797.2014.916957
22. Ali, M.Y., Khawaja, W.S., Bhatti, R.: YouTube usage of faculty of an engineering university of Karachi, Pakistan: implications of media literacy through librarian. Int. Inf. Libr. Rev. **51**(4), 328–337 (2019). https://doi.org/10.1080/10572317.2019.1669938
23. Rodríguez Espinosa, H., Restrepo Betancur, L.F., Aranzazu Taborda, D.: Desarrollo de habilidades digitales docentes para implementar ambientes virtuales de aprendizaje en la docencia universitaria TT - Development of digital skills for implementation of learning virtual environments in university teaching. Sophia **12**(2), 261–270 (2016)
24. Valenzuela, S., Park, N., Kee, K.F.: Is there social capital in a social network site?: Facebook use and college students life satisfaction, trust, and participation. J. Comput.-Mediat. Commun. **14**(4), 875–901 (2009). https://doi.org/10.1111/j.1083-6101.2009.01474.x
25. Zeler, I., Oliveira, A., Malaver, S.: La gestión comunicativa de las empresas vitivinícolas de España en las principales redes sociales / communication management of Spanish wine companies in the main social networks. Revista Int. Relaciones Públicas **9**(18), 161–178 (2019). https://doi.org/10.5783/revrrpp.v9i18.617
26. Malthouse, E.C., Calder, B.J., Kim, S.J., Vandenbosch, M.: Evidence that user-generated content that produces engagement increases purchase behaviours. J. Mark. Manag. **32**(5–6), 427–444 (2016). https://doi.org/10.1080/0267257X.2016.1148066
27. Judd, T., Elliott, K.: Methods and frequency of sharing of learning resources by medical students. Br. J. Edu. Technol. **48**(6), 1345–1356 (2017). https://doi.org/10.1111/bjet.12481
28. Nikkar, K., Parseh, M.J., Ebrahim Samie, M.: Transmission of multimedia content between social networks without reloading. In: 2019 IEEE 5th Conference on Knowledge Based Engineering and Innovation, KBEI 2019, pp. 216–222 (2019). doi: https://doi.org/10.1109/KBEI.2019.8734986
29. Francis Salazar, S.: El conocimiento pedagógico del contenido como categoría de estudio de la formación docente. Actualidades Investigativas en Educación, **5**(2) (2011). https://doi.org/10.15517/aie.v5i2.9139
30. Ruay Garcés, R., Campos Palacios, E.: La plataforma YouTube como estrategia para el autoaprendizaje de la lengua inglesa. Revista Boletín Redipe **8**(12), 129–142 (2019). https://doi.org/10.36260/rbr.v8i12.879
31. Sunaryoa, Y., Supriyati, Y., Lestari, A.: Fun physics learning video by powtoon on energy source materials for senior high school. In: AIP Conference Proceedings, vol. 2320, no. 1 (2021). doi: https://doi.org/10.1063/5.0037499
32. Torres, C., Moreno, G.: Inclusión de las TIC en los escenarios de aprendizaje universitario. Apertura. Revista de Innovación Educativa **5**(1), 48–65 (2013)
33. Tur-Viñes, V., Núñez-Gómez, P., González-Río, M.J.: Kid influencers on YouTube. A space for responsibility. Revista Latina de Comunicacion Social **73**, 1211–1230 (2018). https://doi.org/10.4185/RLCS-2018-1303

Identifying the Political Tendency of Social Bots in Twitter Using Sentiment Analysis: A Use Case of the 2021 Ecuadorian General Elections

Andres Quelal$^{(\boxtimes)}$ (iD), Juan Brito (iD), Mateo S. Lomas (iD), Jean Camacho (iD), Argenis Andrade (iD), and Erick Cuenca (iD)

Yachay Tech University, Urcuquí, Ecuador
{andres.quelal,juan.brito,mateo.lomas,jean.camacho,
argenis.andrade,ecuenca}@yachaytech.edu.ec

Abstract. Sentiment analysis of social network data increasingly represents the real political scenario of many countries, which has turned bots into a powerful tool of influence, mainly due to their high efficiency. This work analyzes the messages on Twitter during the 2021 Ecuadorian presidential elections to determine sentiments and bots detection. We obtained a sample of 35,242 tweets corresponding to each candidate's first and second rounds. Our methodology consists of four phases: first, we perform data collection using the Twitter API; secondly, we preprocess the data; in the third phase, we perform sentiment analysis of the content of the tweets to understand their posture towards a candidate, and finally, we classify the users as bots or not. As a result, we discovered that bots and non-bots people on both sides had more positive feelings towards their respective candidates than unfavorable feelings against the other candidates.

Keywords: Sentiment analysis · Twitter bots · Political tendency · Social media

1 Introduction

Every year, there is a 9% growth in the number of social media users, and half of the internet traffic consists primarily of bots [17]. Part of the content of social media is composed of false or misleading news reports, hoaxes, conspiracy theories, click-bait headlines, junk science, and even satire [18]. In Ecuador, this is not the exception and more important, many of the relevant issues for the general population are received and discussed on social networks. For instance, the most followed users on Twitter in Ecuador respond to a localized and public profile, which means that the leading accounts in the country react to mainly national interests [3].

Although social media communication does not suppose any problem, there is the possibility of massive misinformation and conflicts generated by political

K. Abad and S. Berrezueta (Eds.): DSICT 2022, CCIS 1647, pp. 184–196, 2022.
https://doi.org/10.1007/978-3-031-18347-8_15

and economic interests. These conflicts and the spread of false news often do not only originate from a malicious person or group of people but also respond to a sophisticated set of technologies that include specialized bots that pose as ordinary users through fake accounts.

Twitter's popularity is extensive, giving facilities to do publications through bots, which has reached problems in the platform [4,7]. These social bots have an outsized role in disseminating articles from low-trust sites. The widespread dissemination of digital disinformation has been seen as a severe danger to democratic institutions [18].

Bots include programmed instructions to communicate in digital environments to accomplish tasks such as spam generation, blocking exchange points, launching denial of service attacks, deploying and replicating messages, publishing news, updating feeds, programming malware, phishing, and fraud clicks [16]. In the case of Twitter, many of them post directly through its Application Programming Interface (API). Still, frequently, their publications are disseminated through automation services or applications. It is essential to mention that sometimes the bot profiles lack the account's basic information, such as the username or profile photos [16]. Political bots, for example, are often used in conjunction with three types of political events: elections, scandals turn, and national security crises. Using bots during these situations aims to achieve simple goals such as filling the candidate's "followers" list or complex purposes such as harassing human rights activists or demobilizing citizens [16]. Due to its importance in citizen conversations, Twitter has become the preferred object of studies on the construction of public opinion in Ecuador [5].

If we look deeper at Twitter's role in Ecuador, it respond to mainly national and popular interests, ranging from politics to entertainment [3]. Also, the results of a study by [5] show a close relationship between the cyber-media agenda and the trending topics on Twitter in political and sports content. That wide is the scope of Twitter that during the second round of the presidential elections of Ecuador in 2017, automated accounts or Twitter bots played a central role in positioning campaign hashtags [16]. Taking all this into account, we can see that the utilization of Twitter bots in Ecuador is widespread.

This paper aims to analyze the political trend of tweets in Ecuador during the period of the 2021 presidential elections. This analysis is intended to use sentiment analysis and bots detection techniques. The results are analyzed using various visualizations to represent the political trend in this period. The details of the implementation can be found in the following Google Colaboratoy[1].

2   Related Work

Many works have already studied if social bots on Twitter or other social media have a particular influence over public opinion on politics, science, or different polemic topics. For instance, Pastor-Galindo et al. [15] analyze the impact of bots on Spain's elections during the 2019 campaign period and emphasize specific dates where activity was higher. An important aspect of this work is the

---

[1] https://shorturl.at/dftz6, last access: August 2022.

methodology the authors implement to spot the bots on Twitter and realize if they influenced the elections. Figure 1 shows the methodology adopted by the authors. It shows a pipeline divided into three main processes: data collection, data analysis, and knowledge extraction.

The data collection first sets the query parameters to obtain the tweets from those events related to those topics with a crawler and harvester. Then, the data analysis tests this processed data and the feature discovered over multiple options. This leads to an augmented data set with the individual evaluation of the sentiment analysis. In the final step, they do the knowledge extraction by using this augmented data set on a supervised learning technique to classify their political inclination, whether they are humans or not. Using an unsupervised learning approach, they analyze the friendship graphs, the whole pre-processed data, and the augmented data set they got. All of it lets them identify the possible presence of bots.

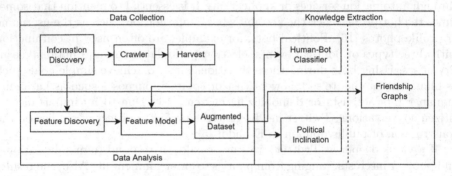

Fig. 1. Research methodology adopted on [15] refereed to elections in Spain.

2.1 Sentiment Analysis

A way to understand the content of users' tweets is text analysis through sentiment analysis. It involves studying tweets' opinions, sentiments, attitudes, and emotions to understand the behavior on social networks of a relevant or trending topic. In Computer Science, there is an area concerned with providing computers with the ability to understand the text and the context of words, called Natural Language Processing (NLP). This area aims to process human language, either speech or text. Sentimental Analysis is part of NLP to understand the writer's purpose, feelings, or emotion from a text.

Many works and papers are dedicated to analyzing sentiment from a tweet's text. For instance, Ibrahim et al. [13] presented a work centered mainly on the sentimental analysis to predict presidential elections. In this work, the authors highlight the importance of cleaning those tweets that computer bots, paid users, and fanatic users could generate. All these kinds of tweets are considered noise and difficult to predict. They use a technique to divide the tweets into sub-tweets using limiters, such as commas, points, question marks, etc. They associate the sub-tweets to the respective politics using their words or names. This score represents the sentiment evaluation; the sub-tweets can be classified as positive or negative to the politician with an associated tweet. Also, using the positive sub-tweets only tends to get more accurate results in predicting any behavior, in this case, who will win elections. This work's value leads principally to how the authors process the data, where phrases get associated with an emotion and a politician. It is mentioned that bots usually talk well only of one of the politicians and bad about the rest.

2.2 Bots Detection

There are some ways to classify/detect if a user is a bot. One technique is using the universal score distribution. On a range [0,1], this score evaluates how likely an account is to be a human or a bot, where 1 is more likely to be a bot and 0 a human. So it is possible to set a threshold to decide in what range we classify them as humans and in what range we classify them as bots. A good range for humans could be: $[0 \leq U_{score} \leq 0.85]$, where the range for bots will be $[0.85 < U_{score} \leq 1]$. This score is calculated based on polarity and subjectivity. Polarity gives us if the sentiment is positive or negative and a value.

There are multiple attempts to detect social bots using machine learning techniques. Some authors use "Blacklists" [21] to extract features of tweets generated by bots and then pass these features to a Decorate classifier [12]. Others prefer comparing the results obtained with more traditional techniques, such as Decision Trees, Random Forest Algorithm, k-Nearest Neighbor Algorithm, Support Vector Machine (SVM), Logistic Regression, Neural Networks, and Naive Bayes Classifier [1, 2, 6, 9, 14, 17, 20]. Moreover, other studies combine some of these previous techniques in the denominated Ensemble Learning, obtaining better results than using only one of them [10, 19]. For instance, Lingan et al. [11] proposed using Deep Q Learning for detecting social bots and influential users in online social networks providing a 5–9% improvement of precision over other existing algorithms. Furthermore, different approaches compare probabilistic techniques (Approximate Entropy, Sample Entropy) along with machine learning for detecting automated behavior on Twitter [8]. Most of the results of these works may also be used to analyze the role of social bots in the context of presidential elections.

3 Methodology

3.1 Data Collection

Data is available from the Twitter platform to request objects or fields such as tweets, users, spaces, lists, media, polls, and locations through its API[2]. Considering the user's information, we can obtain various attributes, such as id, a

---

[2] https://developer.twitter.com/en/docs/twitter-api, last access: August 2022.

screen name (used to communicate online), description, URL, verified (if the user is authenticated) location, list of followers, list of following, list of favorite (used for liked tweets).

The dataset considers the topic's selection, description of the data, and acquisition time. Ecuador Elections 2021 is the input request topic, where the presidential candidates Guillermo Lasso (CREO political party) and Andrés Arauz (UNES political party) are the prominent mentions. We also collect tweets for the vice-presidential candidates' Alfredo Borrero and Carlos Rabascall for CREO and UNES political parties, respectively. The first and second round of the presidential elections from November 30, 2020 to February 2, 2021 is the acquisition period of the dataset. Table 1 shows the query parameters used to collect the dataset.

Table 1. Parameters used in the querys to obtain the dataset of tweets.

Candidate	Guillermo Lasso	Andrés Arauz
Keywords for querys	GuillermoLasso	AndrésArauz
	LassoGuillermo	ArauzAndrés
	"Guillermo Lasso"	"Andrés Arauz"
	Lasso	Arauz
	"Alfredo Borrero"	"Carlos Rabascall"
	Borrero	Rabascall
	AlfredoBorrero	CarlosRabascall
	BorreroAlfredo	RabascallCarlos
Start time 1st round	2020-12-15 T17:00:00Z	2020-12-15 T17:00:00Z
End time 1st round	2021-02-07 T23:30:00Z	2021-02-07 T23:30:00Z
Start time 2nd round	2021-02-07 T17:00:00Z	2021-02-07 T17:00:00Z
End time 2nd round	2021-04-12 T23:30:00Z	2021-04-12 T23:30:00Z
Tweet fields	id	id
	text	text
	created_at	created_at
	author_id	author_id
	public_metrics	public_metrics

The number of tweets generated in one day with the theme Elections of Ecuador in 2021 was enormous, so obtaining all the data for its respective analysis became unrealistic considering the available computational limitations. The solution to this problem was obtaining a certain number of daily tweets. Although it considerably biases the results, it does not remove the possibility of analyzing and drawing accurate conclusions. The decision was made to obtain around 400 tweets per day. These tweets will correspond to each candidate's first and second rounds. A total of 35,242 tweets were collected. The results where stored in a CSV file.

3.2 Data Pre-procesing

The preprocessing and data cleaning process provides a balanced data set. Object attributes such as text were processed using NLP techniques. Tweets' attributes were converted into a usable format for sentiment analysis and bot recognition. For this purpose, data processing methods such as:

- **Punctuation's marks removal:** Twitter messages often contain symbols, numbers, and punctuation such as: $'!"\#\$ \& \backslash'()^{*+,-.1;;} \Leftrightarrow \Rightarrow ?@[11]^\wedge -\{|\} \sim 1$. These preprocessed entities reduce ambiguous and unnecessary expressions for our dataset. All of these punctuation marks were removed using an NLP library. Also, HTML references, mentions, and hashtags were cleaned from our dataset.
- **Tokenization:** The tokenization task aims at splitting a text stream into smaller units called tokens. Tokens are composed of words, phrases, or other meaningful elements that can show a trend of the most common words found in our dataset. For example, the text: *"Durante las elecciones de este 7 de febrero, recuerda cumplir con los protocolos de bioseguridad establecidos."* will become as:

  ['Durante', 'elecciones', 'febrero', 'cumplir', 'protocolos', 'bioseguridad']

- **Stopwords removal:** Some tweet words do not have a significant influence on the sentence. Stopword removal removes common and frequent irrelevant words in our dataset using the NLTK python library.

3.3 Sentiment Analysis

We used Python libraries such as NLTK, specifically TextBlob, to compute the sentiment score. TextBlob is a library that allows complex analysis and operations on textual data.

3.4 Bots Detection

For bot detection, it was used the Botometer platform[3]. However, the API has limitations on the request per day on its free version; nevertheless, the way to detect if an account is a bot or human was the same with other libraries.

4 Results and Discussion

4.1 Statistical Information

Figures 2a and 2b show that the number of accounts that get less than 20 interactions is more than the 70%. In the first and second rounds, we can appreciate the users' interactions do not have a uniform distribution, even though most get

---

[3] https://botometer.osome.iu.edu, last access: August 2022.

20 or fewer actions (tweet, RT, like). Also, it could be expected that get more interactions on Fig. 2b than on Fig. 2a because, on the second round, tension could be even higher than in the first round. Still, accounts from both political sides got similar behaviors.

If we take the average of the sum of all the different interactions (retweet, reply, like, quote) of the bots per game, as reflected, convincing results are not appreciated. The results obtained are generally biased by obtaining a small data set. Many of the possible interactions that bots and people, in general, could have will not be reflected. It is estimated that, on average, there are 2,000 tweets every 10 min; our dataset does not even represent 1% of the entire data set. Another limitation was the fact that the Botometer has restrictions on the number of requests that we can obtain. In this case, it is limited to 500 requests per day; in general, resource limitations prevent us from getting reliable results.

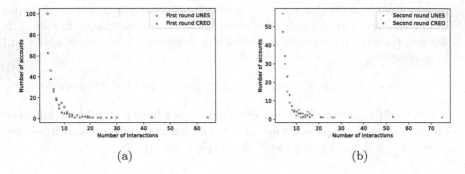

(a)   (b)

Fig. 2. Distribution of accounts with number of interactions in (a) first round and (b) second round.

4.2   Word Cloud Analysis

A practical way to explore the dataset's content is using a Word Cloud visualization. It is a visual representation object for word processing, which shows the frequency of words. For example, our dataset contains reference tweets of two presidential candidates. In Fig. 3a, the Word Cloud representation gives us a better approximation of user opinions in general. Word Cloud helps us understand the users' behavior, where the most used word was "Lasso". In the sentimental analysis, we checked this trend for each candidate. In Fig. 3b, the Arauz word cloud gives us that the most common word was "Andrés Arauz". Some word in this word cloud shows us words controversial events that happened to the candidate.

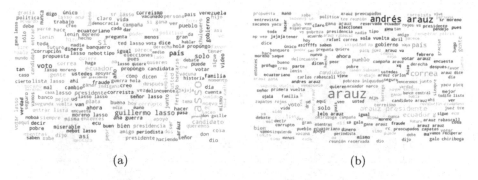

(a)   (b)

Fig. 3. Word Cloud representations of opinions about (a) Guillermo Lasso and (b) Andrés Arauz.

4.3 Sentiment and Polarity Score

Figure 4 shows the volume of tweets per sentiment for every political party. We can see that both parties have a significant volume of positively related sentiments. But the "Neutral" sentiment is as prevalent as positive sentiments, we can see negative sentiments towards parties, but they are not significantly larger than the others.

Table 2 shows in percentages how positive and negative emotions are present in both parties and rounds. They are above 40%, which is an excellent parameter for determining tendencies and intent to vote for that candidate. Both do not differ much, but we must analyze more data to distinguish between parties comprehensively.

Table 2. Sentiment analysis for both candidates in both rounds

Candidate	First round		Second round	
	Positive sentiment	Negative sentiment	Positive sentiment	Negative sentiment
Andrés Arauz	41.99%	23.22%	41.31%	21.35%
Gillermo Lasso	42.44%	22.79%	40.24%	23.60%

In Fig. 5, the polarity score shows a better understanding of user behavior in all presidential elections. Based on the polarity categorization, the scores were classified such that if the score is less than zero, the sentiment is negative, if the score is equal to zero, the sentiment is neutral, and if the score is greater than zero, the sentiment is positive. In relevant events, the decrease in polarity score shows us that users have a negative tendency at this stage. The positive polarity score varies for each stage. The overall trend varies a lot for each date, but it gives us a better understanding of how public opinion was.

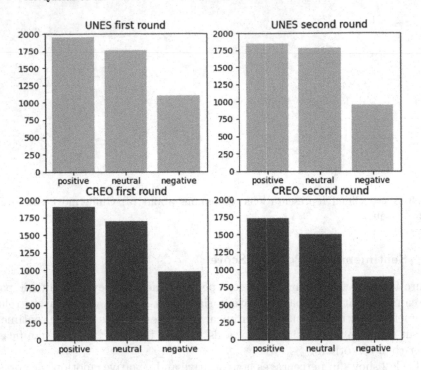

Fig. 4. Volume of tweets per sentiment

4.4   Bots Detection Results

We decided to use Botometer, which is an API that is specialized in the detection of bots. A limitation was the number of daily requests. We split the data set to get a sample to reach some results. There, we got the number of interactions, the politic they are with, and based on the number of interactions, it is viable to infer if they had any relevant participation.

The number of interactions for Andrés Arauz was 8,493 and for Lasso 8,029. In Figs. 6a and 6b, we can appreciate that in different tweets with a certain periodicity, there are some publications with many more interactions. This can represent the publications that turned viral, and as much as Lasso and Arauz, we got a similar number of tweets with more than 4,000 interactions.

Based on that, considering the original data set was of 35.242 tweets, only those users with more than three interactions and a threshold of 0.85, where those users with a score bigger than that were considered candidates to be bots. So we got 17 possible bots: 3 tend to support Guillermo Lasso, and 14 support Andrés Arauz (See Fig. 7). We have to consider that these detected bots are not from the total users of the whole dataset used but instead from a reduced sample. Eventually, this does not say anything about who candidate got more bots, but with these bots spotted, it is possible to look for how many times they interacted.

Presidential Debate Analysis

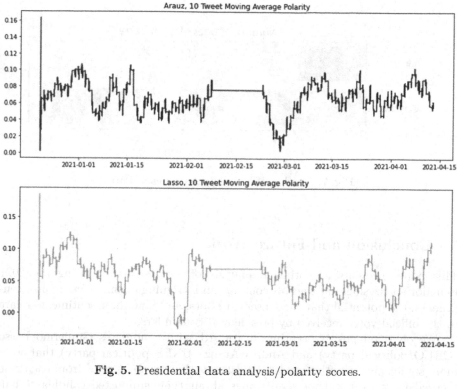

Fig. 5. Presidential data analysis/polarity scores.

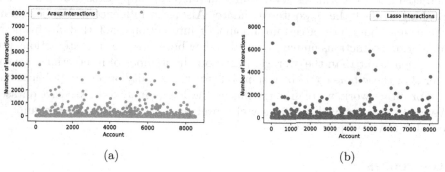

(a)   (b)

Fig. 6. Interactions in a certain tweet by (a) Guillermo Lasso and (b) Andrés Arauz.

In the same way, as in Figs. 2a and 2b, we got the total interactions only of the bot accounts, comparing the amount of interactions. Eventually, a bot tends to get a superior number of interactions in contrast to the people's average interactions; this can be interpreted as a way of influence. Seventeen bots are too few, but those can create a ton of movement on the network and have a direct influence over viral publications; because of that amount of iterations, we can say they get some relevant influence.

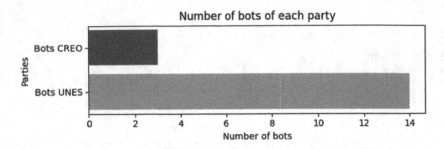

Fig. 7. Number of bots detected of each Party

5 Conclusion and Future Work

This paper presents a sentiment analysis of Twitter users during the 2021 Ecuadorian Presidential Race. It contains an intriguing examination of user sentiments, the potential that these users are bots, and how these sentiments relate to the official votes received by presidential contenders.

We obtained positive sentiments toward both candidates Guillermo Lasso (CREO political party) and Andrés Arauz (UNES political party) that were more significant in both rounds. We can say that the bots used from each side focused more on speaking good things about their supported candidate than speaking against the opposite candidate. Also, the influence of bots can vary where most bots have a certain amount of interactions, not that far from the number of interactions humans do. Still, a few bots have several interactions way more significant than the average. Based on the number of interactions, we can infer that those bots could be responsible for the vitality of certain publications.

For future work, we plan to try this methodology in a more extensive dataset. We could also apply this to a new electoral process before the final results are revealed to try to predict it.

References

1. Alothali, E., Hayawi, K., Alashwal, H.: Hybrid feature selection approach to identify optimal features of profile metadata to detect social bots in twitter. Soc. Netw. Anal. Min. **11**(1), 1–15 (2021). https://doi.org/10.1007/s13278-021-00786-4
2. de Andrade, N., Rainatto, G., Lima, F., Silva Neto, G., Paschoal, D.: Machine learning and bots detection on twitter. Int. J. Sci. Res. (IJSR) **8**, 001–011 (2019)
3. Barredo Ibáñez, D., Arcila Calderón, C., Barbosa Caro, E.: El perfil de los usuarios de Twitter más influyentes en Ecuador y la influencia del mensaje en la captación de seguidores. Observatorio **10**, 219–230 (2016). https://doi.org/10.15847/obsOBS10420161004

4. Chu, Z., Gianvecchio, S., Wang, H., Jajodia, S.: Detecting automation of twitter accounts: are you a human, bot, or cyborg? IEEE Trans. Dependable Secure Comput. **9**(6), 811–824 (2012). https://doi.org/10.1109/TDSC.2012.75
5. Coronel, P., García, J., Vera, M.: Twitter y la opinión pública en Ecuador: discursos, emisores y agendas. In: La Innovación de la Innovación: Del Medio al Contenido Predictivo. Actas del III Simposio Internacional sobre Gestión de la Comunicación (XESCOM 2018), pp. 697–713 (2018)
6. Deekshith, G.: Twitter bots detection using machine learning techniques. Int. J. Res. Appl. Sci. Eng. Technol. **9**, 1536–1541 (2021). https://doi.org/10.22214/ijraset.2021.36637
7. Edwards, C., Edwards, A., Spence, P., Shelton, A.: Is that a bot running the social media feed? Testing the differences in perceptions of communication quality for a human agent and a bot agent on twitter. Comput. Hum. Behav. **33**, 372–376 (2014). https://doi.org/10.1016/j.chb.2013.08.013
8. Gilmary, R., Venkatesan, A., Vaiyapuri, G.: Detection of automated behavior on twitter through approximate entropy and sample entropy. Pers. Ubiquit. Comput. (2021). https://doi.org/10.1007/s00779-021-01647-9
9. Khanday, A.M.U.D., Khan, Q.R., Rabani, S.T.: Identifying propaganda from online social networks during COVID-19 using machine learning techniques. Int. J. Inf. Technol. **13**(1), 115–122 (2020). https://doi.org/10.1007/s41870-020-00550-5
10. Kirn, S.L., Hinders, M.K.: Bayesian identification of bots using temporal analysis of tweet storms. Soc. Netw. Anal. Min. **11**(1), 1–17 (2021). https://doi.org/10.1007/s13278-021-00783-7
11. Lingam, G., Rout, R.R., Somayajulu, D.V.L.N.: Adaptive deep Q-learning model for detecting social bots and influential users in online social networks. Appl. Intell. **49**(11), 3947–3964 (2019). https://doi.org/10.1007/s10489-019-01488-3
12. Melville, P., Mooney, R.J.: Constructing diverse classifier ensembles using artificial training examples. In: Eighteenth International Joint Conference on Artificial Intelligence, pp. 505–510 (2003)
13. Mochamad, I., Omar, A., Alfan, W.F., Mirna, A.: Buzzer detection and sentiment analysis for predicting presidential election results in a twitter nation. In: 2015 IEEE International Conference on Data Mining Workshop (ICDMW), pp. 1348–1353 (2015). https://doi.org/10.1109/ICDMW.2015.113
14. Narayan, N.: Twitter bot detection using machine learning algorithms. In: 2021 Fourth International Conference on Electrical, Computer and Communication Technologies (ICECCT), pp. 1–4 (2021). https://doi.org/10.1109/ICECCT52121.2021.9616841
15. Pastor-Galindo, J., et al.: Spotting political social bots in twitter: a use case of the 2019 Spanish general election. IEEE Trans. Netw. Serv. Manage. **17**(4), 2156–2170 (2020). https://doi.org/10.1109/TNSM.2020.3031573
16. Puyosa, I.: Political bots on twitter in #Ecuador2017 presidential campaigns. Contratexto (27), 39–60 (2017). https://doi.org/10.26439/contratexto.2017.027.002
17. Ramalingaiah, A., Hussaini, S., Chaudhari, S.: Twitter bot detection using supervised machine learning. J. Phys. Conf. Ser. **1950**, 012006 (2021). https://doi.org/10.1088/1742-6596/1950/1/012006
18. Shao, C., Ciampaglia, G.L., Varol, O., Yang, K.C., Flammini, A., Menczer, F.: The spread of low-credibility content by social bots. Nat. Commun. **9**(1) (2018). https://doi.org/10.1038/s41467-018-06930-7
19. Shukla, H., Jagtap, N., Patil, B.: Enhanced twitter bot detection using ensemble machine learning. In: 2021 6th International Conference on Inventive Computation

Technologies (ICICT), pp. 930–936 (2021). https://doi.org/10.1109/ICICT50816.
2021.9358734

20. Souza, S., Rezende, T., Nascimento, J., Chaves, L., Soto, D., Salavati, S.: Tuning
machine learning models to detect bots on twitter. In: 2020 Workshop on Communication Networks and Power Systems (WCNPS), pp. 1–6 (2020). https://doi.
org/10.1109/WCNPS50723.2020.9263756

21. Swe, M.M., Nyein Myo, N.: Fake accounts detection on twitter using blacklist.
In: 2018 IEEE/ACIS 17th International Conference on Computer and Information
Science (ICIS), pp. 562–566 (2018). https://doi.org/10.1109/ICIS.2018.8466499

Implementation of a Lightweight CNN for American Sign Language Classification

Mateo Sebastián Lomas⓪, Andrés Quelal⓪,
and Manuel Eugenio Morocho-Cayamcela⁽✉⁾⓪

Deep Learning for Autonomous Driving, Robotics, and Computer Vision Research
Group (DeepARC Research), School of Mathematical and Computational Sciences,
Yachay Tech University, Hda. San José s/n y Proyecto Yachay,
San Miguel de Urcuqui 100119, Ecuador
{mateo.lomas,andres.quelal,mmorocho}@yachaytech.edu.ec

Abstract. The American sign language is the most popular and widely-accepted sign language for people with hearing difficulties. Computer vision techniques, such as skeleton recognition, depth recognition, 3D model recognition, or deep learning recognition, have helped to develop better systems for sign language classification and detection. Despite the promising results from baseline research efforts, overfitting problems have been detected when the training and testing accuracy are compared. In this work, we propose to exploit the scaling method on EfficientNet, which is a convolutional neural network architecture, in order to uniformly scale all the dimensions of depth, width, and resolution using a compound coefficient. Our results show that the overfitting problem can be solved by incorporating hyperparameter tunning and dropout as a regularization method. We also have the benefit of transfer learning to reduce the training time by reusing the weights of EfficientNet, pre-trained with the ImageNet dataset. Our results are compared with the benchmark paper, proving that our model generalizes better to unseen instances. In the first section of this study, we introduce American sign language meaning, hand gesture recognition, and its related works in the computer vision field. It allows us to mention transfer learning concepts and Efficient Nets architectures. In the second section, we establish the methodology by choosing the B0 model as the architecture selected to test with a Kaggle dataset. Adjusting hyperparameters, we enter in the third section, in the training and testing phase where overfitting problems were solved with high accuracy, finishing talking with contributions and future works.

Keywords: EfficientNet · American sign language · Image classification convolutional neural network · Transfer learning

1 Introduction

A practical study of non-verbal forms of communication evinces a wide field of analysis where technological tools are called to solve hearing problems and

K. Abad and S. Berrezueta (Eds.): DSICT 2022, CCIS 1647, pp. 197–207, 2022.
https://doi.org/10.1007/978-3-031-18347-8_16

reduce the communication barrier. Sign language recognition is a natural non-verbal communication platform that simplifies communication through gestures and visual signs [15]. The American sign language (ASL) is a comprehensive sign language for people who are deaf or have hearing problems [12,13]. Computer vision models that recognize hand gestures depend on robust algorithms and complex image processing techniques. One of the most established hand gesture recognition techniques is deep learning. Unlike touch-based recognition and other classical image processing techniques, deep learning explores artificial neural networks to train and test the learning parameters to predict the results using its multiple convolutional layers. Previous works by Yann LeCun *et al.* [4] on convolutional neural networks (CNN) have cemented the use of intricate structures through multiple layers of processing [4]. From that point, Mohanty *et al.* [8], have worked on CNNs for hand gesture recognition with different imaging conditions. Aly *et al.* [2], implemented a Kinect sensor-based in ASL recognition to capture hand motion using depth images. Subsequently, Morocho-Cayamcela *et al.* [10], proposed an improvement in ASL alphabet prediction accuracy by fine-tuning two CNNs (AlexNet and GoogLeNet) exploiting atypical compensation and transfer learning. Recent works on image classification with pre-trained architectures on ImageNet have produced state-of-the-art models such as CoAtNet-7 with 90.88% accuracy, ViT-G/14 with 90.45%, and meta pseudo-labels (EfficientNet-L2) with 90.2% [17]. The EfficientNet models have approached the state-of-the-art towards an optimal implementation. EfficientNet have also been used on other engineering applications with great success [11]. For that reason, we have decided to base our proposal on that specific architecture. Alexnet and GoogLeNet showed an accuracy result of 99,39% and 95,52%, respectively [10]. Despite the promising results, our hypothesis is that the benchmark model suffers from overfitting.

In this paper, we focus on solving the overfitting problem from previous research efforts by: (1) balancing the depth, width, and resolution of the EfficientNet network, and (2) searching the best hyperparameter configuration for our specific dataset.

2   Related Works

2.1   Classification Techniques for Sign Language Recognition

As far as the state-of-art of ASL recognition is concerned, there are some remarkable artificial intelligence and machine learning classification techniques that have been proved to work better than classical image processing techniques [16]. We summarize the most prevalent ones below:

1. **Neural Networks (NN):** Several works have been presented from 1990. One of the earliest works was proposed by Murakami and Teguchi [14] in 1994. They proposed both postural and gesture recognition system for a 42-symbol finger alphabet and each gesture that corresponds to a word, respectively. The recognition rate was 96% by using their own encoding. On the

Input Image (224x224x32)

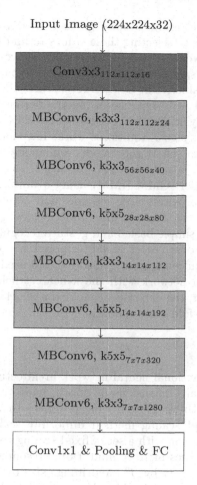

Fig. 1. EfficientNet B0 baseline network

other hand, low-cost sensors such as LMC and Kinect are used with NN architectures (e.g., 3D-CNN, or recurrent networks). In Mohandes *et al.* [7], the authors have proposed a system based on a multilayer perceptron with the naive Bayes classifier, achieving a 98% classification accuracy on Arabic sign language. When referring to 3D architectures; in Shikhar *et al.* [16], the authors used a 3D convolutional network to train and recognize volumetric data such as videos. In 2020, Al-Hammadi *et al.* [1], implemented single and parallel 3DCNN models linking the transfer learning module to overcome the scarcity of labels for the three datasets taken. The feature extraction of the region-based spatiotemporal of these models processes the hand gesture data received. This implementation gets high results in the single mode with a 96.69% accuracy and an excellent recognition rate; the parallel execution receives a 98.12% accuracy. Despite getting great results, hyperparameter problems appear due to selecting these values to find the optimal setting.

2. **Hidden Markov Networks:** Hidden Markov networks are stochastic techniques to scan the spatio-temporal data with dynamic gestures and time signals. One remarkable result is when researchers [19] trained 400 ASL sentences and tested 99 ASL sentences using the parametric hidden Markovian model (PHMM); they achieved an accuracy of 94.23% with isolated signs, and 84.85% in continuous signs. Additional works have focused on improving the hidden networks from the Markov model, enhancing the performance of the vanilla architecture. Fatmit *et al.*. [3] proposed a Gaussian Mixture Model Hidden Markov Model (GMM-HMM) using a novel Myo armbands sensor. This sensor collect orientation, gyroscope, and accelerometer data to infer the hand movement. In 3 users, this model achieving an 81.20% of overall accuracy score with simple basic hand gesture recognition.

3. **k-Nearest Neighbors:** Lee *et al.* [5] proposed a wack-a-mole game with a real-time sign recognition system embedded and used long-short term memory recurrent neural network with the k-nearest neighbour algorithm as a classifier. As a result, the experiment yielded a 99.44% of accuracy rate, and a 91.82% in the five-fold cross validation.

2.2 Efficient Nets

EfficientNet is a convolutional neural network architecture and scaling method that uniformly scales all dimensions of depth, width, and resolution using a compound coefficient. Unlike conventional practices that arbitrary scales these factors, the EfficientNet scaling method uniformly scales the network width, depth, and image resolution with a set of fixed scaling coefficients. For example, if we want to use 2^N times more computational resources, we can increase the network *depth* by α^N, *width* by β^N, and image size by γ^N; where α, β, and γ are constant coefficients determined by the grid-search algorithm on the original model. EfficientNet uses a compound coefficient ϕ to uniformly scale the network width, depth, and resolution in an additional principled way [6].

The compound scaling method is justified by the intuition that if the input image is bigger, then the network needs more layers to increase the receptive field and more channels to capture more fine grained patterns on the bigger image. The EfficientNet-BO network is based on the inverted bottleneck residual blocks of MobileNetV2, in addition to squeeze-and-excitation blocks. EfficientNet also is recognized for transferring their pre-trained weights in a simplified fashion, and can achieve a state-of-the-art accuracy on CIFAR-100 (91.7%), Flowers (98.8%), and 3 other transfer learning datasets with an order of magnitude fewer parameters [6].

2.3 Transfer Learning

We always encounter that neural networks require lots of amount of data to obtain satisfactory results. However, much of these data cannot be obtained or generated due to, in general, the lack of needed data. Here is where transfer learning arises. We can use a similar task with lots of data to help us to solve the desired task that lacks of data. In this manner, a model trained for a related task can be redefined to solve a different task, transferring the knowledge [18].

The intuition behind transfer learning for image classification is that if a model is trained on a large and general enough dataset, this model will effectively serve as a generic model of the visual world [9]. You can then take advantage of the learned feature maps without having to start from scratch by training a large model on a large dataset.

3 Methodology

3.1 Dataset

We will work with the Kaggle ASL alphabet as the dataset. The dataset is a collection of ASL alphabet images. It contains 87,000 images of 200×200 pixels. There are 29 classes in total, where 3 classes contain *space*, *eraser*, and *nothing*.

3.2 NN Architecture

We will use the EfficientNet architecture instead of Alexnet and GoogLeNet used in the reference paper [10]. In addition, our implementation will work with a transfer learning module. Our model is also optimized to reduce the number of parameters to make it efficient to deploy in mobile devices, unlike other models.

3.3 Base Model

We have conducted eight experiments with our optimized EfficientNet model (B0 to B7), under constrained scenarios limited by resolution and depth. One constraint to justify is the shape of the permitted input images to apply to any of these models. Referring to the Keras API implementation, its application follows the resolution: EfficientNet-B0 expects a resolution of 224 pixels, EfficientNet-B1 expects a resolution of 240 pixels, EfficientNet-B2 expects a resolution of 260 pixels, EfficientNet-B3 expects a resolution of 300 pixels, EfficientNet-B4 expects a resolution of 380 pixels, EfficientNet-B5 expects a resolution of 456 pixels, EfficientNet-B6 expects a resolution of 528 pixels, and EfficientNet-B7 expects a resolution of 600 pixels. For our implementation, we will use EfficientNet-B0 as a backbone due to the shape image resolution of the dataset. The overall architecture can be seen in Fig. 1.

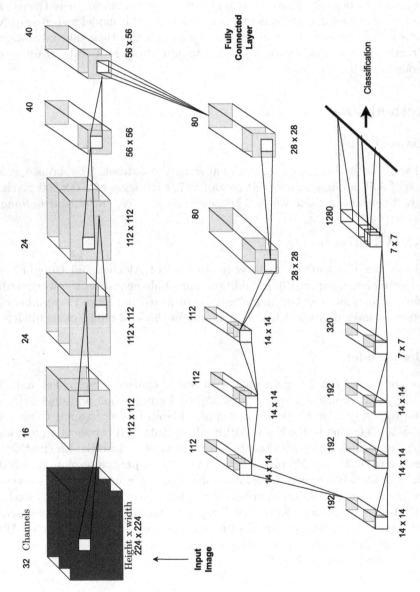

Fig. 2. EfficientNet-B0, EfficientNet first extracts image features through its convolutional layers.

3.4   System Design

In the EfficientNet architecture, the scaling method looks for a small base network and uses the scaling coefficients through MBConv to optimize the accuracy and the FLOPS. Thus, this network baseline avoids complex and expensive modeling.

Compound Scaling Method. The compound scaling method increases the neural network model size by balancing the width α, depth β, and resolution γ values. In EfficientNet B0, the values $\alpha = 1.2$, $\beta = 1.1$, and $\gamma = 1.15$ are the default values according with the original paper.

MBConv. Mainly, MBConv blocks (shown in Fig. 2) add squeeze and excitation optimization to scale-up the network creating EfficientNet. The EfficientNet B0 network contains 18 convolutional layers divided into 9 modules. In the first module, a layer receives an input image of 224×224 pixels, and channels equal to 32. In the second module, a layer reduces the image resolution to 122×122 pixels, and the channels to 16. In the following layers, the image resolution is further reduced and the number of channels increases. The width increases in each layer to improve the accuracy. Finally, in the last module, the fully connected layers outputs an image of size 7×7, and 1280 channels.

Overfitting. An additional regularizer we built in the transfer learning module is *dropout layers*, to help our model to solve the overfitting problems. Two main observations regarding overfitting were described in [17], where the authors proved that the scaling method improves accuracy; but in larger models, this output gain tends to vanish, unbalancing the dimensions of the ConvNet scaling stage.

3.5   Hyperparameter Tunning.

In the final step of our training phase, the hyperparameters were adjusted to maximize the performance of our model. An optimal selection of hyperparameters allows us to improve the accuracy of our model, in addition to reducing training problems such as overfitting. The model was trained using the Adam optimizer and the categorical cross-entropy loss function. A dropout regularizer block with a value equal to 0.2 to avoid overfitting was found empirically to maximize the classification accuracy. Finally, the batch size was set to 32, and the number of iterations to 15 in order to follow the original paper methodology.

4   Results and Discussion

Our results were compared with the benchmark ASL classification network. We verified that the performance of the proposed method solves the overfitting problem. Firstly, the training and testing performance of EfficientNet were

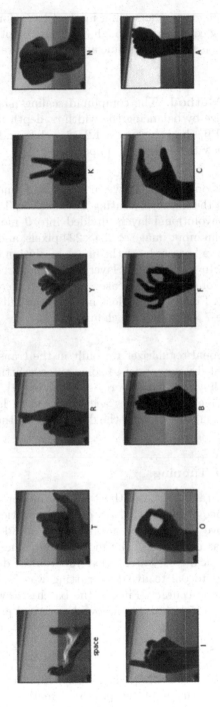

Fig. 3. The sub-captions shows the correct predictions of our ASL recognition model.

Table 1. Training, testing, and validation results of the architectures under study.

Architecture	Training	Testing	Validation
EfficientNet-B0	97.15%	**99.89%**	**95.31%**
InceptionV3	97.81%	96.42%	94.53%
InceptionResnetV2	**99.34%**	96.89%	94.44%

Table 2. Results of EfficientNet-B0 with transfer learning.

Architecture	Training	Testing	Validation
EfficientNet-B0	**96.95%**	**98.79%**	**98.53%**

evaluated and compared with two backbone networks (InceptionV3 and InceptionResnetV2), as well as with the baseline model. A summary of the accuracy values for our experiments is presented in Table 1.

Similar comparison patterns can be found when comparing EfficientNet-B0 with the rest of the architectures. Remarkably, we have found that the InceptionV3 and InceptionResnet models suffer from overfitting. We have also found that EfficientNet-B0 was able to obtain better performance than InceptionV3 and InceptionResnet, as it can be seen in the Table 1. The results of implementing transfer learning to the EfficientNet-B0 architecture with ImageNet are show in Table 2 (Figs. 3 and 4).

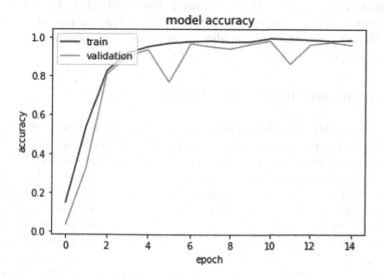

Fig. 4. Train and validation accuracy without Transfer Learning in EfficientNet-B0

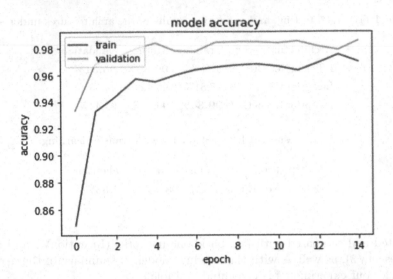

Fig. 5. Train and validation accuracy with Transfer Learning in EfficientNet-B0

In this study, our recognition approach outperformed the AlexNet and GoogL Net-based architectures from the benchmark, in terms of accuracy, and error minimization. The implementation of the additional transfer learning and dropout blocks helped our model to reduce overfitting, and convergence speed. We can see the prediction results in Fig. 5. Our model was trained in a dedicated workstation with 12 GB of RAM allocated, along with a TPU as a hardware accelerators. The performance comparison of training, testing, and validation proved that our model can generalize better to unseen examples. Our model achieved superior results when using transfer learning.

5   Conclusion and Future Works

This paper provides an efficient image classification methodology for the ASL, using EfficientNetB0 as a backbone. Our model is trained on an large dataset in order to improve generalization. We decided to not use data augmentation since the similarities between classes is close. The data processing and pre-training of our model required extra computational resources, which is the primary consideration for any image classification algorithm. Despite these limitations, we managed to use the EfficientNet model in ASL recognition and improve the generalization by avoiding overfitting, and making our model converge faster. Our future plan for this line of research in ASL image classification is to implement ASL live classification with a long short-term memory (LSTM) recurrent network. Besides, a system for recognizing ASL in real-time would be a useful implementation. Lastly, this work can be expanded into a full ASL hand movement communication classifier with complex collection of words.

References

1. Al-Hammadi, M., Muhammad, G., Abdul, W., Alsulaiman, M., Bencherif, M.A., Mekhtiche, M.A.: Hand gesture recognition for sign language using 3DCNN. IEEE Access **8**, 79491–79509 (2020)
2. Aly, W., Aly, S.K.H., Almotairi, S.: User-independent American sign language alphabet recognition based on depth image and PCANet features. IEEE Access **7**, 123138–123150 (2019)
3. Fatmi, R., Rashad, S., Integlia, R., Hutchison, G.: American sign language recognition using hidden Markov models and wearable motion sensors (2017)
4. LeCun, Y., Bengio, Y., Hinton, G.: Deep learning. Nature **521**, 436–44 (2015)
5. Lee, C.K.M., Ng, K.K.H., Chen, C.H., Lau, H.C.W., Chung, S.Y., Tsoi, T.: American sign language recognition and training method with recurrent neural network. Expert Syst. Appl. **167** (2021)
6. Tan, M., Le, Q.V.: EfficientNet: improving accuracy and efficiency through AutoML and model scaling (2019)
7. Aliyu, S., Deriche, M., Mohandes, M.: IEEE 23rd International Symposium on Industrial Electronics (ISIE), Istanbul, Turkey, 1–4 June 2014 (2014)
8. Mohanty, A., Rambhatla, S.S., Sahay, R.R.: Deep gesture: static hand gesture recognition using CNN. In: CVIP (2016)
9. Morocho-Cayamcela, M., Eugenio, W.L., Kwon, D.: A transfer learning approach for image classification on a mobile device. In: Korean Institute of Next Generation Computing, pp. 180–182 (2017)
10. Morocho Cayamcela, M.E., Lim, W.: Fine-tuning a pre-trained convolutional neural network model to translate American sign language in real-time. In: 2019 International Conference on Computing, Networking and Communications (ICNC), pp. 100–104 (2019)
11. Njoku, J.N., Morocho-Cayamcela, M.E., Lim, W.: CGDNet: efficient hybrid deep learning model for robust automatic modulation recognition. IEEE Netw. Lett. **3**(2), 47–51 (2021)
12. National Institute on Deafness and Other Communication Disorders. American sign language (2021)
13. Oudah, M., Al-Naji, A., Chahl, J.: Hand gesture recognition based on computer vision: a review of techniques. J. Imaging **6**(8), 73 (2020)
14. Elakkiya, R.: Machine learning based sign language recognition: a review and its research frontier. J. Ambient Intell. Humaniz. Comput. **12**(7), 7205–7224 (2020). https://doi.org/10.1007/s12652-020-02396-y
15. Safeel, M., Sukumar, T., Shashank, K.S., Arman, M.D., Shashidhar, R., Puneeth, S.B.: Sign language recognition techniques - a review. In: 2020 IEEE International Conference for Innovation in Technology (INOCON), pp. 1–9 (2020)
16. Sharma, S., Kumar, K.: ASL-3DCNN: American sign language recognition technique using 3-D convolutional neural networks. Multimed. Tools Appl. **80**, 1–13 (2021)
17. Tan, M., Le, Q.V.: EfficientNet: rethinking model scaling for convolutional neural networks (2020)
18. Töngi, R.: Application of transfer learning to sign language recognition using an inflated 3D deep convolutional neural network (2021)
19. Vogler, C., Metaxas, D.: Parallel hidden Markov models for American sign language recognition. In: Proceedings of the Seventh IEEE International Conference on Computer Vision, vol. 1, pp. 116–122 (1999)

Use and Product Quality
of Brain-Computer Interface (BCI)
Systems: A Systematic Literature Review

Juan Cobos[1,2], Christiann Moreira[1,2], Paúl Cárdenas-Delgado[1,2],
and Priscila Cedillo[1,2]

[1] Departamento de Ciencias de la Computación, Universidad de Cuenca,
Cuenca, Ecuador
{juan.cobosq94,alexander.moreira,paul.cardenasd,
priscila.cedillo}@ucuenca.edu.ec
[2] Facultad de Ingeniería, Universidad de Cuenca, Cuenca, Ecuador

Abstract. This study presents a systematic review of the literature related to the quality of Brain-Computer Interface (BCI) systems. The main objective of this systematic literature review is to analyze relevant information and what attributes and quality characteristics are used when evaluating the quality of BCI systems. Moreover, some related works are described to contextualize the contribution of this research. In addition, selection and extraction criteria were established to develop this review. In this way, the results showed that Brain-Computer Interface is a comprehensive branch of computer science. Therefore, it has become of great interest and importance in the research field in both industries and academia. Besides, it can be concluded that the most used quality characteristics are efficiency and usability. Finally, it was identified that creating a model quality that covers a research gap in this field is necessary to improve BCI systems quality.

Keywords: Systematic literature review · Quality · Brain computer interaction

1 Introduction

Technological advances and research in the Human-Computer Interaction (HCI) field have become essential to people's lives, facilitating human beings' development in an increasingly globalized society [17]. Due to this, different forms of interaction between users and electronic devices have been developed, such as visual, voice, haptic interaction, and others. Moreover, technological advances are increasingly specific to different groups of people, such as those with physical or cognitive disabilities. For this reason, science seeks to create methods that improve the life quality of persons, and it focuses on priority groups like persons with motor or cognitive disabilities. In this sense, Cerebrovascular accident (CVA), Spinal Cord Injury (SCI), and Amyotrophic Lateral Sclerosis (ALS)

K. Abad and S. Berrezueta (Eds.): DSICT 2022, CCIS 1647, pp. 208–222, 2022.
https://doi.org/10.1007/978-3-031-18347-8_17

are diseases that provoke critical motor disabilities in persons, but their cognitive functions keep well. Thus, is limited the HCI systems that a person can use; therefore, in this specific case is used Brain-Computer Interface (BCI). BCI is a system that measures the activity of the Central Nervous System (CNS) and converts it into an artificial output. The principal aims of BCI are replacing, restoring, improving, increasing, or extending the natural body outputs and achieving changes in the interactions between the CNS and the environment [14].

Consequently, BCI gained significant importance in medicine, HCI, and other research fields [3]. In this sense, BCI systems focus on improving patients' quality of life through rehabilitation or predicting users' intentions to control devices through brain activity. Furthermore, most applications with this technology aim to improve aspects of the user's life, such as communication whit their environment, cognitive abilities, and personal autonomy [8,11].

The initial steps in BCI systems began with Hans Berger, who used EEG in 1992 to classify brain waves [16]. Actually, overal companies, universities, and research centers have invested heavily in the research and development of BCI applications. In addition, today's great entrepreneurs, such as Elon Musk and Mark Zuckerberg, also have invested significant amounts of resources in merging biological and digital intelligence, whereby BCI has become an important research field for human-computer interaction [14].

BCI systems measure Central Nervous System (CNS) activity and convert it into artificial outputs that replace, restore, enhance, or supplement natural outputs by the CNS, allowing persons to interact with the environment. In this sense, one of the objectives of BCI is to create systems that allow the user to have control over different devices, such as computers, prostheses, and others [2]. Moreover, BCI systems analyze and process brain electrical signals like slow cortical potentials, visual evoked potentials, P300 potential, beta or mu rhythms, frequency bands, and others [7]. Besides, in BCI systems, these EEG signals are acquired through a helmet and visualized through software, usually developed by the company that creates the hardware device that captures the signals. Thus, the challenge of BCI systems is application development, as current trends regarding integration into cloud computing, visualization, and real-time processing must be considered [14]. BCI systems can be classified into two groups based on the nature of the input signal: endogenous and exogenous. Endogenous BCI systems depend on the user's ability to control their electrophysiological activity and require intensive training. On the other hand, exogenous BCI systems depend on electrophysiological activity evoked by external stimuli and do not require an intensive training stage [9]. Other authors expand this classification to four types of BCI systems: active, reactive, passive, and hybrid. Active systems obtain their outputs through conscious control by the user. Reactive systems are characterized by offering applications controlled by the user's reaction to an external sensory stimulus: visual, auditory, haptic, or olfactory. Passive systems do not directly control a target device, but the acquisition and analysis of neural activity are made to decipher the user's cognitive state. Finally, hybrid systems are characterized by merging active and reactive BCI mechanisms to improve system performance [4].

On the other hand, the software quality features and the ergonomy of hardware are essential aspects to consider to developing any technology. Software quality refers to the degree of performance of the characteristics that a computer system must meet. These characteristics guarantee that the client has a reliable system, which increases his satisfaction with the built system's functionality and efficiency [6]. Another definition of the Institute of Electrical and Electronics Engineers (IEEE) mentioned that software quality is "the degree to which a system, component or process meets the specified requirements and the needs or expectations of the client or user". In this sense, the BCI system must consider these quality features, and for this reason, it is essential to review how is the state of the art of quality of the BCI system.

Hence, this research collects the features of product quality and quality of use considered for developing Brain Computer-Interface systems since it can be noted that no tool has been created that allows developers to evaluate the existing quality of BCI systems [16]. Next, some results related to BCI systems and literary reviews carried out by other authors are detailed. Besides, the search method used to carry out the systematic literature search focused on the research topic is described. In addition, the results obtained from this literature review are detailed. Moreover, the future work section explains how this research will continue. Finally, in the last section of this work, the conclusions and results obtained from this research are detailed.

2   Related Work

This section presents related contributions, other literature reviews, and works related to BCI quality.

Kalagi et al. [9] present a review that collects information based on non-invasive EEG signals used in systems BCI. This review collects information based on non-invasive EEG signals used in BCI systems. The authors focus on providing information on EEGs, brain activity, EEG artifacts, and the basic structure of a BCI system. They describe each topic mentioned and provide information to enrich knowledge based on BCI systems. Still, the authors do not address the essential quality issues related to this system. In addition, it is necessary to mention that this work does not provide information about the process that the authors carried out to collect the data.

Several BCI systems have been developed to facilitate the communication of seniors with motor disabilities; for example, Kundu, [10] presents a systematic review of the BCI orthographic systems. This element plays an essential role in facilitating communication of seniors with motor disabilities, and it also includes orthographic paradigms, feature extraction, and classification techniques used in BCI systems. Furthermore, this article analyzes the advantages and limitations of the different spelling paradigms and machine learning algorithms.

Furthermore, Vaid et al. [15] present a review of EEG signals and BCI systems. This article covers fundamental topics such as the types of brain signals and the structure of BCI systems. Besides, it describes each of the stages that follow a BCI system, analyzes the acquisition of signals, and the processing that must be given to them to obtain important information about user intentions.

Similarly, Alberto et al. [1] present a literary review of video games based on BCI, in which a total of 50 related articles were reviewed. The objective that the authors raised was to identify the problems and difficulties at the time of designing, developing, and using games with brain activity reading devices. The review concluded that there are many challenges to overcome in the BCI area because this area is relatively new; they also highlight the lack of information on the development process of video games. In addition, this work describes some of the quality attributes that go into BCI-based games.

On the other hand, it has studies that address BCI systems application within to be systematics review. For example, Beraldo et al. [5] integrate the non-invasive BCI with a Robot Operating System (ROS) to control it mentally. The ROS Middleware Framework is a non-invasive BCI system that provides a common infrastructure and several platform-independent packages. However, ROS is still far from an adopted standard in the BCI community due to a lack of standardization, making it almost impossible to verify, replicate, and validate the experimental results. Therefore, the authors propose an objective to show the benefits of integrating a last-generation BCI and ROS system to control a telepresence robot without considering the quality aspects that involve the system's usability.

Finally, Martínez-Cagigal et al. [12] address information about the structure of a BCI system and its types. The objective of this research is that people with ALS can control web applications through EEG signals emitted by their brain; for this, they have applied an asynchronous threshold that monitors the user's attention and determines if they are paying attention to the stimulation caused by the monitor. The web browser development is made up of three stages: the first acquisition, to register and pre-process the EEG signal; the second is the processing, where the stimuli and evoked potentials of the user P300 are detected and finally, the web browsing, where the translate the user's intention into reality. They used five control users and sixteen people with ALS for its validation. The authors concluded that the browser is simple to use because the precision obtained in the evaluation was 95.75 for control people and 84.14 for sick people. Moreover, this research explains the entire development process of a BCI system; nevertheless, at no stage do they address quality properties that must be taken into account for the final product.

3   The Systematic Literature Review

A systematic review of the literature seeks to follow a scientific, repeatable, and replicable method to collect information on a specific topic [13]. Therefore, following a set of tasks is necessary to get a solid foundation and possible gaps in the study. For this case, the issue is related to the quality of use and product quality in BCI technology systems. Therefore, this study follows the Montagud et al. [13] methodology, which covers the following phases: (i) planning the review, (ii) conducting the review, and (iii) reviewing the report. The activities concerning the planning and the conducting of our systematic review are described in the following subsections. The report of the review stage is presented in Sect. 3.3.

3.1   Planning the Review

Below are the subtasks or activities that are part of the planning stage: (i) Definition of the research questions, (ii) The strategy to follow for the search for studies, (iii) Establish the criteria for the selection of primary studies, (iv) Evaluation of the quality of the studies, (v) Establish the strategy of extraction of data, (vi) Define the synthesis strategy.

Research Question. The objective of the systematic review is to know how BCI systems are defined, their limitations, and the challenges faced by developers. At the same time, it seeks to collect information on metrics that can be used when evaluating the quality of use and product quality in systems BCI. Below, the research questions generated with their respective justification are presented.

- RQ1. In what contexts, with what tools, and what type of users are BCI applications aimed at?
- RQ2. What architectures, tools, and methodologies have been created around BCI, and how has their development been carried out?
- RQ3. What characteristics of use and product quality are addressed in BCI applications to offer acceptable quality both in the area of quality in use and quality in the product?
- RQ4. What phase is the development of the study and what type of validation does this study use, and what kind of study is it?

Data Sources and Search Strategy. The first stage of the methodology proposed by Montagud et al. [13] refers to planning. At this stage, the keywords to identify possible primary studies are defined; the keywords obtained are shown in Table 1. In addition, using the keywords obtained, a search string was generated and used to search electronic databases or digital libraries. The resulting search string is "("Brain-Computer Interface" OR "BCI" OR "Brain-Machine Interface" OR "Direct Brain Interfaces") AND ("Software Quality" OR "QOS" OR "Quality" OR "Quality Model")." In this step, the inclusion and exclusion criteria are applied to collect the most significant number of articles related to the study area; these are explained in the following sections.

3.2   Conducting the Review

Moreover, the search terms, the electronic databases, and the search period are defined in this stage. The search terms were generated based on the research questions presented previously for this research. Besides, as shown in Table 2,

Table 1. Keywords used to search string.

Sub-cadena	Conector
BCI	OR
Brain computer interface	AND
BMI	OR
Brain machine interface	AND
DBIs	OR
Direct brain interfaces	OR
Software quality	OR
QOS	OR
Quality	AND

the search was carried out in electronic databases and digital libraries. These two digital libraries were selected because they obtained the best results focused on the research topic and the search string. In order to increase the results range, a manual search was carried out in journals, conferences, and workshops. Therefore, it was to obtain the most significant number of articles referring to the subject of the review. Furthermore, the period considered for selecting articles corresponds from 2010 to 2021. Since according to the European Commission, BCIs have become a research interest topic in recent years. Besides, in 2010/2011, Comisión Europea funded the coordination action Future BNCI program.

Table 2. Database used in the literature review.

Number	Digital library	
1	ACM Digital Library	
2	IEEE Xplore	
	Conference Title	Acronym
C1	International Winter Workshop on Brain-Computer Interface	BCI
C2	International Symposium on Computer, Consumer and Control	IS3C
C3	IEEE Symposium on Computational Intelligence and Games	CIG
C4	Annual International Conference of the IEEE Engineering in Medicine and Biology Society	EMBC
C5	Simposio CEA de Bioingeniería, Interfaces Cerebro-Máquina	CEA
	Journal Title	Ranking
J1	Brain-Computer Interface	Q1

Extraction Criteria. In this stage will answer each sub-question raised in the research. The strategy will ensure that data extraction criteria are met and facilitate classification. The complete list of extraction criteria is presented in Table A at the following URL: https://n9.cl/laxbj.

Two researchers analyzed each paper to decide the inclusion of each article obtained from the search. It was taken count inclusion, and exclusion criteria were applied; thus, it was analyzed the title, abstract, and keywords of each paper. If discrepancies in the primary studies selection appeared, a consensus was reached to guarantee the selection of valuable articles for the proposed research.

Studies that met at least one of the following inclusion criteria were included:

– Studies that present information regarding BCI and quality systems.
– Studies that present information on treatments or interpretation of brain signals using computer-oriented BCI.
– Studies that present information on how to implement a BCI system.
– Studies that present information on the structure of BCI systems.

Studies that met at least one of the following exclusion criteria will be excluded:

– Introductory articles for special editions, books, and workshops.
– Duplicate reports of the same study in different sources.
– Short articles of less than five pages.
– Articles that are not written in English or Spanish.

Quality Assessment. Two aspects have been considered to evaluate each study's quality: i) The relevance of the conference or journal in which the article is published. In this case, the articles have been classified into three categories, as shown in the web annex, Table B: https://n9.cl/laxbj. ii) The number of citations the article has. The classification is also done in 3 categories: high, medium, and low. Citations are considered according to Google's academic citation count. In addition, to not penalize potentially valuable papers, they have been classified according to the year, as shown in the web annex on Table C and Table D. The URL to access the web annex is https://n9.cl/laxbj.

3.3   Results of the Systematic Review

After searching the digital libraries, 115 articles were obtained. Subsequently, the inclusion and exclusion criteria were applied, resulting in 38 papers being selected. Finally, these papers were distributed: 13 corresponded to the ACM library and 25 to the IEEEXplore library.

Methods of Analysis and Synthesis. The analysis methods and synthesis show the systematic review results; the statistical tables show individual results of each criterion concerning the number of studies that speak or are related to that subject, which is shown in this link: https://n9.cl/xkgtj.

Results by Year. Then it is present in Fig. 1, the number of selected articles by year of publication. Regarding this, they can highlight three years, 2016, 2017, and 2018, because, in these three years, it has the highest average of publications. The year with the most significant number of articles is 2017, with six articles and the years 2010 and 2013 are those with the fewest publications with one article. It should be noted that within this literature review, no relevant articles were found in the years 2020 and 2021.

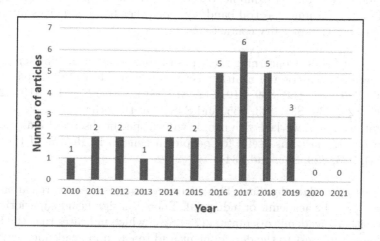

Fig. 1. Articles selected by years of publication.

Discussion Criteria per Criteria. This section analyzes the papers reviewed and their results in the extraction criteria matrix.

EC1. Research Context: The results obtained from the systematic review indicate that the most used research context in the set of articles is the technologies that use the processing of brain stimuli (63.16%). In addition, the quality of life and HCI contexts can also be highlighted, with 34.2% and 31.6%, respectively. Finally, the least used context was rehabilitation and training, with 7.89%; only three articles (S22, S27, and S29) covered a context different from EC1.

Articles S01, S06, S07, S09, S11, S14, S16, S18, S20, S23, S24, S31, S32, S33, S34, S38, use the context of technologies that use the processing of brain stimuli and also to develop These investigations used a helmet or electrodes as a tool.

As mentioned in previous chapters, the BCI aims to improve the quality of life of people who have a particular disease; a clear example of what is mentioned are articles S07, S10, S16, S17, S19, S21, S23, S26, S28, S35, S36, S37, S38, in which the second most used context predominates, quality of life.

EC2. Tool Used. In the second extraction criterion, 63.2% of the reviewed articles, S01, S03, S06, S07, S09, S10, S11, S14, S16, S18, S20, S22, S23, S24, S26, S27, S28, S29, S31, S32, S33, S34, S37, and S38 use a helmet or electrodes as a tool; it is essential to point out that most helmets used in BCI contain electrodes in their structure, the same ones that are used to take the user's brain signal. Finally, the second most used tool was the processing software, 52.63% of the articles used at least one processing software, making it the second most used tool.

Some items like S06, S07, S11, S18, S20, S22, S24, S29, S31, and S33 used the tools mentioned above. Finally, four items, S21, S25, S30, and S35, used other tools or no tool at all; for example, S25 covers the development of an algorithm focused on the Gamma spectral band. On the other hand S30 gives information on the construction of a dry contact electrode.

EC3. Type of Users. Concerning the types of users used in the different research articles, the participation of healthy users stands out in 65,79% of papers (S01, S02, S05, S06, S07, S08, S09, S10, S11, S12, S13, S14, S15, S18, S19, S21, S24, S25, S27, S28, S30, S31, S33, S35, and S38). On the other hand, 36,84% of the investigations found worked with people with a specific disease. Finally, they are working on BCI systems useful for people in general in 15,79% of the articles (S03, S04, S23, S29, S32, and S34).

EC4. Scope of the Investigation. This criterion analyzes the research approach; in this case, it can be academic or industrial. There is a significant superiority of the articles with an academic orientation (73.68%), which indicates that the BCI is a technology of interest to the development and research in academic institutions. On the other hand, the following articles (S07, S21, S23, S27, S28, S29, S30, S31, S35, and S37), have an industrial orientation; most of these articles focus on products that are on the market or that they will come out soon. In addition, many articles with an academic orientation focus on motor imagination, for example, the following articles (S01, S02, S03, S04, S05, S06, S08, S09, S11, S13, S15, S16, S17, S18, S20, S22, S26, S32, S38).

EC5. Stages of a BCI System Architecture. For this criterion, four BCI system architecture stages i) Signal was considered: Acquisition, ii) Signal Processing, iii) Feedback, and iv) Application - User interaction. The most used BCI system architecture stage was the signal processing stage; this stage was found in the following articles S01, S02, S04, S05, S06, S07, S08, S09, S11, S12, S13, S14, S15, S16, S17, S18, S19, S22, S23, S24, S26, S27, S30, S31, S33, S34, S35, S37, and S38. On the other hand, the second stage most used was signal acquisition; 68.42% of the articles reviewed included this stage. Concerning application-user Interaction and signal processing stages are used in a large number of articles related to the motor imagination paradigm or motor perceptual system paradigm; in this context, it finds the following articles S01 S02, S03, S04, S05, S06, S07, S08, S09, S11, S13, S15, S16, S17, S18, S22, S26, S30, S31, and S38. Finally, feedback was the most minor used stage in the different investigations; 9 articles, S10, S19, S20, S26, S28, S30, S31, S33, and S37, used it.

EC6. Applied Techniques. This criterion analyzes the several paradigms that can be used in BCI systems; selecting the adequate paradigm depends on the objective of the BCI system. Four paradigms were considered for this criterion: i) Task in particular, ii) Motor Imaging - Perceptual Motor System, iii) Neuroimaging and iv) P300 Potentials. In this review, the paradigm most used in the selected articles is the motor imagination, 60.53% of the articles (S01, S02, S03, S04, S05, S06, S07, S08, S09, S11, S13, S15, S16, S17, S18, S20, S22, S26, S28, S30, S31, S32, and S38) use this paradigm. On the other hand, the neuroimaging paradigm is the second most used in the selected articles, S06, S07, S11, S18, S23, S24, S26, S27, S28, S29, S30, S33, S34, S35, S36, S37 and S38 use it. Finally, it is noteworthy that S25 is the only article that does not explain the tool used in its study.

EC7. Quality of Use Characteristics. This criterion considered five characteristics to help to evaluate the quality of use of the software, these were: i) Effectiveness, ii) Efficiency, iii) Satisfaction, iv) Safety, and v) Usability. In this sense, the articles review showed that efficiency is the most used characteristic; 20 articles (S01, S02, S03, S04, S05, S06, S07, S08, S09, S10, S11, S12, S15, S17, S18, S19, S22, S28, S30, and S36), used it. On the other hand, usability is the second most used feature, articles S02, S03, S04, S10, S12, S13, S14, S15, S16, S17, S18, S19, S20, S23, S24, S27, S32, and S36 mentioned of this characteristic. Likewise, satisfaction is the third most mentioned characteristic in the articles; 17 mention it. Finally, no feature is mentioned to evaluate the quality of use in BCI systems in articles S25, S31, S33, S34, S35, and S38.

EC8. Quality of Product Characteristics. For this criterion, three characteristics were considered: i) Useful, ii) Desirable, and iii) Attainable. In this review it could identify the utility as the characteristic most used; the articles S01, S03, S04, S05, S06, S07, S08, S09, S10, S12, S13, S14, S15, S16, S17, S18, S20, S22, S24, S26, S27, S28, S30, S32 S33, S36, and S37, taken into account this characteristic. Similarly, desirability is the second most used characteristic in the articles; this seeks to relate that software must generate a desire to use said product; in articles S01, S05, S06, S07, S21, S23, S35, and S38; this feature is mentioned. Finally, reachability was found in 13.16% of the articles.

EC9. Study Phase. This criterion involves the study phases described in each of the articles; it can highlight that 63.16% of articles (S01, S02, S03, S04, S05, S08, S11, S12, S13, S14, S15, S16, S17, S19, S20, S21, S22, S23, S24, S25, S29, S32, S34, and S38), explain the analysis phase of their research. On the other hand, 20 articles (S01, S02, S03, S04, S05, S06, S07, S08, S09, S10, S11, S12, S13, S14, S15, S16, S17, S18, S22, and S37) explain the design phase of their research. Finally, the implementation phase was explained in 50% of the reviewed articles, while the testing phase was explained in 11 articles (S03, S05, S07, S09, S10, S18, S19, S22, S26, S27, and S28).

EC10. Type of Validation. This criterion analyzes the validation type used in the different articles reviewed. The validation through experiments is the most used;

25 articles apply this type of validation in their research. On the other hand, in articles, S01, S03, S04, S05, S06, S07, S08, S09, S11, S13, S14, S18, and S19, surveys are used for the validation. Moreover, the quasi-experiment is used in 15.79% of papers. Finally, the prototype was the minor used type of validation; S07 was the only article that used it. In addition, comparing EC11 with EC12 criteria, we can see that the experiment is used mainly in new studies; thus, only eight articles (S06, S10, S18, S20, S26, S27, S31, and S36) of those reviewed are articles that continue a study and use the experiment as a form of validation.

EC11. Type of Study. This criterion analyzes if articles as new studies or extensions of a previous study. In this way, results show that 78.95% of the articles reviewed are new topics, and only articles S06, S10, S18, S20, S26, S27, S31, and S36 are the continuation of a previously developed study.

Relations Between Criteria. The bubbles presented in Fig. 2, Fig. 3, and Fig. 4 shows a comparison between some criteria, and it was considered the principal results.

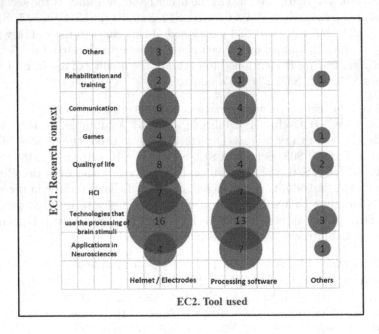

Fig. 2. Comparison between EC1: Research context and EC2: Tool used.

Figure 2 shows the relationship between the tools used and the context in which each was applied. In this sense, it is possible to highlight the contexts that use the processing of brain stimuli and quality of life since they use all the tools found in the different investigations.

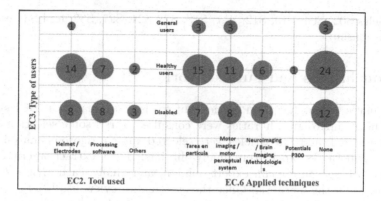

Fig. 3. Comparison between EC3: Type of users and EC2: Tool used and EC6: BCI paradigms.

Figure 3 shows the relationship between EC2 and EC3, where it can highlight that articles S01, S06, S07, S09, S10, S11, S14, S18, S24, S27, S28, S31, S33, and S38, work with healthy users and using a helmet/electrodes as a tool, this tool is used for all possible users of the EC3. In contrast, the other tools are not used in the category of users in general.

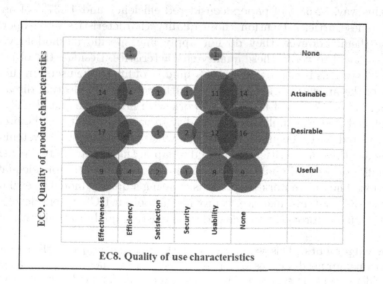

Fig. 4. Comparison between EC9: Quality of product characteristics and EC8: Quality of use characteristics

Figure 4 shows the relationship between the quality of use and product quality characteristics, highlighting the relationship between usability and desirability;

the articles S02, S04, S10, S12, S17, S18, S23 S24, S27, S32, and S36 establish this relationship.

4   Conclusions and Future Work

A systematic review has been carried out focused on quality in BCI systems. Thus, the leading digital libraries were consulted. First, some selection criteria were considered, and 115 articles were selected; after a rigorous analysis based on those criteria, 38 papers were finally obtained. Then, extraction criteria were established based on domain expert opinion, and finally, each article was analyzed based on these criteria. Once the systematic review has been completed, the BCI systems researching area state is clear, and it is known what the current studies are. Moreover, it has been able to identify the essential developed applications and the applying areas. Furthermore, it has been an able identity that most research has an academic approach (73.68% of the articles); and the rest have an industrial approach. In addition, it is also important to mention that only eight articles are the continuation of others previously developed. In this way, after these first steps, and based on the amount of obtained papers, BCI systems are a vast research area and attractive to both industry and academia. Moreover, according to the systematic review results, it can be concluded that the most used quality characteristics in BCI systems are efficiency and usability. In this way, 52.63% of papers considered efficiency and 47.37% of usability. Despite, these articles mention those quality characteristics and superficially evaluate them; however, they do not apply any specific methodology or use a quality model to verify these quality characteristics. Besides, the objective of many BCI systems is to provide a better quality of life to the users. In this sense, 36.84% of the articles work with people with motor or intellectual diseases. On the other hand, 65.79% of the articles work with healthy people. Finally, it can be concluded that the application of quality in use and quality in the product is not considered with adequate importance when developing BCI systems; thus, this was identified as a critical point and a gap in this research area; considering that quality of use and quality of the product is fundamental for adequate user interaction. The future work proposed is creating a quality model to evaluate the quality of BCI systems; likewise, it provides a tool for BCI system developers to assess the quality properly and consider all existing quality attributes.

Acknowledgements. This work is part of the research projects: "Fog Computing applied to monitoring devices used in assisted living environments. Case study: platform for the elderly" and "Design of architectures and interaction models for assisted living environments for elderly people. Case study: ludic and social environments". Hence, the authors thank to DIUC of Universidad de Cuenca for its academic and financial support.

References

1. Alberto, J., Dávila, V., Macías, J.V., Lamas, M.V.: Videojuegos basados en BCI (Interface cerebro computadora): Revisión Sistemática Literaria Zacatecas View project **9**, 10–23 (2017). https://www.researchgate.net/publication/324506899
2. Araujo, M., González, N., Pose, F.: Evaluación y detección de potenciales evocados sobre una interfaz cerebro computadora. Ingeniería Biomédica **7**(October) (2016). http://www.scielo.org.co/scielo.php?script=sci_arttext&pid=S1909-976220 13000200006
3. Arboleda Clavijo, C., Garcia, E., Posada, A.: Diseño y construcción de un prototipo de interfaz cerebro-computador para facilitar la comunicación de personas con discapacidad motora. Revista EIA, pp. 105–115 (2009)
4. Aricó, P., Borghini, G., Di Flumeri, G., Sciaraffa, N., Colosimo, A., Babiloni, F.: Passive BCI in operational environments: insights, recent advances, and future trends. IEEE Trans. Biomed. Eng. **64**(7), 1431–1436 (2017). https://doi.org/10. 1109/TBME.2017.2694856
5. Beraldo, G., Antonello, M., Cimolato, A., Menegatti, E., Tonin, L.: Brain-computer interface meets ROS: a robotic approach to mentally drive telepresence robots. In: Proceedings of the IEEE International Conference on Robotics and Automation, pp. 4459–4464 (2018). https://doi.org/10.1109/ICRA.2018.8460578
6. Bosse, S., Muller, K.R., Wiegand, T., Samek, W.: Brain-computer interfacing for multimedia quality assessment. In: 2016 IEEE International Conference on Systems, Man, and Cybernetics, SMC 2016 - Conference Proceedings, pp. 2834–2839 (2017). https://doi.org/10.1109/SMC.2016.7844669
7. Gutiérrez-martínez, J., Cantillo-negrete, J., Cariño-escobar, R.I., Elías-viñas, D.: Una Herramienta Para Apoyar La Rehabilitación De Pacientes Con Discapacidad Motora. Investigación en Discapacidad **2**(2), 62–69 (2013). https://www. medigraphic.com/pdfs/invdis/ir-2013/ir132c.pdf
8. Hornero, R., Corralejo, R., Álvarez González, D.: Brain-Computer Interface (BCI) aplicado al entrenamiento cognitivo y control domótico para prevenir los efectos del envejecimiento. Lychnos **8**, 29–34 (2012)
9. Kalagi, S., Machado, J.: Brain computer interface systems using non- invasive electroencephalogram signal: a literature review, pp. 1578–1583 (2017)
10. Kundu, S.: Brain-Computer interface speller system for alternative communication: a review. Elsevier. https://www.sciencedirect.com/science/article/pii/S1959 031821000944?casa_token=xD1_QuOfdpUAAAAA:DSV547FS2tDHrykHebjR-5h1 pim32p-NWGfEfPW8f9xA6dfdLLvtbvSSWTOIUlb7PbUUL2lBGtn
11. Lance, B.J., Kerick, S.E., Ries, A.J., Oie, K.S., McDowell, K.: Brain-computer interface technologies in the coming decades. Proc. IEEE **100**(SPL CONTENT), 1585–1599 (2012). https://doi.org/10.1109/JPROC.2012.2184830
12. Martínez-Cagigal, V., Núñez, P., Hornero, R.: Spectral regression kernel discriminant analysis for P300 speller based brain-computer interfaces. In: Ibáñez, J., González-Vargas, J., Azorín, J.M., Akay, M., Pons, J.L. (eds.) Converging Clinical and Engineering Research on Neurorehabilitation II. BB, vol. 15, pp. 789–793. Springer, Cham (2017). https://doi.org/10.1007/978-3-319-46669-9_129
13. Montagud, S., Abrahão, S.: A systematic review of quality attributes and measures for software product lines. Softw. Qual. J. **20**(4), 425–486 (2012). https://doi.org/ 10.1007/s11219-011-9146-7
14. Saha, S., et al.: Progress in Brain Computer Interface: challenges and Opportunities. Front. Syst. Neurosci. **15**(February), 1–20 (2021). https://doi.org/10.3389/ fnsys.2021.578875

15. Vaid, S., Singh, P., Kaur, C.: EEG signal analysis for BCI interface: a review. In: International Conference on Advanced Computing and Communication Technologies, ACCT 2015-April, pp. 143–147 (2015). https://doi.org/10.1109/ACCT.2015. 72
16. Vela-Dávila, J., et al.: Aplicación de Estándares y Procesos en áreas de Desarrollo de Software Dentro de las Universidades. ecorfan.org (2017)
17. Zapata, L., Karam, J., Gutiérrez, D.: La tecnología y su impacto en la vida cotidiana. Revisión y comentarios del libro: "Silicon Valley vs Hollywood: cuando las empresas de tecnología y sus medios se confunden". Palermo Bus. Rev. **17**, 43–53 (2018). https://www.palermo.edu/economicas/cbrs/pdf/pbr17/PBR_17_03.pdf

Author Index

Printed in the United States
by Baker & Taylor Publisher Services